The Uses
of the Old Testament
in the New

The Uses
of the Old Testament
in the New

by

Walter C. Kaiser, Jr.

MOODY PRESS

CHICAGO

Library of Congress Cataloging in Publication Data
Kaiser, Walter C.
   The uses of the Old Testament in the New.

   Bibliography: p.
   Includes indexes.
   1. Bible. O.T.—Quotations in the New Testament.
2. Bible. O.T.—Relation to the New Testament.
3. Bible—Hermeneutics. I. Title.
BS2387.K33   1985   225.4'8   85-4885
ISBN 0-8024-9085-9

   1 2 3 4 5 6 7 Printing/RR/Year 90 89 88 87 86 85

Printed in the United States of America

To Ken and Carol Meyer
and
Warren and Lenore Benson,

for demonstrating the love of Christ and enthusiastic joy in
His service on the occasion of our completing five years of
working together as an administrative team in theological
education

Contents

Preface

The method of Bible study creating the most debate today is known as *redaction criticism* or *redaction history*. This method "traces the path the unit [of Scripture] has taken from the time it was first written down until the time it achieved its final literary form."[1] Bluntly stated, this method assumes that individual units of the biblical text, as well as some biblical books, have not come down to us with the same text and form in which they were originally written.

A close rival in contemporary religious news is another method known as *canon criticism*. This method also relocates the context in which an Old Testament text can be best understood, for among its many emphases is the assertion that an Old Testament text cannot be understood apart from the context of the whole Christian canon—especially its relationship to the New Testament.

No less significant for our day was an earlier approach to the biblical texts that investigated the use of Old Testament quotations in the New Testament. In our judgment it is impossible to understand many aspects of the present debate over the legitimate use of redaction and canonical criticism (and there are many dubious assumptions and conclusions in both of those approaches[2]) without appreciating the fact that several of these scholars began their stream of thought with

1. Klaus Koch, trans., S. M. Cupitt, *The Growth of the Biblical Tradition* (New York: Scribner's, 1969), p. 58.
2. For some preliminary analyses on these two methods see Roland M. Frye, "Literary Criticism and Gospel Criticism," *Theology Today* 36 (1979):207–19.

this problem of the way that the New Testament uses Old Testament quotations. There are certainly many other factors that enter into this discussion, but we wish to highlight one that should have been thought out and judged more critically, that is, the use of Old Testament quotes in the New Testament. When a majority of contemporary scholars concluded that the Old Testament text could be (and indeed was) interpreted very permissively by the New Testament writers, the door was opened for a similar charge that the gospel writers of the New Testament likewise indulged in a corresponding interpretive freedom in their handling of the units of teaching available to them from other sources. It is that turn of events that we regret and now attempt to reverse by returning to what we believe might have been the signal for the breaking of the dam—at least for many who had, until then, held to a high view of Scripture.

Even before the turn of the century this issue was the subject of many publications, but with the discovery of the unique method of interpretation uncovered in several of the Dead Sea Scroll commentaries following their discovery in 1947, and with the new interest in rabbinic commentary, New Testament scholarship underwent a very dramatic metamorphosis. Bluntly stated once again, the autonomy of the New Testament writer (or even the autonomy of the contemporary reader of the New Testament) in his method of citing Old Testament texts was given the approving nod by almost all scholars over the rights and meanings of the Old Testament writer who claimed to have stood in the Council of God and to have had a revelation entrusted to him that he understood and wanted to share.

This book, in part then, is an attempt to understand how such a state of affairs came about. Rather than dealing with the issue in an abstract or detached way, we have attempted to go directly to the texts themselves. Too frequently the topic has been surveyed in essay form. But even in those rare cases where detailed and serious exegesis of the biblical text was a key feature, the New Testament text was obviously the area where these writers exhibited their greatest comfort zones. What has been missing is an extended analysis of the cited Old Testament text with its own context and exegesis. It is our sincere hope that we have offered a contribution in this key area of Old Testament exegesis and context.

It is the New Testament use of the Old Testament texts for apologetic or argumentative reasons that has suffered the most in this recent debate. If we were allowed just one question to symbolize our entire work, it would be this: In their attempt to show that the Messiah and many of the events in the first century church had indeed been anticipated by the Old Testament writers, have the New Testament writers fairly cited the Old Testament quotations according to their real truth-intention and original writer's meaning?

The case we want to assemble here is similar to the one that the prophet Isaiah mounted. His challenge to the inanimate idols of his day was:

> Declare to us the things to come,
> tell us what the future holds,
> so we may know that you are gods.
> (Isa. 41:23, NIV*)

Again:

> Who then is like me? Let him proclaim it
> Let him declare and lay out before me
> What has happened ...
> and what is yet to come—
> Yes, let him foretell what will come ...
> Did I not proclaim this and foretell it long ago?
> (Isa. 44:7–8, NIV)

Or:

> Concerning things to come,
> do you question me about my children,
> or give me orders about the work of my hands?
> (Isa. 45:11b, NIV)

And:

> Declare what is to be, present it—
> let them take counsel together.
> Who foretold this long ago,
> who declared it from the distant past?
> Was it not I, the Lord?
> (Isa. 45:21, NIV)

Finally:

> I foretold the former things long ago,
> my mouth announced them and I made them known;
> Then suddenly I acted, and they came to pass....

* *New International Version*

> Therefore I told you these things long ago;
>   before they happened I announced them to you
> so that you could not say,
> "My idols did them."

(Isa. 48:3, 5a–b, NIV)

It was in this tradition that the apostles wrote and boldly preached. They appear to be absolutely convinced that the Old Testament had clearly anticipated many of the verities and events they proclaimed. Can their claims be upheld? Or, did they so massage the Old Testament text that it suddenly printed out new meanings previously unattested, but in the contemporary tradition of rabbinic midrash or Qumran *pesher?* That is our central question in this monograph.

Before we turn to the case itself, I must append here several pleasant acknowledgments. Special thanks must be given to the publishers listed at the end of this preface for their permission to use either part or the entirety of the articles previously printed in a number of journals or *Festschriften.* It is also a pleasure to acknowledge the skilled and dedicated efforts of my administrative assistant, Mrs. Lois Armstrong, and Luann Kuehl, faculty secretary, and the long hours spent on the computer recording the indices by my youngest son Jonathon Kevin and my wife Margaret Ruth. I am also grateful to President Earl Radmacher, the faculty, and the student body of Western Conservative Baptist Seminary in Portland, Oregon, for their kind invitation and generous reception to give the Bueermann-Champion lectureship in February 1983, where some of the key chapters of this book were given for the first time. I must also express my appreciation to my graduate assistant Stephen L. Childers, who did a major share of compiling my working bibliography, and to Dana Gould of Moody Press for his encouraging resourcefulness in seeing this manuscript through all its stages.

It is our desire that this volume may stimulate a new segment of contributors to this ongoing conversation on the proper hermeneutical use of the Old Testament in the New Testament.

Acknowledgments

I wish to express my thanks to these publishers for permission to quote from their materials.

DALLAS THEOLOGICAL SEMINARY
"The Promise Theme and the Theology of Rest," *Bibliotheca Sacra* 130 (1973):135–50.
Portions of "The Promised Land: A Biblical-Historical View," *Bibliotheca Sacra* 138 (1981):302–312.

EISENBRAUNS
"The Promise of God and the Outpouring of the Holy Spirit," in *The Living and Active Word of God*, ed. Morris Inch and Ronald Youngblood (Winona Lake, Ind.: Eisenbrauns, 1983), pp. 109–22.

GRACE THEOLOGICAL SEMINARY
"The Promise of the Arrival of Elijah in Malachi and the Gospels," *Grace Theological Journal* 3 (1982):221–33.

THE EVANGELICAL THEOLOGICAL SOCIETY
"The Promise to David in Psalm 16 and Its Application in Acts 2:25–33 and 13:32–37," *JETS* 23 (1980):219–29.
"The Davidic Promise and the Inclusion of the Gentiles (Amos 9:9–15 and Acts 15:13–18): A Test Passage for Theological Systems," *JETS* 20 (1977):97–111.
"The Current Crisis in Exegesis and the Apostolic Use of Deut. 24:4 and 1 Cor. 9:8–10," *JETS* 21 (1978):3–18.

Moody Press

"The Abolition of the Old Order and the Establishment of the New: Psalm 40:6-8 and Hebrews 10:5-10," in *Tradition and Testament: Essays in Honor of Charles Lee Feinberg*, ed. John S. Feinberg and Paul D. Feinberg (Chicago: Moody, 1981), pp. 19–37.

Thomas Nelson Publishers

Portions from "The Single Intent of Scriptures," in *Evangelical Roots: A Tribute to Wilbur Smith*, ed. Kenneth S. Kantzer (Nashville: Nelson, 1978), pp. 23–41.

Abbreviations

ALOUS	*Annual of Leeds University Oriental Society*
ANET	*Ancient Near Eastern Texts*, ed. J. B. Pritchard
ATR	*Anglican Theological Review*
BETS	*Bulletin of the Evangelical Theological Society*
BDB	Brown, Driver, and Driggs, *A Hebrew-English Lexicon of the Old Testament*
CBQ	*Catholic Biblical Quarterly*
ExpT	*Expository Times*
JBL	*Journal of the Society of Biblical Literature*
JETS	*Journal of the Evangelical Theological Society*
JSNT	*Journal for the Study of the New Testament*
JSOT	*Journal for the Study of the Old Testament*
JSS	*Journal of Semitic Studies*
JTS	*Journal of Theological Studies*
KJV	Kings James Version
LXX	The Septuagint version of the Old Testament in Greek
NASB	*New American Standard Bible*
NEB	*New English Bible*
NIV	*New International Version*
NovT	*Novum Testamentum*
NT	New Testament
NTS	*New Testament Studies*
OT	Old Testament
OTS	*Old Testament Studies*

RB   *Révue Biblique*
RSV   *Revised Standard Version*
SJT   *Scottish Journal of Theology*
TDNT   *Theological Dictionary of the New Testament*
VT   *Vetus Testamentum* (Supplements, *SuppVT*)
USQR   *Union Seminary Quarterly Review*
WTJ   *Westminster Theological Journal*
ZAW   *Zeitschrift für die alttestamentliche Wissenschaft*

1

Introduction to the Uses
of the Old Testament in the New

The use of the Old Testament (hereafter OT) in the New Testament (hereafter NT) has captured the interests of a wide spectrum of biblical scholars since the time of Jerome.[1] The subject, along with its modern bibliography, has continued to grow so large that it defies any convenient treatment in a single monograph.[2] Nevertheless, the relationship between the OT and the NT stands as one of the foremost, if not the leading, problems in biblical research of this century.[3]

FREQUENCY OF CITATIONS

The importance of this problem can be observed in the sheer frequency of the OT quotations and allusions in the NT. How large this number actually is depends on how an allusion is defined and identified. Whereas explicit quotations are easier to identify because they are often preceded by an *introductory formula* such as, "That it

---

1. Matthew Black, "The Christological Use of the Old Testament in the New Testament," *NTS* 18 (1971–72): 1.
2. Principal items in the earlier literature are cited by L. Venard, "Citations de l' Ancien Testament dans le Nouveau Testament," *Dictionnaire de la Bible: Supplément,* ed. L. Pirot (Paris: Librairie Letouzey, 1934) II:23–51; Krister Stendahl, *The School of St. Matthew and Its Use of the Old Testament* (Lund: C. W. K. Gleerup, 1954), pp. 218–38; and Robert H. Gundry, *The Use of the Old Testament in St. Matthew's Gospel with Special Reference to the Messianic Hope* (Leiden: Brill, 1967), pp. 235–40.
3. For a similar evaluation, see Lester J. Kuyper, "The Old Testament Used by the New Testament Writers," *Reformed Review* 21 (1967): 2.

might be fulfilled" and "This was to fulfil what the Lord had spoken by the prophet," allusions to the OT often elude the reader. Allusions may be clauses, phrases, or even a single word, and, therefore, we may not always be sure that the NT writer deliberately intended that the OT connection should be made in the minds of his readers. Some of this wording may only have been fortuitous or accidental without a conscious allusion intended. An example of overlapping language where no allusion was intended may be seen in Jeroboam I's flight to Egypt in 1 Kings 11:40 ("Solomon tried to kill Jeroboam, but Jeroboam fled to Egypt ... and stayed there until Solomon's death") and that of the holy family in Matthew 2:13–15.[4] But other wording deliberately recalls key words, promises, and incidents found in the OT such as the words heard at the baptism of Jesus: "You are my Son, whom I love" (overtones of Psalm 2:7 with echoes from Genesis 22:2); "with you I am well pleased" (the same ascription given to the Servant of the Lord in Isaiah 42:1). Thus, whereas we are clear on the presence of allusive quotations, we are not certain about the exact extent or actual number of all such instances. That will account, in the main, for the differences among scholars as to the number of OT quotations in the NT.

In 1884 C. H. Toy[5] identified 613 OT quotations and allusions in the NT, whereas Wilhelm Dittmar[6] counted 1,640, and E. Hühn[7] topped everyone with a count of 4,105. A rough count of the references in Nestle's Greek Testament[8] yields about 950 quotations and allusions, and the United Bible Society's Greek text lists over 2,500 NT passages from nearly 1,800 OT passages.[9]

NUMBER OF FORMAL QUOTATIONS

More realistic counts can be obtained from limiting oneself to formal quotations of the OT introduced in the NT by introductory formulas. Accordingly, H. M. Shires[10] found 239 quotes drawn from

---

4. This illustration is suggested by Robert H. Gundry, "Quotations in the NT," in *The Zondervan Pictorial Encyclopedia of the Bible*, 5 vols., ed. Merrill C. Tenney (Grand Rapids: Zondervan, 1975), 5:7.
5. C. H. Toy, *Quotations in the New Testament* (New York: Scribner's, 1884).
6. W. Dittmar, *Vetus Testamentum in Novo* (Gettingen, 1899, 1903).
7. E. Hühn, *Die AT Citate und Reminiscenzen im Neuen Testamen* (Tübingen, 1900).
8. D. Eberhard Nestle, *Novum Testamentum Graece* (New York: American Bible Society, 1952), pp. 658–71. Also see the 312 OT quotations listed and discussed in six categories in Gleason Archer and Gregory Chirichigno, *Old Testament Quotations in the New Testament* (Chicago: Moody Press, 1963), esp. pp. xxv–xxxiii.
9. Kurt Aland, Matthew Black, Bruce Metzger, and Allen Wikgren, eds., *The Greek New Testament* (New York: United Bible Societies, 1966) pp. 897–920.
10. Henry M. Shires, *Finding the Old Testament in the New* (Philadelphia: Westminster, 1974), p. 15.

185 different OT passages. In addition to those referenced quotations, he has 198 unacknowledged quotations taken from 147 OT texts plus another 1,167 instances of rewording or paraphrasing reflecting 944 OT passages. His combined total is 1,604 NT citations of 1,276 different OT texts. Roger Nicole had a similar number of direct quotations. He concluded that there were 250 direct quotations with another 45 instances that also depended directly on the OT to make a total of 295 unquestionable separate references.[11] Louis M. Sweet also counts approximately 300 direct quotations.[12] Thus, it is safe to conclude that there are approximately 300 formal citations in the NT from the OT in addition to an almost incalculable influence on the language, modes of expression, and thought in the NT. Earl Ellis estimates that approximately one-third of all the NT citations are found in Paul's epistles— 93 OT references.[13] Over against the Pauline usage stands the book of Revelation, which probably contains more OT imagery and phrases than any other NT writing, yet it does not contain a single formal quotation from the OT!

Both the direct and the allusive quotations, however, are valuable for biblical studies. The former often can inform us about the specific text forms that were being used by the writers. Whether those writers had easy access to synagogue scrolls or even, in some cases, copies of individual books, as Robert Gundry has argued,[14] or if they depended solely on their memory, as Henry Shires preferred,[15] cannot be settled with any finality. But allusions must not be passed off too quickly, for, as Gundry points out, "an allusive quotation rather reflects the language and phrase-forms with which the writer is most familiar and in which he habitually thinks."[16] Thus, the interweaving of the phrases from Scripture with one's own words revealed the literary style as well as the fabric of thought of the NT writers. It also reflected a "thorough acquaintance with and a reverent meditation upon the Old Testament," as Fitzmyer observed.[17]

11. Roger Nicole, "New Testament Use of the Old Testament," in *Revelation and the Bible*, ed. Carl F. H. Henry (Grand Rapids: Baker, 1958), p. 137.
12. Louis M. Sweet, "Quotations: New Testament," in *International Standard Bible Encyclopedia*, 5 vols. (Grand Rapids: Eerdmans, 1939), 4:1516.
13. Earle E. Ellis, *Paul's Use of the Old Testament* (Grand Rapids: Eerdmans, 1957), p. 11; and *idem*, "A Note on Pauline Hermeneutica," *NTS* 2 (1955–56):127–33 (now reprinted as *idem*, "Midrash Pesher in Pauline Hermeneutics," in *Prophecy and Hermeneutic in Early Christianity* (Grand Rapids: Eerdmans, 1978), pp. 173–81.
14. Robert H. Gundry, *The Use of the Old Testament in Matthew*, p. 3.
15. Henry M. Shires, *Finding the Old Testament in the New*, p. 16.
16. R. H. Gundry, *The Use of the OT in the New*, p. 3.
17. Joseph A. Fitzmyer, "The Use of Explicit Old Testament Quotations in Qumran Literature and in the New Testament," *NTS* 7 (1960–61):298. He labels this style: *le style anthologique*.

TYPES OF FORMAL QUOTATIONS

The writers of the NT sometimes present in the form of a single citation an assemblage of phrases or sentences drawn from two or more OT sources. This method is sometimes referred to as the *haraz* method. Thus, when our Lord expelled the merchants from the Temple, He exclaimed: "It is written, 'My house shall be called a house of prayer: but you have made it a den of robbers'" (Matt. 21:13; cf. Mark 11:17; Luke 19:46). The first part of His citation was drawn from Isaiah 56:7, whereas the second half came from Jeremiah 7:11. Romans 11:8-10 appropriates three OT texts, namely, Isaiah 29:10; Deuteronomy 29:4; and Psalm 68:23ff. Such chain-stringing of quotes can also be seen in Luke 1:17 (using Mal. 3:1 and 4:5-6); Acts 1:20 (using Pss. 69:25 and 109:8); Romans 9:25-26 (from Hos. 2:23 and 1:10); Romans 9:33 (using Isa. 28:16 and 8:14); Romans 11:26-27 (from Isa. 59:20-21 and 27:9); Romans 15:9-12 (from Pss. 18:49; 117:1; Deut. 32:43; Isa. 11:10); 2 Corinthians 6:16 (using Lev. 26:11-12 and Ezek. 37:27); and Galatians 3:8 (using Gen. 12:3 and 18:18). The longest chain of quotes appears to be in Romans 3:10-18, where a single introductory formula, "as it is written," is followed by verses from Psalms 14:1-3 (paralleled by Ps. 53:1-3); 5:9; 140:3; 10:7; Isaiah 59:7-8 and Psalm 36:1.

A few citations present the unique problem of an unknown OT source. In the whole NT, there are only four clear instances of this category. Matthew 2:23: "He will be called a Nazarene"; John 7:38: "Out of his belly shall flow rivers of living water"; Ephesians 5:14: "Awake, O sleeper and arise from the dead, and Christ shall shine upon you"; and James 4:5: "The spirit that dwells in us lusts to envy" are the usual examples of this phenomena. Whereas approximate language may be found for most of those four citations, they nowhere occur in those exact words and, therefore, are "quotations of substance"[18] of the OT or "concise summaries of the teaching of various parts of the older Scriptures."[19]

TEXT TYPES EMPLOYED

What text type does the NT prefer when citing the OT? The substantial majority of these quotes and allusions reflect the Septuagint (hereafter LXX). Of course, there are some quotes that conform to

18. Franklin Johnson, *The Quotations of the New Testament from the Old Considered in the Light of General Literature* (Philadelphia: American Baptist, 1896), pp. 410-15.
19. Frederic Gardiner, *The Old and New Testaments in Their Mutual Relations* (New York: James Pott, 1885), p. 310.

the Hebrew (i.e., the Masoretic text) such as Matthew 2:15, 18; 9:13; 12:7; 27:46. But there are citations that vary from both the Hebrew and the Greek, for example, Matthew 4:7; 13:14, 15; 19:4 and others that reflect elements of both the Hebrew and the Greek, such as Matthew 15:4*a,b;* 19:5, 18, 19; Mark 12:36; John 10:34.

That the LXX was the principal Bible of the early church can hardly be refuted if one is to judge on the basis of the text form of the OT most frequently used throughout the entire NT in quotations. D. M. Turpie concluded that the NT writers departed from the LXX far less than from the Masoretic text.[20] H. B. Swete was able to show that the LXX recension agreed more frequently with Alexandrinus than with Vaticanus even though, in some cases, Theodotion was supported against the LXX.[21] That judgment has continued as the fairest assessment of text types, for Krister Stendahl concluded: "Swete's statement about the relation between the New Testament and the Septuagint holds good today; indeed, it has become apparent that it has more solid foundations than Swete himself could have known."[22]

"The use of the LXX in quoting," comments Roger Nicole, "does not indicate that the New Testament writers have thought of this version as inspired in itself."[23] The only point at which the text cited need be totally authentic, according to the high views of Scripture fostered by the Reformers and their doctrinal heirs today, is where that word or limited word set *on which the argument hinges* in those passages when the appeal to the OT is for the purpose of authorita tively supporting the doctrine, practice, or view being presented in the NT. The rest of the citation may be a free, paraphrastic summary of the general essence or substance of the OT passage. Hence, no decisions may be made about the "inspired" text form based on the recensional form of the OT texts used in these NT quotes.

The precise reasons for the wide variations in the exactness of the text form in the NT citations are not always known. Numerous explanations have been suggested by C. H. Toy, D. M. Turpie, F. Johnson, and H. Gough.[24] Among the reasons usually given in the past are: quotations from memory, translation problems of moving from Hebrew or Aramaic to Greek, and the accessibility of varying recen-

20. D. M. Turpie, *The Old Testament in the New* (London: 1868, 1872). See also the fine survey article by B. F. C. Atkinson, "The Textual Background of the Use of the Old Testament by the New," *Journal of Transactions of the Victorian Institute* 79 (1947):39–69.
21. H. B. Swete, *Introduction to the Old Testament in Greek* (Cambridge: U. Press, 1900), pp. 395, 403.
22. Krister Stendahl, *The School of St. Matthew*, p. 171.
23. Roger Nicole, "New Testament Use," p. 143.
24. H. Gough, *The New Testament Quotations* (London: Walton and Maberly, 1855). The other three writers and their works have all been cited previously.

sions of the Greek Bible such as LXX A or LXX B. But since the
discovery of the Dead Sea Scrolls, wherein the *pesher* method of
exegesis is found, it has become much more common for scholars to
explain the variations between the OT Hebrew form of the text and
its context with the apparent or real variations in the NT as stemming
from exegetical causes. In the pesher method, the quoter or commentator simply incorporated into the body of his quotation his own
application and modern interpretation. Whereas older studies had
confined themselves to noting such exegetical adaptations of older
texts as changes in person, number, tense, mode, and voice of verbs,
or substitutions of pronouns for nouns and the like, more recent
scholarship has tended to drop its concern for the original context
from which the text was drawn or for the truth-intention of the OT
author in favor of the more modern emphasis on *ad hoc* renderings
of those citations or meanings that stress the reader's views and needs
as being more normative than any prior claims of the quotation in its
own OT setting. Whether this latter and more modern explanation
will stand up to the demands of the texts themselves must be seen
later on in this work. But note well that the prevailing mode of
scholarship has decided this question already as a *fait accompli.*
Krister Stendahl, Earle Ellis, and Robert Gundry, to name only a few,
feel that such a *pesher* exegetical factor convincingly accounts for
the material divergence between the Hebrew OT text and the Greek
NT.

CLASSES OF OT QUOTATIONS

The exegetical explanation for the variations that occur between
the original text and context of the OT quotation and its adaptation
in the NT raises the whole area of the ways in which writers made
use of the OT. It is clear that the OT texts are being cited for more
reasons than to authorize a particular stance or teaching as canonical.
What is the scope of their uses? What hermeneutical methods did the
NT writers employ? And are those same methods exegetically and
theologically acceptable today?

Frederic Gardiner listed four general classes in which the NT used
the OT quotations. They were:

1. For purposes of argument,
2. As expressions of general truth belonging alike to all ages,
3. As illustrations, and
4. Simply as sacred and familiar words expressing, without regard
   to their original use, that which writers wished to say[25]

25. Frederic Gardiner, *The Old and New Testaments*, p. 312.

This appears to be a likely enough list and one that adequately covers all the phenomena of NT citations of the OT.

Joseph Fitzmyer examined forty-two OT passages as used at Qumran and decided on these four classes:

1. The *literal* or *historical* class, in which the OT is quoted in the same sense it was intended by the original OT writers;
2. The *modernization* class in which the OT text originally had reference to an event contemporaneous with that OT text, but which was nevertheless vague enough to be applied to some new event;
3. The *accommodation* class, which modified or deliberately changed the OT context to adapt it to a new situation or purpose;
4. The *eschatological* class, which promised or threatened something that was to be done in the *eschaton*, an event still future to those using the quotation.

Fitzmyer illustrates each of those categories in the NT after surveying the Qumran evidence for the same fourfold division of classes. The literal or historical sense of OT passages can be found in the Scriptures Christ quoted to Satan in His temptation experience (Matt. 4:4, 6, 7, 10; Luke 4:4, 8, 10, 12 quoting Deut. 8:3; Ps. 91:11; Deut. 6:16; 6:13). Also, John 6:31 quotes Psalm 78.24 about feeding the fathers in the desert with manna the same way the NT uses it. Again, John 10:34 makes the same point about men being called "god(s)" as Psalm 82:6. There are likewise numerous points of univocal meaning between Stephen's speech in Acts 7 and his resumé of Israel's history (e.g., Acts 7:3 quoting Gen. 12:1).[26]

As examples of NT modernization of OT texts, Fitzmyer[27] points to Matthew 4:15–16. To validate the Galilean ministry of Christ, the words of the Immanuel prophecy (Isa. 8:23—9:1) with their promise of a great light in Galilee and liberation from the Assyrian menace are used. The words are also general enough in Isaiah 61:1–2 to be used by Christ in His synagogue reading of Luke 4:16–21 and applied to Himself. In a similar fashion, Isaiah 49:8 is used by Paul in 2 Corinthians 6:1–2 of a welcome time and a day of deliverance—not Isaiah's day of return from captivity, but the time of his own preaching and ministry among the Corinthians.

Fitzmyer feels that Christ's appeal in Exodus 3:6 (or chaps. 15–16) to substantiate the resurrectability of the dead is a clear case of

26. Joseph A. Fitzmyer, "The Use of Explicit OT Quotations," pp. 308–9.
27. Ibid., pp. 315–16.

accommodating a NT text,[28] for there is no reference at all to resurrection in the statement, "I am ... the God of Abraham, the God of Isaac and the God of Jacob." Therefore, the original sense of the context has been disregarded, claims Fitzmyer. Another case is Paul's appeal to Isaiah 52:5, where God's name is subjected to abuse and dishonor because of the Babylonian captivity and the sad state of affairs for the Jews. Yet, Paul's use of this text in Romans 2:23–24 has disgrace coming to God's name because the Jews who boast about the law do not observe it. Likewise, Paul's use of Psalm 68:19 in Ephesians 4:8 atomizes the text to extract the phrases "he went up" and "he gave" for his own novel use, thereby wrenching it from its context.

The eschatological class has fewer examples in the NT than other classes.[29] Fitzmyer portrays Paul as looking forward in time in Romans 9:26–27 as he quotes Isaiah 59:20–21 and 27:9 to explain why only a partial blindness has come to Israel, which lasts until all the heathen have come in, and then all Israel will be saved. Or, Matthew's quoting, "Depart from me, I never knew you" from Psalm 6:9 while projecting it into "that day" when many will say "Lord! Lord!" (Matt. 7:23). Likewise, Romans 12:19, "Vengeance is mine, I will repay, says the Lord" (citing Deut. 32:35) is put in an eschatological setting by Paul.

Fitzmyer is careful to avoid the impression that those four categories exhaust all the uses of the OT in the New,[30] but all four are represented and parallel the Qumran use of the OT. He concluded that both Qumran and the NT used the OT *in general* as literal exegesis in opposition to the allegorical schools of Philo and Alexandria, even though noncharacteristic allegorization did occur at Qumran and in the NT. Thus, it is not *strictly a literal* exegesis if by that we intend the original meaning and context of the words quoted, but it is an exegesis based on the words quoted even though their historical settings meant very little to the NT writers.[31] We will wish to examine that conclusion in the chapters that follow. Fitzmyer's third class, the accommodation class, is especially suspicious and needs to be examined more closely in the NT.

In one more list of classes, Jack Weir offers us five NT methods for interpreting the OT.[32] They are:

---

28. Ibid., pp. 324–25.
29. Ibid., pp. 329–30.
30. Ibid., pp. 306, 330, n 2.
31. Ibid., pp. 330–31.
32. Jack Weir, "Analogous Fulfillment: The Use of the Old Testament in the New Testament," *Perspectives in Religious Studies* 9 (1982):67–70.

1. The *literal historical* method, in which the OT quotations have the same meaning in the New as they had in their original contexts;
2. The *pesher* method applied OT texts directly to contemporary events of the NT writer apart from any consideration of their original historical setting, often modifying those OT texts in the process to fit the new theological and historical needs of the community;
3. The *typological* method focuses on six kinds of divinely ordained and preestablished similarities between the OT "type" and the NT "antitype," namely, persons (Adam), institutions (sacrifices), offices (priesthood), events (the Exodus), actions (lifting up the brazen serpent), and things (Tabernacle);
4. The *allegorical* method, such as the Hagar and Ishmael treatment in Galatians 4:21–31 and the Melchizedek episode in Hebrews 7:1–10, focuses on the theological content while regarding the historical setting of the OT text and the truth-intention of its author as only imagery and drapery through which that theological idea may be presented; and
5. The *theological* method sets NT theological motifs such as the purpose of God, the covenant, salvation-history, or Christology against the OT background, not in any mechanical or legalistic manner, but within broad, general traditions. This method must not be restricted to a single motif nor must the horizon of one Testament be chosen over the other, for the two Testaments in dialectic create a new context that results in more than the sum of the parts of both

Those then are the choices before us. Again, we must raise our most direct questions against Weir's *pesher*, allegorical, and theological methods while we attempt to sharpen our definition on his literal and typological methods. This point is especially critical when we come to those OT passages that are cited to establish a fact or doctrine. We cannot withhold our full support to Frederic Gardiner, who concluded in 1885 that:

> in all quotations which are used argumentatively, or to establish any fact or doctrine, it is obviously necessary that the passage in question should be fairly cited according to its real intent and meaning, in order that the argument drawn from it may be valid. There has been much rash criticism of some of these passages, and the assertion has been unthinkingly made that the Apostles, and especially St. Paul, brought up in rabbinical schools of thought, quoted Scriptures after a rabbinical

and inconsequential fashion. A patient and careful examination of the passages themselves will remove such misapprehension.[33]

THE "TESTIMONY BOOK" HYPOTHESIS

One more aspect of NT citations must be tackled: the alleged existence of a collection of OT prooftexts gathered into *testimonia* as an anti-Jewish apologetic that later served as the source for the *Vorverständnis* and exegesis of the early church as it wrote the NT with a keen eye on these "testimony books." J. Rendall Harris argued that such collection must have existed and antedated all extant Christian writings.[34] Harris postulated his testimonia theory to explain four problems in OT citations in the New: (1) The attribution of citations to wrong authors (e.g., Mark 1:2–3 ascribes Malachi [3:1] to Isaiah [40:3] and Matthew 27:9–10 attributes to Jeremiah [LXX, 18:1] a text from Zechariah [11:13]); (2) the "formula quotations" in Matthew in which ten of his citations (four distinctive ones in the infancy narratives and five in common with the other synoptics) have a special introductory formula and identify more closely with the Hebrew text and not with the LXX; (3) citations that diverge from the commonly used text of the LXX suggested to Harris the previous existence of those quotations in a *testimonia* collection; and the chief reason, (4) composite quotations where quotations are strung together without intervening comments or identification of their author or authors, such as in Romans 9:25–29; 10:15–21; 11:8–10; 11:26; 11:34–35; 15:9–12; 2 Corinthians 6:16–18, and are often organized around a *stichwort*, such as "heathen," "stone," or the like.[35]

The name *testimonia* was borrowed by Harris from a subtitle of a work by the third-century church father Cyprian.[36] Cyprian's work, in its first two books, is a collection of OT passages compiled for an apologetic purpose *adversus Iudaeos*. From the fourth cave of Qumran has come a similar collection entitled "4 Q *Florilegium*" (a *florilegia* is an anthology or collection) containing at least two OT passages (2 Sam. 7:11–14 and Amos 9:11) introduced by the introductory formula "as it is written." Another Qumran fragment is "4 Q Testimonia" and contains these biblical passages: Deuteronomy 5:28–29; 18:18–19; Numbers 24:15–17; and Deuteronomy 33:8–11 along with the curious

33. Frederic Gardiner, *The Old and New Testaments*, pp. 317–18.
34. J. Rendall Harris, *Testimonies*, 2 vols. (Cambridge: Cambridge U., 1916, 1920).
35. J. Rendall Harris, 1:18. Whereas the idea did not originate with F. C. Burkitt, he was the first to use the name *testimonia* to identify a systematic collection of OT texts; F. C. Burkitt, *The Gospel History and Its Transmission* (Edinburgh, 1907), p. 126 as cited by Joseph A. Fitzmyer, "'4 Q Testimonia' and the New Testament," *Theological Studies* 18 (1957):521–22.
36. Cyprian, *Ad Quirinum: Testimoniorum libritries.*

nonmessianic and not entirely scriptural section provisionally entitled "4 Q Psalms of Joshua." In addition to those two Qumran texts, C. H. Roberts published a Greek text in 1936 bearing the identification, "John Ryland's Papyrus, Greek Number 460."[37] That two-column fragment, when put together with two other scraps from an Oslo papyrus codex published by G. Rudberg in 1923,[38] contains the following fourth-century A.D. collection of OT verses in Greek: Isaiah 42:3–4; 66:18–19; Isaiah 52:15; 53:1–3, 6–7, 11–12; an unidentified verse; Genesis 26:13–14; 2 Chronicles 1:12; and Deuteronomy 29:8, 11. Thus, there is some circumstantial evidence favoring the existence of such a collection as Harris wished to identify with Papias's *Logia*, which antedate the NT.

Harris's proposal, offered in 1916 and 1920, while exercising great influence, waited for the searching criticism of C. H. Dodd in 1957.[39] In spite of the significance of this proposal, Dodd rejected the testimony book hypothesis; that is, that there was a primitive anthology of isolated prooftexts to be used in controversy with the Jews. Dodd's counterproposal did acknowledge that there was a real consensus, although largely oral, behind the repeated use of OT texts. Dodd focused on fifteen important texts used more than once in the NT. Those and related texts tended to fall into three groupings: (1) apocalyptic-eschatological texts; (2) texts on the new Israel; and (3) Scriptures on the Servant of the Lord, the righteous Sufferer. Dodd then argued that those citations reflected "a certain method of biblical study,"[40] for the isolated texts were not meant as prooftexts (much less an anti-Jewish apologetic as Harris wanted it); instead, those citations were pointers to the larger contexts in which they were found. Thus, Matthew's citation of Isaiah 7:14 in Matthew 1:23 probably had in mind Isaiah 6:1—9:7, even as the phrase "God with us" (Isa. 8:8, 10) and the frequent use of Isaiah 6–9 elsewhere in the NT shows. Thus, these shorter citations were only outcroppings and signs that pointed to the larger contexts from which those quotes came.

A. C. Sundberg found that Dodd's proposal was just as vulnerable as Harris's *testimonia* hypothesis.[41] Sundberg pointed out that 42 percent of the 423 OT chapters cited in the NT were cited by more than one NT writer, whereas 71 percent of the 56 chapters of Isaiah quoted in the NT are also quoted by more than one NT writer. Also,

---

37. C. H. Roberts, *Two Biblical Papyri in the John Rylands Library Manchester* (Manchester, 1936), pp. 47–62.
38. As cited by Joseph A. Fitzmyer, "4 Q Testimonia," p. 528.
39. C. H. Dodd, *According to the Scriptures: The Substructure of New Testament Theology* (London: Nisbet, 1957).
40. Ibid., p. 126.
41. Albert C. Sundberg, Jr., "On Testimonies," *Novum Testamentum* 3 (1959):268–81.

more than a third of 101 Psalms cited in NT are found in more than one NT writer.[42] Furthermore, those OT books which on Dodd's assumptions comprised the Bible of the early church did not actually appear predominately in the entire NT. Sundberg's thesis tended to undermine Dodd's main contention that most OT quotations in the New were dependent on their OT context for a proper understanding. Instead, what Sundberg discerned as divergent uses of the same text argued against any theory of a common exegetical method. His argument, in part, went this way:

> II Sam. vii. 14 is interpreted in Heb. i:5 as God speaking to Jesus ...; however, Rev. xxi 7 relates this saying to faithful Christians. Ps. ii 1 is related in Acts iv 25–27 to the events of Jesus' trial and crucifixion; in Rev. xii 18 it is related to the final judgment. The preaching of peace from Isa. lii 7 is depicted in Acts x 36 as fulfilled by Jesus but Paul relates the saying to the preaching of the gospel by Christians (Rom. x 15; cf Eph. vi 15).... The prophecy in Zech. xii 10 is quoted in Jh. xix 37 as a prediction of the piercing of Jesus' side after his death...; Rev. 1:7 uses the same passage as a prediction of the second coming (cf Matt. xxiv. 30).[43]

The effect of Sundberg's contribution tended to move biblical research away from Harris's search for an exact source for most, if not all, of the OT quotations in the New in favor of a new focus on the *manner* and *purpose* of appropriating the OT. Two men modified Dodd's stance: Krister Stendahl,[44] who analyzed OT quotations in Matthew with a view to recovering their function and setting both in Matthew and in the pre-Matthean tradition, and Barnabas Lindars,[45] who saw a "shift of application"[46] and a "modification of text"[47] for apologetical purposes to support the changing situation of the church and its emerging *kerygma*.[48]

Aside from the attempts of both of those writers to read a development of primitive Christian kerygma in and through the OT quotations (a highly risky business, to say the least), their fundamental significance for our purposes here is their agreement on the impact of Qumran *pesher* exegesis on the NT writers. Both Stendahl and Lindars formulated their concepts of early Christian exegesis from

42. See Tables I and II in A. C. Sundberg, Jr., "On Testimonies," pp. 272–73.
43. Ibid., pp. 278–79.
44. Krister Stendahl, *The School of St. Matthew.*
45. Barnabas Lindars, *New Testament Apologetic: The Doctrinal Significance of the Old Testament Quotations* (Philadelphia: Westminster, 1961).
46. Ibid., pp. 17–24.
47. Ibid., pp. 24–28.
48. Ibid., p. 30.

what they believed they observed in the function and use of OT quotations. Consequently, in their view, texts were chosen and, at times, even modified to fit the historical and theological needs of the community.

For Lindars, as with Dodd, the primary meaning must be ascertained by referring to the whole passage. Furthermore, passages have been selected where the events of redemption are the regulative factor and provide the key to the meaning of Scripture.[49] Nevertheless, the events contemporary with the NT writer are the realities to which the OT pointed, and this method of exegesis is bound to lead to "a certain amount of wresting the text, to say the least."[50] Deliberate alterations and modifications are introduced by the NT writers to elucidate the obscurities in the text and to highlight the convictions of the NT writers. Such practices constituted a "school of exegesis." Thus, we have to be concerned with three things here: (1) the NT citations of the OT as representing a theological tradition centering on redemption, (2) a "school" of exegesis, and (3) a *pesher* method of interpretation which that school employs.

Earle E. Ellis, while admitting the apostle Paul did not use the *pesher* method extensively in his citations of the OT, also argued that Paul often did integrate his exposition into the substance of the quotations themselves.[51] He then quoted Manson approvingly who said:

> We are long accustomed to distinguish carefully between the text which—in more senses than one—is sacred, and the commentary upon it and exposition of it. We tend to think of the text as objective fact and interpretation as subjective opinion. It may be doubted the early Jewish and Christian translators and expositors of Scripture made any such sharp distinction. For them the meaning of the text was of primary importance; and they seem to have had greater confidence than we moderns in their ability to find it. Once found, it became a clear duty to express it; and accurate reproduction of the traditional wording of the Divine oracles took second place to publication of what was held to be their essential meaning and immediate application.[52]

THE ARGUMENTATIVE USE OF THE OT

Enough has been said to see the shape of the problem before contemporary biblical scholarship. The issues are massive and wide-

49. Ibid., p. 17.
50. Ibid., p. 15.
51. Earle E. Ellis, *Paul's Use of the OT*, pp. 145–48.
52. T. W. Manson, "The Argument from Prophecy," *JTS* 46 (1945):135 as cited by Earle E. Ellis, *Paul's Use of the OT*, p. 146.

ranging. For our part, however, at the heart of the whole debate lies those passages from the OT appropriated by the New in which their purpose is to establish doctrine or fact. In those argumentative texts, the NT writers used the OT apologetically with a view to convincing intransigent Jewish listeners that neither Christ nor Christianity was some new or unrelated artiface of men on the contemporary scene. It, in fact, was exactly what could have been expected—and that in detail—had the OT writers been heeded. The constant challenge was—search the Scriptures, for these are the authenticating credentials that validate Christ, His claims, and this group of believers.

Whereas both Jewish and Christian believers often would trifle with the Scriptures for devotional and meditative purposes, one would be hard-pressed to find any apologetic value in appealing to such procedures as *midrash, pesher,* allegory, or the like to validate the claims of what was regarded as an intrusion of an outside force.

Can that thesis be sustained? If we were to isolate some of those texts used argumentatively, would it be possible to show that their OT contexts had not been violated? That they, indeed, were used in the NT in a manner consistent with the single truth-intention of the original author? That claims for *pesher* and *midrash* in those texts were unwarranted? That their use of typology, and phenomena such as corporate solidarity, generic, and apotelesmatic prophecy[53] were not antithetical to those claims for single authorial intention of the OT meanings? It is those issues that we will address in this monograph.

---

53. *Apotelesmatic* comes from two Greek words, *apo,* "from," and *telein,* "to end"; hence, that view of predictive events that sees the present fulfillments as part and parcel of the final result or complete fulfillment.

PART 1

THE APOLOGETIC USE
OF THE OLD TESTAMENT
IN THE NEW

Introduction

Does the method of interpreting Scripture that Jesus and the apostles taught us differ from the principles that contemporary interpreters regard as sound exegesis? Or, are the methods of Jesus and the apostles of the NT closer to the practices of rabbinic midrash and Qumranian pesher? And, if they are, should we also follow that Christological and apostolic lead and reproduce their kind of exegesis[1] when we read or study the Bible?

To avoid confusion we are restricting our attention to that class of OT texts that are cited "for the purposes of argument."[2] It is in those texts more than in any other that we would expect the meaning of the OT text to be the same as the NT meaning. If this meaning could not be the agreed platform from which the discussion began, then what was the sense in appealing to OT texts that could be arbitrarily inflated with meaning to carry all sorts of subjective interpretations?

The NT writers believed that the OT writers spoke in such definite and recognizable ways that they anticipated the appearance, saving work, and ministry of One whom the NT writers identified as Jesus. Accordingly, Peter boldly declares in Acts 3:18: "What God foretold by the mouth of all prophets, that his Christ should suffer, God thus fulfilled." Therefore, it was no accident or the mere working of chance

1. Richard Longenecker formulated this question best in his article "Can We Reproduce the Exegesis of the New Testament?" *Tyndale Bulletin* 21 (1970):3–38; also see his *Biblical Exegesis in the Apostolic Period* (Grand Rapids: Eerdmans, 1975).
2. See the section "Classes of Old Testament Quotations" in our introductory chapter.

17

that had brought about those circumstances, but God Himself had worked the fulfillment of the OT! Likewise, in a large number of other cases, the events of the NT conformed to what "he spoke by the mouth of his holy prophets of old" (Luke 1:68-79) and "promised beforehand through his prophets in the Holy Scriptures" (Rom. 1:2). In fact, Jesus severely rebuked the disciples on the road to Emmaus for their failure "to believe all that the prophets had spoken" (Luke 24:25), for "everything *must* be fulfilled that was written about [Christ] in the law of Moses, the prophets, and the Psalms" (Luke 24:44).

The apostle Paul's preaching illustrated that same confident apologetic use of the OT. In Thessalonica, "he argued with them from the Scriptures [OT] explaining and proving that it was necessary for Christ to suffer and to rise from the dead" (Acts 17:2-3). In his announcement of the gospel, he repeated this same refrain: "Christ died for our sins in accordance with the Scriptures, he was buried, and he was raised on the third day in accordance with the Scriptures" (1 Cor. 15:3-4).

Paul's stance (as that of any other NT speaker or writer) was not that he was in his own person the center of gravity or the force that held together this new truth and gave it status, authority, and pertinence in the church. Instead of imposing on the OT his own judgment of its meaning, he strenuously contended that all fair interpreters of a straightforward reading of the text would agree that his claims for Jesus had already been anticipated by the law, the prophets, and the writings!

But, of course, that may actually be begging the question. Were the NT authors reading the OT text "straightforwardly," or did they unlock the "mysteries" (*rāzim*) the prophets recorded even as the teacher of righteousness did for his followers at Qumran in the Dead Sea community in which Habakkuk 2:1 was interpreted this way:

> And God told Habakkuk to write down the things that are going to come upon the last generation, but the fulfillment of the end-time he did not make known to him. And when it says, *so that he can run who reads it,* the interpretation of it concerns the Teacher of Righteousness, to whom God made known all the mysteries of the words of his servants the prophets.[3]

F. F. Bruce, along with many other current exegetes, believes that the apostle Peter stated a "strikingly similar"[4] doctrine to the Qumran teacher of righteousness in 1 Peter 1:10-12. In Bruce's view, "Peter's

---

3. From 1Qp Hab vii. 1-5 as cited in Maurya P. Horgan, *Pesharim: Qumran Interpretations of Biblical Books* (Washington, D.C.: Catholic Biblical Association, 1979), p. 12.
4. F. F. Bruce, *Biblical Exegesis in the Qumran Texts* (London: Tyndale, 1960), p. 76.

claim is, in effect, that things had been concealed from the prophets—things vitally affecting the interpretation of the words which the prophets spoke—[but which things] had been revealed to himself and to his fellow apostles."[5]

No text has appeared more frequently in the argument against the prophets' right to say first of all what they intended their texts to mean than 1 Peter 1:10–12, which says:

> Concerning which salvation the prophets, who prophesied of the grace that was to come to you, inquired and searched diligently, searching what, or what manner of time [NIV, "the time and circumstances"] to which the Spirit of Christ, which was in them, was pointing when he predicted the sufferings of Christ, and the glory that should follow. Unto whom it was revealed, that not unto themselves, but unto us they did minister the things, which are now reported to you by them that have preached the Gospel unto you.

The disputed Greek phrase in this *crux interpretum* is *eis tina ē poion kairon.* The *Revised Standard Version,* the *Berkeley,* the *New American Standard Version,* the *Amplified Bible,* and the footnote in the *New English Bible* all translated this phrase to the effect that the prophets inquired and searched for "what *person* or time" (emphasis ours) was indicated in the Scriptures they were writing. This rendering of the Greek text would vindicate the widespread belief that the prophets "wrote better than they know,"[6] leaving the mysteries of their exact referents for NT authors to unlock just as the teacher of righteousness functioned in the Qumran community. On the other hand, the King James Version, Goodspeed, Williams, the *New English Bible,* and such paraphrases as *The Living Bible,* Phillips, and Wuest all have the prophets puzzling only over the *time,* but not the *person,* indicated in their prophecies.

However, this question is not unsolvable; it can be decided by an analysis of the grammar and syntax of those verses. We must ask this question: Can one dissociate *tina* from *kairon* and render it "in reference to *whom,*" or must *tina* and *poion* both be left to modify *kairon?*

Greek grammarians respond overwhelmingly in favor of the second option. A. T. Robertson cites Acts 7:49 as an instance of this tautological usage where *tis = poios.*[7] Blass, DeBrunner, and Funk likewise

5. Ibid.
6. For a full discussion of this slogan, see Otto Friedrich Bollnow, "What Does It Mean to Understand a Writer Better Than He Understood Himself?" *Philosophy Today* 23 (1979):16–28, and Walter C. Kaiser, Jr., *Toward an Exegetical Theology* (Grand Rapids: Baker, 1981), pp. 34–36, 111–14.
7. A. T. Robertson, *A Grammar of the Greek New Testament in Light of Historical Research,* 4th ed. (Nashville: Broadman, 1923), pp. 735–36.

suggest that *tis* may be combined with *poios* as "a tautology for emphasis" with the resulting translation of searching for "what time."[8] That same opinion is set forth by Arndt and Gingrich, who render it as "what time or what kind of time."[9] Many of the most influential commentators, such as Charles Briggs, Edward G. Selwyn, and John Edward Hunther could be cited as favoring the same position.[10]

Definite corroboration for understanding *eis tina ē poion kairon* as handling only a single question as the object of the prophets' searching and inquiring (for the time) rather than treating two questions (the person *and* the time) can be obtained from the prophet's own words in this very context. There were five things the prophets were certain of when they wrote their texts. They knew they were predicting that: (1) the Messiah would come; (2) the Messiah would suffer; (3) the Messiah would be glorified (in kingly splendor); (4) the order of events 2 and 3 was that the suffering came first, and then the glorious period followed; and (5) this message had been revealed to the prophets not only for their own day, but also for a future generation such as the church of Peter's audience (v. 12).

What then were the prophets all stirred up about in their searching and inquiring? It was the question of *time*—the same issue on which we, too, are still ignorant. The fact that the prophets' visions and prophecies were appointed "for many days to come" (Ezek. 12:27), or for "that time" (Zeph. 3:20), only led all the more to the question What time? or When shall these things be? (Luke 17:20; Acts 1:6–7). Nevertheless, even though the precise time was unknown, there still were those who knew that they were waiting for the Messiah. Among such knowledgeable people were Simeon (see his *nunc dimittus* in Luke 2:25–33) and Anna, who represented "those who were waiting for the consolation of Israel" (Luke 2:36–38). They managed to do what the stubborn "fools" on the road to Emmaus could have done, but failed to do (Luke 24:25–27).

Therefore, 1 Peter 1:10–12 does not teach that these men were curious, yet often ignorant as to exact impact or meaning of what they wrote and predicted. Theirs was not a search for the *meaning* of

8. F. Blass and A. DeBrunner, *A Greek Grammar of the New Testament*, rev., trans. R. W. Funk (Chicago: U. of Chicago, 1967), p. 155, §198.
9. W. F. Arndt and F. W. Gingrich, *A Greek-English Lexicon of the New Testament* (Chicago: U. of Chicago, 1957), p. 691, s.v. *poios*.
10. Charles Biggs, *International Critical Commentary on I Peter* (Edinburg: T & T Clark, 1901), pp. 107-8; Edward G. Selwyn, *The First Epistle of St. Peter* (London: Macmillan, 1955), pp. 134–38; and John Edward Hunther, *Critical and Exegetical Handbook to the General Epistles* (New York: Funk and Wagnall, 1887), pp. 218–24. Richard Schultz has called my attention to the same construction, only in reverse order, in Dionysius (or Longinus); *poia de kai tis autē*, "what and what manner of road is this?" (*On the Sublime*, XIII, 2 in *The Loeb Classical Library*, Aristotle XXIII, p. 199.)

what they wrote; it was an inquiry into the *temporal* aspects of the *subject*, which went beyond what they wrote. It must be carefully noted that the scope of the subject is invariably larger than any set of verbal meanings contributed by a given writer of Scripture to that subject. Nevertheless, the writers can and do have an *adequate* understanding of the subject on which they write even if it is not a *comprehensive* control of all the particulars and parts that belong to that subject.

The importance of this discussion on whether the prophets "wrote better than they knew" is extremely critical when it comes to treating those passages from the OT that the NT writers cite to establish a fact or doctrine as one that was known and announced centuries before its NT fulfillment. Frederic Gardiner already in 1885 anticipated much of the current tendency in scholarship to attribute those citations to various kinds of rabbinical modifications of the meaning of a text or shifts in meaning by some major reorientation of those texts. In Gardiner's view, the reverse was true. We have already noted that he judged that:

> In all quotations which are used argumentatively in order to establish any fact or doctrine, it is obviously necessary that the passage in question should be fairly cited according to its real interest and meaning, in order that the argument drawn from it may be valid. There has been much rash criticism.... that the Apostles, and especially St. Paul, brought up in rabbinical schools of thought quoted Scriptures after a rabbinical and inconsequential fashion. A patient and careful examination of the passages themselves will remove such misapprehension.[11]

The apostles were so confident of their equating the person, ministry, and office of Jesus with those OT anticipations that they could, at times, threaten their audiences as Peter did on the porch of the Temple:

> Repent then, and turn to God, so that your sins may be wiped out, that times of refreshing may come from the Lord, and that he may send the Christ, who has been appointed for you—even Jesus. He must remain in heaven until the time comes for God to restore everything, as he promised long ago through his holy prophets. For Moses said, "The Lord your God will raise up for you a prophet like me from among your own people; you must listen to everything he tells you. Anyone who does not listen to him will be completely cut off from among his people." (NIV, Acts 3:19–23 with citation from Deut. 18:15, 18, 19)

11. Frederic Gardiner, *The Old and New Testaments in Their Mutual Relations* (New York: James Pott, 1885), pp. 317–18.

This certainly is miles apart from such estimates as those of R. S. McConnell, who concluded that the "Old Testament prophecies were not regarded as authoritative in themselves.... Rather the prophecies which were important were determined by the life of Jesus."[12] However, the apostles betray no evidence that they were under some compulsion to make the details of the life of Christ fit some predetermined schema forced on the OT by giving the OT a different sense than what it originally had and then building their case on the assumption that the original passage had the same sense they had attributed to it.

In an attempt to remove the argument from the hands of OT exegetes who seem to assure us of such minimal messianic references, many resort to appealing to Daniel 12:6-9 in an attempt to show that the prophets did not understand the import of what God suggested to their minds. Often, when these understandably disturbed interpreters are shown that the dependence on 1 Peter 1:10-12 for this "mystery" hypothesis is blocked by fair exegesis, they will then flee to Daniel 12:6-9 for refuge.

> And one of them said to the man clothed in linen, which was upon the waters of the river, How long shall it be to the end of these wonders? And I heard the man clothed in linen, which was up on the waters of the river, when he held up his right hand and his left hand unto heaven, and swore by him that liveth for ever and ever that it shall be for a time, times and an half; and when he shall have accomplished to scatter the power of the holy people, all these things shall be finished. And I heard, but I understood not: then said I, "O my Lord, what shall be the end of these things?" He replied, "Go on your way, Daniel, because the words are closed up and sealed until the time of the end." (Dan. 12:6-9)

So there it is, say many: "I heard, but I understood not." However, before we conclude too much, let us ask, What was it that Daniel did not understand? Was it the words he was speaking?

Not at all! First, the words he did not understand were those of the angel and not his own! Second, the fact that these words of the angel were to be "closed up and sealed until the time of the end" was no more a sign that these events were to remain *unexplained* until the end time than was the equivalent expression used in Isaiah 8:16, "Bind up the testimony, seal the law." There, as here, the "sealing" of the

---

12. R. S. McConnell, "Law and Prophecy in Matthew's Gospel: The Authority and Use of the Old Testament" (Theologische Dissertationen, II Babel: Friedrich Reinhardt, 1969), p. 138 (emphasis his) as cited by Douglas J. Moo, *The Old Testament in the Gospel Passion Narrative* (Sheffield: Almond, 1983), p. 380.

testimonies was a reference primarily to the *certainty* of the predicted
events. Third, Daniel's question in verse 8 involved a temporal question: "What shall be the end of these things?" One of the angels had
asked in verse 6, "How long shall it be to the end of these wonders?"
But Daniel asked a different question: What would be the state of
affairs at the close of the time, times, and an half? However, God gave
him no further revelation on this question. Therefore, the "sealing up"
of the prophecy only indicated its *certainty,* not its hiddenness.

Daniel, nevertheless, did understand what was being shown him.
So clear was Daniel's understanding of the meaning of his prophecy
and so dramatic was its effect on him that he "was overcome and lay
sick for some days" (RSV,* Daniel 8:27).

We conclude that Daniel did understand all aspects of his prophecy
except in two areas: (1) the temporal aspects (an exclusion we share
even to this present day and one noted as well in 1 Peter 1:10–12); and
(2) the request for added information beyond what had already been
revealed to him.

There is, of course, a sense in which we now do understand the
predictions of the prophets and apostles better than they did. Consider
the difference between a man who visits a country and describes it
and one who writes about it only from the perspective of extensive
studies, but who never personally visited that country. Surely, such a
distinction contributes little to the question about an author's understanding of his own meanings. What we have in this illustration is the
confusion between fullness of consequences or fullness of a total
subject and the validity, truthfulness, and accuracy of all contributions to that subject. And should that lead to the argument that God
is the real Author of Scripture, it would still make no important
difference. God did not make the writers omniscient. Rather, He
imparted just as much revelation as they needed to make their
message effective for that moment in history and for the future
contributions to the whole process of revelation.

This introduction to the apologetic use of the OT could be extended,
but more benefit can come from considering three alleged difficult
cases (Psalm 16; Hosea 11:1; and Jeremiah 31:15) than from all the
theoretical discussions. For example, did the psalmist in Psalm 16:10
make a prediction about the Messiah when he said, "Thou wilt not
leave my soul in hell, neither wilt thou suffer thine Holy One to see
corruption"? Or, was the psalmist merely expressing a devout sentiment that might very properly be expressed by any devout man in
any age, given the proper conditions? Can we show from the OT
context, grammar, and syntax that the speaker or writer intended as
much as the apostle Peter obviously derived from it in Acts 2:29–33?

* *Revised Standard Version.*

2
Foreseeing and Predicting the Resurrection
Psalm 16 and Acts 2:29–33

Few psalms simultaneously raise as many important methodological and theological questions as does Psalm 16. Yet, it was this
psalm that received one of the honored places in the early Christian
church when it served as one of the scriptural bases for Peter's
message on the day of Pentecost and Paul's address at Antioch of
Pisidia.

However, in spite of the high estimate given to this psalm, exegetes
must squarely face the hermeneutical and theological questions arising from the distinctively messianic use made of it. Were the various
fulfillments that the apostles attributed to this text explicitly present
in the psalmist's purposes and consciousness when he wrote the
psalm? Or, was there some valid system or legitimate principle of
interpretation that, while it exceeded the author's known truth intentions, nevertheless was acceptable to God as well as to sympathetic
and potentially hostile listeners?

THE NATURE OF THE MESSIANIC HOPE

THE SINGLE MEANING OF THE TEXT

The absolute necessity of establishing a single sense to any writing,
much less to Scripture, has been acknowledged by all interpreters—

occult or double sense we introduce an element of uncertainty in the sacred volume, and unsettle all scientific interpretation."[1]

Likewise Louis Berkhof argued: "Scripture has but a single sense, and is therefore susceptible to a scientific and logical investigation.... To accept a manifold sense ... makes any science of hermeneutics impossible and opens wide the door for all kinds of arbitrary interpretations."[2]

Unfortunately, many like Berkhof will turn right around and say almost in the same breath: "Scripture contains a great deal that does not find its explanation in history, nor in the secondary authors, but only in God as the *Actor primarius*."[3]

This raises the whole question of how far the psalmist (or any writer of Scripture) understood his own words and to what degree he was conscious of the way in which his words would be fulfilled if they pointed to some future development. Psalm 16, however, is an ideal psalm for a discussion of this question because Peter did authoritatively comment on this very question of the psalmist's understanding and precise consciousness of the future fulfillment. Therefore, we believe the dictum as stated most simply by John Owen will best unlock the depths even of the messianic psalms: "If the Scripture has more than one meaning, it has no meaning at all."[4]

THE FAILURE OF MODERN RATIONALISM

Many fear that the result of this kind of insistence will be the minimal results of a T. K. Cheyne whose blunt words summarize the results and attitude of another school of interpreters: "All these psalms are (let me say it again, for it concerns modern apologists to be frank) only messianic in a sense which is psychologically justifiable. They are, as I have shown, neither typically nor in the ordinary sense prophetically messianic."[5]

The difficulty evidenced in this approach is that it has failed to do justice to the Scripture writers' own sense of connection with an antecedent body of writings and the build-up of phrases, concepts, events, and expectations. Furthermore, most adherents to this view insist on declaring the historical setting and internal claims of the text to be totally or partially fraudulent in favor of more "modern" but subjectively imposed settings, writers, and occasions. The risks for

1. Milton S. Terry, *Biblical Hermeneutics* (Grand Rapids: Zondervan, n.d.), p. 413.
2. L. Berkhof, *Principles of Biblical Interpretation* (Grand Rapids: Baker, 1950), p. 57.
3. Ibid., p. 133.
4. J. Owen as cited by Terry, *Hermeneutics*, p. 493.
5. T. K. Cheyne, *The Origin and Religious Contents of the Psalter* (London: Kegan Paul, 1891), p. 340.

this kind of philosophy, which says that "the text is guilty until proven innocent," are extremely high.

Others will protest that in Jewish exegesis, Psalm 16 was not traditionally understood to refer to the Messiah, but was interpreted as the prayer of a godly man seeking preservation from death. Thus S. R. Driver concluded:

> The Psalm contains ... a great declaration of the faith and hope of an Old Testament saint.... But when we study it in itself, and consider it carefully in its original import, we see that v. 10 will not support the argument which the Apostles built upon it, and that the Psalm cannot be appealed to, in the way in which they appealed to it, as a proof of the resurrection of Christ.[6]

This is the issue that needs to be explored. It will be our contention here that Peter is most insistent that his use of Psalm 16:8–11 was not novel or self-imposed understanding but one that was first made by David himself.

The rationale for this kind of preunderstanding on the part of the NT writers varies among contemporary scholars. Some attempted to explain this alleged gap between the OT writer's meaning and the apparently new use made of that OT text by the Christian community and the apostolic writers as a new work of the Holy Spirit. That is the point of Prosper Grech:

> The Holy Spirit is not only the author of the written word, but also of its interpretation. Earle Ellis remarks [*Paul's Use of the OT* (London: 1957), 25ff] rightly that although all Scripture is the work of the Spirit, if it is not interpreted according to the Spirit, it remains *gramma*, not *graphē*.[7]

In other words, the text has been invested with a pregnant meaning whose plenary senses (*sensus plenior*) are known to the Holy Spirit and released as He will to those who are spiritually prepared to receive them.

The text most frequently cited as a basis for this teaching is 1 Corinthians 2:14: "The natural man receives not the things of the Spirit of God, for they are foolishness to him; neither can he know them, because they are spiritually discerned." Is this, then, to be used

---

6. S. R. Driver, "The Method of Studying the Psalter: Psalm 16," *Expositor*, Seventh Series, 10 (1910):37.
7. Prosper Grech, "The 'Testimonia' and Modern Hermeneutics," *NTS* 19 (1972–73):321.

as some kind of precedent for bypassing the otherwise dreary tools employed in exegetical skills?

Daniel Fuller[8] has shown the weakness of that whole line of argumentation. The word "to receive" (*dechomai*) in 1 Corinthians 2:14 means "to welcome with pleasure, willingly, and earnestly." Had the word been *lambanō*, then the idea would have been simply "to receive something." Furthermore, the word for "know" (*ginōskō*) means not just perceiving a thing as such but "embracing things as they really are."[9] Thus, there are not two or more logics, meanings, and interpretations that are to be found in Scripture—as if one was apparent and objectively realizable while the others were spiritual, mysterious, and occasionally available. Is this not a confusion of the doctrine of revelation with the doctrine of illumination at this point?

To insist that the Holy Spirit interrupts the hermeneutical process with a new—even messianic—meaning is to proudly argue that another divine revelation has taken place in the interpreter's experience while he, the exegete, was looking at an ancient text. And that precisely was Barth's argument: The locus of revelation was a believer waiting for a divine encounter as he bent over the Holy Scriptures. But surely Barth and those holding to these plenary views are confounding the necessary work of the Holy Spirit in illumination, application, and personally applying a text with the original scope and content of that text in the singular act of revelation to the writer.

Is this error that far removed from contemporary philosophical exegetical systems such as Georg Gadamer's theory, which stresses the reader's perception of the text to the detriment of the author who first penned that text? According to Gadamer, the text is to be read from the reader's own horizons, situations, and questions that he brings to that text. Thus, a fusion is made between the text (as stripped from its author and his meanings) and the outlook of the reader. Rather than accepting the charge that such a procedure is arbitrary or even subjective, Gadamer believes it is more than tolerable because both the written text and the reader share the same real world that shaped both text and reader. Accordingly, when the reader interrogates the text with his own previously devised questions, the text "explains" the reader as much as the reader makes the text speak.

But all of this discussion leaves untouched the matter of validation: which "reading" of the text is valid. But then, of course, we have just spoiled everything and mentioned that word no one in the last third of the twentieth century is supposed to talk about: "truth." Yet, is not

---

8. Daniel P. Fuller, eds. W. W. Gasque and W. S. LaSor, "The Holy Spirit's Role in Biblical Interpretation," *Scripture, Tradition, and Interpretation* (Grand Rapids: Eerdmans, 1978), pp. 190–93.
9. Ibid., p. 191, as cited by Fuller from *TDNT*, 1:690.

that the same issue for all pneumatic theories of meaning as well? How can I validate my meaning that I now attribute to the Holy Spirit? And if the apostles claim they found such plenary meanings in the OT only by aid of the Holy Spirit in them as authors of Scripture, why must they appeal to the OT or to their audiences for approval of that which they say has already been received among their listeners?

AN ALTERNATIVE SOLUTION TO THE MESSIANIC PSALMS PROBLEM

We would urge, as a solution to the problem of retaining a single meaning to the text while doing full justice to legitimate messianic claims, that a blend of views between the ancient Antiochian concept of *theōria* and Willis J. Beecher's[10] concept of promise (or epangelical) theology be adopted.

According to Antioch, God gave the prophets (in our case the psalmist) a vision (*theōria*, from *theōrein*, "to look, gaze at") of the future in which the recipient saw as intimate parts of one meaning the word for his own historical day with its needs (*historia*) and that word for the future. Both the literal historical sense and the fulfillment were conceived as one piece. Both were intimate parts of one total whole work of God.

Beecher, in our view, added to this emphasis on a single meaning vision for the present and distant future by stressing the fact that more was involved in this vision than the word spoken prior to the event and the fulfilling event itself. There was the common plan of God in which both the word, the present historical realization, and the distant realization shared. Often these parts of the plan of God, known as his covenantal promise, were generic or corporate terms (such as "seed," "my son," "Servant of the Lord," "first-born") that were deliberately used to include the historical antecedents as well as the realities yet to come. Also, the promise embraced yet another perspective in its single meaning: the means that God used to fulfill that word in the contemporary environment of the prophetic speaker and the result or even series of results that issued forth from that word as they lined up with the past and the future. For every historical fulfillment of the promise was at once a fulfillment and a sample, earnest or guarantee of whatever climactic event it likewise often pointed forward to by virtue of the wholeness and singularity of meaning in that word. We believe such to be the case in the psalm we have selected as a sample of a more consistent hermeneutical handling of the messianic feature in the psalmist's words.

10. W. J. Beecher, *The Prophets and the Promise* (Grand Rapids: Baker, 1975 [1905]).

PSALM 16

THE AUTHOR AND CONTENTS OF THE PSALM

Whereas few commentators have laid much stress on the fact that the title designates David either as the author ("from David") or the one praised in the psalm ("to David"), Franz Delitzsch[11] and E. W. Hengstenberg[12] have listed numerous points of contact between the phrases used in this psalm and other better known Davidic hymns. They include: verse 1—Pss. 7:1; 11:1: "in you I take refuge"; verse 5—Ps. 11:6: "my portion, my cup"; verse 8—15:5; 10:6: "I shall not be moved"; verse 9—4:8: "dwell securely"; verse 10—4:3: "your favored one"; verse 11—17:7, 15; 21:6; 109:31: "at your right hand"; "joy of your presence." This evidence is very compelling, but when the NT apostles also attribute the psalm to David the matter should pose no further concern, for both lines of argument now match.

This psalm of David is called a *miktām,* a superscription that is only found in six psalms (Pss. 16, 56–60). Three of those six were written as three of the eight fugitive psalms; psalms composed under the stress David suffered while he was being pursued by Saul in the wilderness. Attempts, such as that of Mowinckel, to derive the term *miktām* from the Akkadian *katāmu,* "cover" or "atone for,"[13] have not been convincing. This term is also possibly used in Isaiah 3:8, according to the improbable corrected Hebrew text that changes *miktāb,* "scripture" or "inscription," to *miktām* in psalms of thanksgiving for recovery from an illness. But the term remains obscure and it does not seem to add anything distinctive to our understanding of the psalm's historical setting or literary genera apart from the known company it shares with David's three fugitive psalms and two others collected together in Psalms 56–60.

The special events in David's life that occasioned this psalm are much more difficult and probably will never be known for certain. Three major suggestions for its placement are (1) a severe sickness after David had finished his own cedar palace (Delitzsch); (2) his stay

---

11. F. Delitzsch, *The Psalms* (Grand Rapids: Eerdmans, 1955), 1:217.
12. E. W. Hengstenberg, *The Psalms* (Edinburgh: T. & T. Clark, 1851), 1:231.
13. Sigmund Mowinckel, *The Psalms in Israel's Worship,* trans. D. R. Ap-Thomas, 2 vols. (Nashville: Abingdon, 1967), 2:209. See also Peter C. Craigie, *Word Biblical Commentary: Psalms 1–50* (Waco, Tex.: Word, 1983), 19:154, n.1a for five additional surmises as to what *miktām* means. Craigie notes that four of the six psalms are associated with times of crisis.

at Ziklag[14] among the Philistines (2 Sam. 30) when he may have been tempted to worship idols (Hitzig); and (3) David's word under the influence of Nathan's prophecy (2 Sam. 7) about his future dynasty, kingdom, and throne (Lange's *Commentary*). If we had to side with one view, we would choose the last one because of the scope of Nathan's prophecy and the linkage made in Psalm 16.

The contents of Psalm 16 are as follows. Rather than expressing any sudden emergency, the psalmist is jubilant with a joy and happiness that knows few bounds. David has placed himself under the overlordship of his suzerain, Yahweh (v. 1), whom he describes as his "portion" (v. 5) and his "inheritance" (v. 6). There is not another good in addition to the Lord. Thus David delights in the company of fellow worshipers of God (v. 3), but he detests all whose lips and lives serve false gods (v. 4). From such a fellowship and enjoyment of God comes counsel, admonishment, and protection (vv. 7–9). And then the most remarkable consequence of all as the psalmist suddenly reverts to the imperfect tense in verse 9b: He, who is God's "holy one" (*ḥāsîd*), rests confidently in the fact that neither he nor God's everlasting "seed" (here called *ḥasid*) will be abandoned in the grave, but the God who has made the promise will be the God in whose presence he will experience fullness of joy and pleasures forever.

THE EXEGESIS[15] AND INFORMING THEOLOGY TO PSALM 16

The Psalmist begins with no vague subjective plea such as "Save me, for I believe you can!" Neither does he plead any merit based on what he had done for God, but as W. Robertson Smith pointed out, "He pleads a covenant relation to God."[16]

THE COVENANT RELATIONSHIP

The word *ḥāsâ*, "I have committed myself to you," as used in a secular sense in Judges 9:15 and Isaiah 30:2, meant that a vassal

14. The title to Psalm 16 calls this psalm a *miktām*, which is the name also used of Psalms 56, 57, and 59—all written during David's exile and Saul's persecution of him. However, *miktām* is probably only a musical term and not one that denotes kinds of content because the style, sentiment, and expressions are different from those found in Psalm 16 (so De Wette had argued according to Hengstenberg, *Christology of the Old Testament* [abridged by T. K. Arnold; Grand Rapids: Kregel, 1970], 78).
15. In addition to the usual commentaries, we found these articles on the psalm: W. R. Smith, "The Sixteenth Psalm," *Expositor* 4 (1881) 341–372; S. R. Driver, "The Method of Studying the Psalter: Psalm 16," *Expositor*, Seventh Series, 10 (1910):26–37; H. W. Boers, "Psalm 16 and the Historical Origin of the Christian Faith," *ZAW* 60 (1969):105–110; A. Schmitt, "Ps. 16, 8–11 als Zeugnis der Auferstehung in der Apostelgeschichte," *BZ* 17 (1973):229–248. J. Lindblom, "Erwägungen zu Psalm XVI," *VT* 24 (1974):187–95; M. Mannati, "Remarquest sur Ps. XVI. 1–3," *VT* 22 (1972):359–61.
16. Smith, "Sixteenth Psalm," p. 342.

attached himself to a suzerain in order to enjoy his protection. Here the term pointed in a religious context to the covenant that God had made with the psalmist and his people. Thus he took refuge in that covenant and God.

So enjoyable was this relationship that the psalmist found that he had no other good or wealth apart from God. Everything he recognized as being of value or worth, God actually contained in Himself, hymned the psalmist.

THE PORTION AND INHERITANCE

What had been measured out to David according to God's grace was a "portion" or "inheritance" that was nothing less than Yahweh Himself. It was in the same sense that Yahweh had been declared to distinctively be the Levites' "portion" and "inheritance" (Num. 18:20, 24) in that they received no assignment in the division of the territory of the land. Later, in Jeremiah 10:16, the Lord will be described as the "portion" of the whole nation of Israel. It comes as no surprise, then, to find that Psalms 119:57 and 142:5 present individual believers addressing God as "my portion." Likewise, what had been measured out by lines or measuring tapes[17] were not "portions" in this world but the "inheritance" of spiritual joys, chief among which was God Himself in His presence, grace, and fellowship.

"Therefore," concludes the psalmist in verse 9, "my flesh shall rest secure because you will not abandon (or leave) me to Sheol (or "in the grave"); you will not permit your "holy one" (*ḥăsîdkā*) to experience corruption." One of the most frequently asked questions is whether those clauses are a reference to the hope for the psalmist's future resurrection or rather an expression of his confidence that God will watch over his earthly body as well as his spirit and preserve him from physical harm and death.

"THE FAVORITE ONE" (*ḥāsîd*)

The answer to this question will depend, in our view, more on the identity, meaning, and significance of the "favorite one" (*ḥāsîd*) than upon a discussion of the words for "security," "grave," and "corruption." In fact, the reason this passage should ever have been linked to the Messiah along with the Davidic speaker rests on the proper

---

17. See the same phrase in Joshua 17:5. J. J. Perowne, *The Book of Psalms* (Grand Rapids: Zondervan, 1966 [1878]), 1:194, says: "The line was said to 'fall' as being 'thrown' by lot! See Micah 2:5." For the theology of this term see W. C. Kaiser, Jr., *Toward an Old Testament Theology* (Grand Rapids: Zondervan, 1978), pp. 126–30, esp. n.12.

understanding of the term *hāsîd*.[18] As a messianic term, it is only surpassed by "Servant of the Lord" and "Messiah" in the OT.[19]

Despite a large measure of skepticism among current scholars, we believe *hāsîd* is best rendered in a passive form,[20] "one to whom God is loyal, gracious, or merciful" or "one in whom God manifests his grace and favor," rather than in an active form as "one who is loyal to God." In form it may be either active or passive; it is the context that will make the final decision.

In Psalm 4 David claimed that he was Yahweh's *hāsîd:* "Realize that Yahweh has set apart for himself a *hāsîd*" (Heb., 4:4) Accordingly, all attempts to frustrate David by evil deeds would be futile. The reason for this confidence can be found in Psalm 18:26 (2 Sam. 22:25), a psalm where David celebrates the Lord's deliverance from all his enemies: "With a *hāsîd*, you (O Lord) will manifest yourself *hāsîd*" (the *hithpael* form of the verb). Thus a *hāsîd*, a "favored one," denoted a person in whom God's divine graciousness was specially manifested. More often than not, the special lovingkindness intended was that which the Lord first announced to Abraham, to Israel, and to the dynasty of David.

One of the key passages that connects our term *hāsîd* with David is Psalm 89:20–21 (English, vv. 19–20). "Of old you spoke to your favored one in a vision and said: I have set the crown on a hero, I have exalted from the people a choice person. I have found David my servant (a messianic term in Isaiah) with my holy oil and I have anointed him (another messianic concept)." What else can we conclude except that in the psalmist's view Yahweh's *hāsîd*, king, servant, and anointed one are one and the same in the person, office, and mission of David?

As early as Moses' era (Deut. 33:8) there is a reference to "the man of thy *hāsîd* whom thou (Israel) didst test at Massah" (a reference to Ex. 17, where water came from the rock). The only "man" who was tested and put to the proof in Exodus 17:2, 7 was the Lord! Could not this clear association of the Lord with the term *hāsîd* have been the background against which David also understood the term of himself as it is now granted in a new revelation? Likewise, Hannah spoke of

---

18. *Hāsîd* occurs thirty-two times and only in poetic texts, never in prose. Besides twenty-five examples in the Psalms it appears in Deuteronomy 33:8; 1 Samuel 2:9; 2 Samuel 22:26 (duplicated in Ps. 18:26); Proverbs 2:8; Jeremiah 3:12; Micah 7:2; 2 Chronicles 6:41 (duplicated in Ps. 132:9). In seventeen cases it is plural, eleven times it is singular; and four times there are variant readings.
19. This is the judgment of Beecher, *Prophets*, p. 313.
20. The noun and adjectival pattern, according to Hupfeld, on Psalm 4:4 is like *'āsîr*, "one who is bound, a prisoner," or *qāsîr*, "what is gathered, the harvest"; so BDB, p. 339.

the coming *ḥāsîd*, "the horn of his anointed one" (1 Sam. 2:9–10), the same association of concepts made in Psalm 89:17–21.

Rowley argues[21] that the most decisive evidence in favor of the active meaning is that the word is used of God in Psalm 145:17 and Jeremiah 3:12. But those instances are no different from Deuteronomy 33:8, for the *ḥāsîd* is not only the one to whom favor comes because of some distinctive office or mission but also the one in whom such favor resides. Because Yahweh was Himself *ḥāsîd*, Israel was invited to return to Him (Jer. 3:12), just as He was "righteous in all his ways and *ḥāsîd* in all his deeds" (Ps. 145:17). In other words, Yahweh is first declared to be just and *ḥāsîd* before He begins to manifest such characteristics to others.

Neither are the seventeen examples of the plural form, "favored ones," a problem for one messianic view. The oscillation between the one and the many is exactly what we observe in such parallel examples as "seed," "anointed one," "servant," and "first-born."

In Psalm 16, then, David is God's *ḥāsîd*, "favored one," yet not David as a mere person but David as the recipient and conveyor of God's ancient but ever-renewed promise. Therefore, as Beecher concluded:

> The man David may die, but the *hhasidh* is eternal. Just as David is the Anointed One, and yet the Anointed One is eternal; just as David is the Servant, and yet the Servant is eternal; so David is the *hhasidh*, and yet the *hhasidh* is eternal. David as an individual went to the grave, and saw corruption there, but the representative of Yahaweh's [*sic*] eternal promise did not cease to exist.[22]

The Masoretic text has the plural form, "thy favored ones," whereas the marginal reading is singular. In this instance the margin with its singular form is to be adopted because it is supported by the largest number of manuscripts and the best.[23] Whereas the plural reading is the more difficult text and, therefore, that which the canons of textual

---

21. H. H. Rowley, *The Faith of Israel* (London: SCM, 1956), p. 130 n.1: "It is quite impossible to suppose that when God says [in Jer. 3:12] 'I am *ḥāsîdh*' he means that he has been treated with *ḥesedh*, because the whole burden of the verse is that he has not."
22. Beecher, *Prophets*, p. 325.
23. See Hengstenberg, *Christology*, 76 n.6; 77 nn.2, 3; Perowne, *Psalms*, p. 200 n.d. C. B. Moll, *The Psalms: Lange's Commentary* (New York: Scribner, Armstrong, 1872), p. 126, added this explanation: "The Masora likewise says, *yod* is not pronounced. Thus, if this had read in the MSS *ḥᵃsîdekā* as now likewise some, and especially ancient Spanish Codd, have it, this is not to be regarded as plural, but as singular, and indeed so that it is not so much to be regarded as the so-called emphatic plural or plural of majesty (...after the ancient interpreters) as rather the *yod* is to be considered as, Gen. xvi. 5; Ps. ix. 14; Jer. xlvi. 15, as a sign of the seghol."

criticism would ordinarily favor, the weight of the external evidence overbalances any use of that rule in this situation.

THE PATH OF LIFE (VV. 9B–11)

The fact that David had a direct consciousness that God was his Lord and his inheritance not only cheered his heart but also allowed his body (*bāśār*)[24] to share in this joy as well. His "body would dwell in safety" (v. 9*b*) mainly because Yahweh's *ḥāsîd* would not experience the "pit" (from the root *šûaḥ*, "to sink down") or "corruption" (from the root *šāḥâ*, "to go to ruin")

It is difficult to decide between the renderings "pit" and "corruption." Most interpreters will agree that our word *šaḥat* does occur in Job 17:4 meaning "corruption" where it stands in parallelism to *rimmâ*, "worm," and that all the ancient versions render our passage "corruption." But that ends the agreement. The parallelism appears to favor "pit"; yet "corruption" is every bit as fitting[25]—especially if *šeʾôl* is uniformly rendered "grave," as it should be, and not "the underworld" or "pit."[26]

The expression "to see corruption" may be determined by the opposite phrase, "to see life" (= "to abide, to remain alive").[27] Likewise, the preceding clause, "to abandon" (*ʾāzab*), with the preposition *le* signifies "to give up to (another)" as if the grave were here personified as an insatiable animal that will be overpowered.[28]

David expects to arrive safely with his immaterial and material being in the presence of God, just because God has promised the future of his "favored one" (*ḥāsîd*). The God who was the God of the living and not of the dead would be David's God in life and in death, lighting the path to life with its pleasure and joy afterwards in the presence of God.

The "path of life" for the psalmist was "eternal life" even as Dahood has argued from Ugaritic sources where *ḥayyîm*, even for that early and—for some—primitive age, was used in parallelism with "immortality."[29]

24. My student, Ken Burdick, has suggested the remote possibility that *bāśār* might mean here "kindred, blood-relation" (BDB, 142, def. 4), as in Genesis 37:27; Isaiah 58:7. David's hope then would be that his posterity would not be cut off. The text seems to parallel "heart" and "glory" or "liver" too closely for that suggestion.
25. Moll, *Psalms*, 126, says: "The ancient Jews have had so little doubt (that *šaḥat* meant 'corruption'), that from it has originated the rabbinical fable, that the body of David has never decayed."
26. For confirmation of this thesis see R. L. Harris, "The Meaning of Sheol as Shown by Parallels in Poetic Texts," *BETS* 4 (1961):129–35; A. Heidel, *The Gilgamesh Epic and Old Testament Parallels* (Chicago: University Press, 1946), pp. 180ff.
27. Perowne, *Psalms*, p. 201.
28. Hengstenberg, *Christology*, p. 77, n.5.
29. M. Dahood, *Psalms*, The Anchor Bible (Garden City, N.J.: Doubleday, 1965), 1:91.

PETER'S AND PAUL'S USE OF PSALM 16

Our argument has been that the identity, office, and function of the "favored one" (*ḥāsîd*) is critical to a proper understanding of the single meaning of the psalmist. Another confirmation of the adequacy of this view can be found in Paul's message at Antioch of Pisidia where he boldly connected "the holy and sure blessings of David" (*ta hosia David ta pista*) as announced by Isaiah 55:3 with the quote from Psalm 16:10 that "thou wilt not let thy 'Favored One' see corruption" (LXX, *ou dōseis ton hosion sou idein diaphthoran*).

Isaiah is as clear as Paul was on the fact that "the sure mercies of David" were not David's acts of mercy toward God but rather the results of God's grace being poured out on David as a recipient of the unfolding promise of God. Whereas Andrè Caquot[30] and W. A. M. Beuken[31] have argued for a subjective genitive, H. G. M. Williamson[32] has handily demonstrated that an objective genitive is what Isaiah intended here. David was God's man of promise who received the renewal of the covenant (2 Samuel 7) that was made with Abraham, Isaac, and Jacob and that included those gifts (the root is *ḥesed*) that Yahweh had faithfully promised to bestow on Israel and through Israel to all the nations on the face of the earth. Thus it involved no hermeneutical error for Paul to connect the psalmist's *ḥāsîd*, "favored one," with Isaiah's *ḥasdê*, "mercies" (or, better, "graces"). He clearly understood the essence of the OT promise or blessing of God.

Most recent NT commentators, however, see it differently. Paul is interpreted as using the rabbinical practice of associating passages merely on the basis of similar catchwords. The most quoted passage is from Lake and Cadbury:[33]

> When the Rabbis found a phrase which could not be explained by any ordinary method in its own context they interpreted by "analogy," that is, they found the same word in some other place where its meaning was clear, and interpreted the obscure passage in the light of the intelligible one. Here, *hosia* is unintelligible; therefore the writer takes another passage in which the adjective *hosios* is used substantially, Ps. xvi. 10, "thou wilt not give thy holy one—*hosion*—to see corruption," and introduces it by *dioti*, to show that this is the justification for his interpretation, and that by perfectly correct Rabbinical reasoning *ta*

30. A. Caquot, "Les 'Graces de David' a pos d'Isaie 55:3b," *Sem* 15 (1965):45–59.
31. W. A. M. Beuken, "Isa. 55:3–5: Reinterpretation of David," *Bijdragen* 35 (1974):49–64.
32. H. G. M. Williamson, "'The Sure Mercies of David': Subjective or Objective Genitive?" *JSS* 23 (1978):31–49.
33. K. Lake and H. J. Cadbury, *The Beginnings of Christianity* (London: Macmillan, 1933), 4:155–56.

hosia means the Resurrection.... It is very important to notice that the whole argument is based on the LXX and disappears if the speech be not in Greek.

But if what we have argued above is correct, such as the writer's intention when he used *ḥāsîd* or employed the objective genitive, then the exegesis of Lake and Cadbury is entirely wrong. The case does not depend on Paul's use of Greek in that speech anymore than the claim that *ta hosia ta pista* is unintelligible. Moreover, when Paul introduces Psalm 16:10 with *dioti*, "therefore," he "clearly marks out that which follows as an inferential clause, adduced to demonstrate that the resurrection was a part of the realization of the holy and sure blessings promised to David."[34]

In fact, rather than being unintelligible the situation was just the reverse for, as Lövestam[35] explained, Paul had already (Acts 13:23) made reference to the blessings God had given to David. There can be little doubt that Paul's citation of Isaiah refers to the covenant promised to David. Lövestam correctly conjectures that the rendering of Isaiah 55:3 as *ta hosia* may have been motivated by a desire to use Greek words similar in sound to the Hebrew originals.

Peter in Acts 2:25–33 does not fare any better at the hands of his commentators. In fact, S. R. Driver opined:

> It is difficult not to think that the application of the words to Christ found in Acts ii. 25–31, xiii. 35–37 was facilitated by the mistranslations of the Septuagint.... But the apostles used arguments of the kind usual at the time, and such as would seem cogent both to themselves and to their contemporaries.[36]

Yet that conclusion hardly does justice to Peter's claim that David was a "prophet"[37] who did indeed "foresee" (*proidon*) and also knowingly spoke about (*peri*) the resurrection of Messiah when he wrote Psalm 16 (Acts 2:30–31). Acts 2:25 carefully introduces the quotation from Psalm 16:8–11 with the phrase, "David says with reference to (*eis*) him," rather than "concerning (*peri*) him" (which would have meant

34. A. M. Harman, "Paul's Use of the Psalms" (Th.D. thesis, Westminster Theological Seminary, 1968), p. 40.
35. E. Lövestam, *Son and Saviour: A Study of Acts 13:32–37* (Copenhagen: Munksgaard, 1961), pp. 71–87. He adds on p. 84: "With regard to Ps. 16:10 ... it is expressly combined with the promise to David: David's covenant is quoted there as foundation and justification for the psalm saying's reference and application to Jesus' resurrection. This is of importance for the understanding of the connection of the quotation from Ps. 16:10 with the promise to David in Acts 13:34f."
36. Driver, "Method," p. 36.
37. J. A. Fitzmyer, "David, Being Therefore a Prophet (Acts 2:30)," *CBQ* 34 (1972):332–39.

that the total reference was of the Messiah alone). But Peter is most insistent that his understanding of Psalm 16 is not a novel interpretation: It was David's own view. Thus, any belief that the psalm had been accommodated to contemporary fancies or subjected to a reinterpretation fails to grapple with the apostle's own claim: Psalm 16, not Peter (or Paul), made those claims for Christ and his resurrection.

The charge by H. W. Boers[38] that Acts 2:24 is the real evidence that Psalm 16 was reinterpreted with its word "pangs (*ōdinas*) of death" as if the Hebrew read *hēbel*, "pain" or "pang," instead of *hebel*, "cord, rope, line" (the plural of both Hebrew words being indistinguishable), must likewise fail. In Boers's eyes it was the word association of Psalm 16:6 ("lines have fallen to me in pleasant places") with verses 8–11 of that chapter that caused the Lord's disciples to refer it to Jesus' death, for the same word was used in Psalm 18:5 ("the lines of death surround me") and was understood as a reference there to the death of Jesus. Thus he contends that Psalm 16:8–11 was originally interpreted as predicting the death, not the resurrection of Jesus. Only later, we are assured by Boers, did the church reverse itself and see Jesus' resurrection in Psalm 16.

However, Peter does not pretend to quote Psalm 16:6 in Acts 2:24. The artificiality of the suggestion is most evident from the ponderous conclusions Boers attached to this tenuous exegesis. Even if Psalm 18:5 is also quoted in Acts 2:24 (and it may be so), Peter's failure to start his citation at verse 6 rather than the verse 8 that he chose certainly should put this suggestion to rest. Rather, Peter felt his exegesis rested squarely on the revelatory word given to David.

One final objection may be noted. Many have contended that the focus of Peter's argument is the word "corruption" (*diaphora* for the Hebrew *šāhat*), which he derives from the LXX translation in the same way he had used that same Greek translation for *lābetah* ("secure") as meaning "in hope" (*ep elpidi*). According to this line of argumentation, Peter shifted the meaning from David's original sense of resting in God's protection and assurance that he, David, would not die in the immediate crisis to picturing Christ's confident expectation in a resurrection from Sheol. Thus, what had only been *present* safety, goes this argument, was converted into a *future* hope from the power of the grave. In the words of S. R. Driver:

> It is difficult not to think that the application of the words to Christ found in Acts ii.25–31, xiii.35–37 was facilitated by the mistranslations of the Septuagint ("shall dwell in hope," "wilt not leave my soul in

---

38. Boers, "Psalm 16," p. 108.

Hades," and "to see corruption").[39] "But the apostles," continued S. R. Driver, "used arguments of the kind usual at the time, and such as would seem cogent both to themselves and to their contemporaries."[40]

Of course, that is exactly the point in contention! Would such a line of argumentation on so critical a point of difference be at once acceptable to the Christian interpreters and the strongly dissenting Jewish exegetes? We cannot accept such an assumption!

Neither is the argument helped any further by Peter Craigie's conclusions:

> With respect to the initial meaning of the Psalm, it is probable that this concluding section should not be interpreted either messianically or in terms of personal eschatology.... Yet it is apparent that in the earliest Christian community, the psalm was given a messianic interpretation.... This change in meaning ... is an example of the double meanings which may be inherent in the text of Scripture. The new meaning imparted to the text suggests not only progress, but contrast.[41]

But why must we argue that the special nature of Scripture forces us to posit double or multiple meanings for any given text? For some, the answer will lie in their inability to see how such "lofty" NT values could have possibly been conceived, much less understood, by OT saints. For others, the answer will rest where C. S. Lewis laid it.

> If the Old Testament is a literature thus "taken up," made the vehicle of what is more than human, we can of course set no limits to the weight or multiplicity of meanings which may have been laid upon it. If any writer may say more than he meant, then these writers will be especially likely to do so. And not by accident.[42]

Both answers are faulty. The first answer has such strong discontinuity between the revelation of the OT and the NT that it devalues the Old to increase the stock and provide a high view of revelation for the New. How will that square, however, with Paul's estimate ("All Scripture is inspired by God") and the divine claims for the contents of both Testaments? And the second answer begins too low by assuming that what is truly human (as Scripture is in the same sense that Christ in His incarnation was likewise truly human) must thereby be infected in its raw materials with the "merely natural," "naivety,"

39. S. R. Driver, "Method of Studying," p. 36.
40. Ibid.
41. Peter C. Craigie, *Word Biblical Commentary*, 19:158.
42. C. S. Lewis, *Reflections on the Psalms* (New York: Harcourt, Brace, 1958), p. 117.

"error," "contradiction," and "even wickedness."[43] It is only when those raw materials in all their humanity, goes Lewis's argument, are "taken up" and "upgraded" that we will be able to see beyond this "lower" or "merely human literature."[44]

Surely C. S. Lewis has failed to understand what the writers of Scripture claimed for themselves: a divine concursus between their human skills and the Holy Spirit's gift of the message and its meaning. One of the most precise statements on the mode of inspiration, which showed how the divine Spirit and the human author received and recorded the "deep things of God," is found in 1 Corinthians 2:13: "Words taught, not by wisdom, but by the Spirit." That representation clearly excludes all mechanical forms of dictating the words of Scripture or the use of "merely natural," "raw materials." Instead, there was such a living assimilation of the writer's own style, vocabulary, and literary *gattung* that the resulting truth was exactly what the Holy Spirit "taught." Paul's choice of the word *didaktos* ("taught") and the sphere of the Spirit's teaching *logois* ("words") shows that the writers of Scripture experienced the work of the Holy Spirit to the point of verbalizing their message and that the truth became part and parcel of their own person, style, and vocabulary.[45]

Did Peter apparently mistake the original meaning or deliberately add a new meaning when he stressed "corruption," "shall dwell in hope," and "will not leave my soul in hell"? No! He did not, for the word *Sheol* is, as we have already argued above, merely the poetic for the prose word "grave" and the word often rendered "pit" is best rendered "corruption" (*šahat*). In this case, "corruption" is only another way of referring to the grave and to its effects. The LXX translations were giving the Greek dynamic equivalents rather than a woodenly literal translation of the Hebrew text.

Once again, we must warn the Christian church that Peter's view clearly states that David's prophetic status allowed him to have a clear prevision of Christ's resurrection. Such a strong affirmation blows to bits all kinds of theories about hidden, double, multiple, or increased meanings or senses (meaning) of the text.

CONCLUSION

Without injecting any contrived artifices of dualism, docetism, or spiritual hermeneutics, we believe that David, as the man of promise

43. Ibid., p. 111.
44. Ibid., p. 116.
45. For more details, see Walter C. Kaiser, Jr., "A Neglected Text in Bibliology Discussions: 1 Corinthians 2:6–16," *Westminster Theological Journal* 43 (1981):301–19, esp. pp. 315–17. Note the contributions of F. L. Godet and H. A. W. Meyer to this discussion in the footnotes of the article cited here.

and as God's *ḥāsîd* ("favored one"), was in his person, office, and function one of the distinctive historical fulfillments to that word that he received about his seed, dynasty, and throne. Therefore, he rested secure in the confident hope that even death itself would not prevent him from enjoying the face-to-face fellowship with his Lord even beyond death, because that ultimate *ḥāsîd* would triumph over death. For David, this was all one word: God's ancient but evernew promise.

3

Respecting the Old Testament Context: Matthew's Use of Hosea and Jeremiah

Hosea 11:1 and Jeremiah 31:15

Enter into a discussion of the NT citations of the OT and, before long, someone is bound to raise the example of Matthew's use of Hosea 11:1: "Out of Egypt have I called my Son." Thus, it would seem appropriate to begin with a discussion of Matthew 2:15 and to link it with Matthew 2:18, where we find Rachel weeping for her children at Ramah.

MATTHEW'S USE OF THE OLD TESTAMENT

Once again estimates vary on the precise use Matthew makes of the OT, but based on a conservative count, there are sixty-five formal citations of the OT in Matthew. Interest, however, usually centers on the eleven quotations called *formula-citations*, with four of the eleven occuring together in a dense-pack in Matthew 2 and without precedent anywhere else in the gospels.[1]

These formula-citations or fulfillment-citations are introduced by a formula that observes that the NT event took place "in order to fulfill" the OT passages being cited. For example, Matthew 1:22 has this formula, "in order that it might be fulfilled which was spoken through the prophet, saying." The German term, *Reflexionszitate*, appearing as early as the 1889 commentary on the synoptics by H. J. Holtzmann,

1. Raymond E. Brown, *The Birth of the Messiah* (Garden City, N.Y.: Doubleday, 1977), p. 219.

emphasized that these quotations had been added to the gospels as a "personal reflection." A more felicitous and descriptive term has now replaced it, *Erfühlungszitate*, that is, "fulfillment citations,"[2] or as we are calling them, formula-citations.

In addition to composing a unique category, these formula-citations generally reflect an underlying Hebrew text from the OT rather than from the LXX, which is ordinarily reflected in the majority of the synoptic's citations. Thus, it has become customary for some scholars to seek a close affinity between those eleven formula-citations and the *pesher* method of interpretation found at Qumran.

Nowhere is the significance of the *pesher* thesis more critical than in Matthew 2. The prominence of the OT in Matthew 2 has led many to conclude that Matthew embellished his OT quotations, just as many of the stories about the great teachers of Israel tended to be elaborate and to use grandiose terms. The effect of such reasoning would lead to labeling Matthew's narratives in Matthew 2 as imaginative constructions based on general OT motifs and texts. They would be "pious fictions" foisted on Matthew's readers for the elevation of the Messiah, His life, and His claims.

But how could such flagrant fabrication of events and facts lead to such high goals? It is one thing to construct such eulogizing embellishments after the targeted audience has granted that the person is whom he claims or pretends to be, but it is another situation altogether when the audience is admittedly skeptical and reluctant to grant anything good about the leader whom the group or writer wishes to argue for or present in the best light. This later situation calls for toughmindedness, hard fact, and hard exegesis of the plain, straightforward anticipations in the grammar and syntax of one's own accepted religious documents if any obstacles of rejection of the thesis are to be overcome. We believe that Matthew was writing for an outside (i.e., nonbelieving) audience as well as for the community of faith. The gospel was more than a catechetical handbook or even a liturgical guide—it was a tract written to move toughminded resisters to conclude that Jesus was the promised Messiah from God. If that were so, then all such embellishment would be recognized for what it was: worthless as an evangelistic or apologetic tool and singularly unconvincing.

Thus, the issue at stake for the current crop of biblical interpreters is this: Did Matthew in his formula-citations indicate that an OT text was fulfilled by the words and deeds of Jesus much as the Qumran commentary on Habakkuk began with the introductory formula *pesharaw sal*, "it's interpretation bears upon," that is, with *pesher*

2. Ibid., pp. 96–97, n.1.

exegesis? Did Matthew use these standard practices of the *pesher* methodology:

1. Merge pertinent OT texts into one grand "prooftext"?
2. Adapt the OT texts into the grammar of the NT context and application?
3. Choose more suitable renderings of known OT texts or targums?
4. Create *ad hoc* interpretations?

The two texts in Matthew, 2:15 and 18, may be used as test examples from a section of Matthew, which is at the eye of this storm. The infancy narratives have long been assailed for their lack of credibility, that is, "Matthew makes stories up," opines M. D. Goulder.[3] But when many of these negative estimates of the infancy narrative are traced back to their source, a good deal of it is to be laid at the feet of Matthew's alleged indulgence in a special kind of interpretive selection and translations of his OT texts according to the *pesher* method. This thesis cannot be sustained when the texts are fairly evaluated in light of their OT contexts, and the grammar and syntax employed. This remains to be demonstrated here.

THE MESSAGE AND PURPOSE OF MATTHEW 2

Matthew 2 is not, properly speaking, a birth or even an infancy narrative.[4] The stories in this chapter are about Joseph, the Magi, and Herod. The aim, instead, is theological, apologetic, and serves as a prolegomena to the story proper, which begins in Matthew 3.

Accordingly, four pericopae that make up Matthew 2 each center on a formula-citation: (1) the visit of the magi—quoting Micah 5:2; (2) the escape to Egypt—quoting Hosea 11:1; (3) the slaughter of the children—quoting Jeremiah 31:15; and (4) the settlement in Nazareth—quoting what is either an unidentifiable OT quotation or a general substance citation, "He shall be called a Nazarene."

What, then, was the message and purpose of those four OT citations? Was it as Stendahl[5] argued, that is, to be found in the geograph-

---

3. M. D. Goulder, *Midrash and Lection in Matthew* (London: SPCK, 1974), p. 33 as cited by Richard T. France, "Herod and the Children of Bethlehem," *Novum Testamentum* 21 (1979):98. In footnote 2 on the same page, France lists the opinions of two others, nontheological specialists, who claim the incident of massacre of the innocents by Herod is "but myth or folklore" and "a complete fabrication."
4. So argues Richard T. France, "The Formula-Quotations of Matthew 2 and the Problem of Communication," *NTS* 27 (1980–81):234.
5. Krister Stendahl, *"Quis et Unde?* An Analysis of Matt. 1–2," in *Judentum Urchristentum Kirche:* Festschrift für Joackim Jeremias, ed. Walther Eltester, Beihefte zur Zeitschrift für die neutestamentliche Wissenschaft (Berlin: Alfred Töpelmann, 1964):94–105.

What, then, was the message and purpose of those four OT citations? Was it as Stendahl[5] argued, that is, to be found in the geographical names? Matthew 2, as Stendahl saw it, was written to answer two
embarrassing questions raised in John 7:41–42: (1) How can Messiah
come from Galilee? and (2) Does not Scripture say that the Christ will
come from David's family in Bethlehem where David lived? Thus,
Matthew 1 had focused on *personal* names around David's name with
the catch number being *fourteen*—a number based on the very
numerical value of "David" in Hebrew.[6] Even the four "irregularities"
of the women with unsavory reputations (Tamar, Rahab, Ruth, and
Bathsheba) were overcome by the intervention of God. But when we
come to the second chapter of Matthew, *geographical* names take
over.

But if the embarrassment is simply over the Galilean connections
of Jesus, is it not easy to see why Matthew found it necessary to
introduce *Egypt* or even the Magi from the *East* into the narrative?[7]
Does not the *prima facia* evidence suggest that the formula-citations
were to promote the point that what was happening to this child had
been anticipated by the Scriptures belonging to the same audience
that had found the acceptance of such a Jewish Messiah most difficult? Can that point be sustained?

Most are willing to concede that Matthew 2:5–6 and the use of
Micah 5:2 does count as a straightforward prediction that Messiah
would be born in Bethlehem, located in Judah. The surface meaning
is that Bethlehem was the predetermined place of origin for the
Messiah. There is not a shade of arbitrary exegesis or a *pesher* method
of handling that text.

Whereas Matthew has introduced three deliberate changes into his
wording of that text,[8] none of them affect the clear surface meaning
of the text that Christ's birth in Bethlehem did count as evidence for
His messianic claims. What changes were introduced were supple-

5. Krister Stendahl, *"Quis et Unde?* An Analysis of Matt. 1–2," in *Judentum Urchristentum Kirche:* Festschrift für Joackim Jeremias, ed. Walther Eltester, Beihefte zur
Zeitschrift für die neutestamentliche Wissenschaft (Berlin: Alfred Töpelmann,
1964):94–105.
6. דָּוִד (*dwd*), that is, 4 + 6 + 4 = 14 (*daleth* being the fourth letter in the alphabet and
waw being the sixth).
7. A point made by R. T. France, "The Formula-Quotations," pp. 237–39.
8. Ibid., pp. 241–42. They are: (1) "land of Judah" instead of the ancient name for
Bethlehem, Ephrathah; (2) reversing Bethlehem's insignificance to "by no means
least"; and (3) substituting God's charge to David, "who will shepherd my people
Israel" for the last words of Micah 5:2, "whose origins are from of old, from
eternity." The only other difference is Matthew's "rulers" of Judah instead of
Micah's "clans" or "thousands" of Judah; however, the textual difference between
these two readings is actually minimal and depends only on the pointing (i.e.,
vowels) of the same consonants.

introduction of another text bearing on the same office and its function as it was divinely commissioned to a previous holder of that office. But all three alterations had no effect on the plain meaning of the text. The NT writer did not need to resort to any contortions or twisting of texts or meaning to get Messiah's birthplace in the land of Judah, or more specifically, in Bethlehem, formerly known as Ephrathah.

MATTHEW'S USE OF HOSEA 11:1

Perhaps the most widely known example of the NT citing an OT text is the case of Matthew 2:15 with its quotation from Hosea 11:1, "Out of Egypt have I called my Son." In this instance, there is no alteration in the wording; it apparently is an independent and accurate translation of the Hebrew text, for the LXX reads on Hosea 11:1, "Out of Egypt I summoned his children (plural!).

THE ISSUES

There are, however, a number of problems surrounding Matthew's appeal to this passage: (1) Why does he quote Hosea 11:1 when the Holy Family goes *into* Egypt in verse 15? Should he not have waited until verse 20 if he wished to stress their *coming out* of Egypt?; (2) Is Hosea 11:1 a prophecy or in any sense a prediction of this event that overtook Joseph, Mary, and Jesus? Is not Hosea merely referring to a past historical act of God in the Exodus? Perhaps Matthew's hermeneutical method here betrays a use of *pesher, sensus plenior,* typology, or some other option than direct prophecy; and (3) What is the significance of Matthew's fulfillment formula, and what is his purpose in quoting this text? Each of those three issues must be answered if the riddle of this text is to be unravelled.

The problem that encompasses all of those is this: Did Matthew properly use Hosea 11:1 or did he abuse both Hosea's context and meaning? Many, such as Dewey M. Beegle, agree that:

> the sense of the passage and the intention of the prophet point backward, not forward. There is not the slightest hint that the statement was intended as a prophecy ... there was apparently a definite cause-and-effect relationship in the mind of Matthew, and so he quoted the passage as being authoritative proof from the Old Testament for an event in the life of Jesus. Although unintentional, is not his use of Hosea 11:1 in a sense a distortion of the context? Is Matthew's appeal to Hosea

actually true to the sense of the passage when he picks words out of
context and uses them for another purpose in the New Testament?[9]

Is this, then, an "unintentional ... distortion" where Matthew merely
"picks words out of context and uses them ... ?"

THE CONTEXT OF HOSEA 11:1

Hosea's prophecy may be structured along these lines: (1) An introductory and autobiographical section that symbolically mirrors the
tragedy of Israel's spiritual harlotry against Yahweh, Hosea 1–3; (2) A
pivotal court scene in 4:1 in which three charges are preferred against
Israel in their revolt against God and in which three charges form the
backbone of the rest of the prophecy with each, however, ending on
a bright, optimistic note for the future: (a) "no knowledge of God"
(4:2—6:3); (b) "no covenantal love" (hesed; 6:4—11:11); and (c) "no
truth" (11:12—14:9). The passages of hope for the future come in each
case at the end of the sections: 6:1–3; 11:1–11; 14:1–9. They are
generally forward looking and incorporate an eschatological view of
better times in the future as reason for hope in the present distress.

It is from the optimistic conclusion of the second charge that
Matthew has taken his quotation. Israel's failure to exercise and
demonstrate hesed, "covenantal love," or "loyal fidelity" to her Lord is
evident everywhere. What hesed she does evidence is like the morning
cloud and the early morning dew—it quickly disappears (Hos. 6:4).
Meanwhile treachery (6:6–11), perversity (7:1–2), conspiracy (7:3–7;
four out of the last six kings of northern Israel were murdered!),
stupidity (7:8–13), and duplicity (7:14–16) all persist in outrageous and
alarming ways in Israel. Instead of being God's luxuriant and produc-
tive vine (10:1), she bore fruit for herself and to the degree that she
prospered, so did the multitude of Israel's idols and pagan altars (10:1–
2) increase! It was time for Israel's fallow ground to be broken up so
that righteousness and hesed could be sown once again (10:12).

But in Hosea 11 a stark contrast interrupts this long indictment
that had begun in 6:4 and continued until 10:15. The persevering love
and election of God is placed in juxtaposition to the loveless condition
of the citizens of Israel. In fact, Yahweh cared for them even as they
turned from Him (11:2–4); He simply refused to give up on them
(11:8–11). The watchword here is God's love manifest in his preserva-

9. Dewey M. Beegle, Scripture, Tradition and Infallibility (Grand Rapids: Eerdmans,
1973), p. 237. Likewise, James Barr, Old and New in Interpretation (London: SCM,
1966), says, "Thus the word of Hosea, 'Out of Egypt have I called my son,' could
be taken as predictive, although in the original context it is clearly related to the
past (Matt. 2:15)," p. 125.

tion of His undeserving people. Repeatedly, Hosea stressed God's love for His people (1:10–11; 2:16–23; 3:4–5; 6:1–3; 11:1–11; 14:1–9). Similarly, in Matthew's infancy narrative there is stress on God's *preservation* during the child's early years (1:20; 2:13–18). However, by itself this thematic approach establishes little more than an analogous relationship between the two events. Something else must have been involved.

THE DESIGNATION "MY SON"

It is in the deliberate application of what had become by now a technical title, "My Son," that the correlation between Hosea 11:1 and Matthew 2:15 begins to become most direct. The term was first used in Exodus 4:22–23 of Israel. There she was called "my firstborn son ... my son."[10] The whole community was pointedly designated by a singular noun, thereby allowing for the many to be represented in the One and the One to stand for the many in the same way the term *Seed* had already functioned and the parallel term *Firstborn* would come to function in both the OT and NT.

Eventually, "My Son" was connected with the coming scion of the house of David (2 Sam. 7:14), even the One whom the God of heaven would install as His righteous king in Zion as ruler over all the earth and nations (Ps. 2:7), the Son of the Holy One and whose name is unknown (Prov. 30:4). This designation, "My Son," became a technical term and an appellation that could be applied either collectively to the nation as the object of God's love and election or specifically to that final representative person who was to come in Christ. Almost all interpreters observe this important connecting link.[11]

Matthew appealed to Hosea, first, because for him Jesus was "the Son" absolutely. Three times Matthew speaks of Jesus as "the Son" (Matt. 1:21, 23) and twelve times as "the Son of God." The title "My Son" was just as messianic as "Seed" in Genesis 3:15; 12:7. Even prior to the Exodus, Israel as God's "son" and "firstborn" had been designated the heir of all things. This usage of the Son of God as the Father of Israel is also found in Deuteronomy 1:31; 32:6; Jeremiah 3:19; 31:9, 20, and once more in Hosea, Ephraim is called "a son" who is not wise (13:12–13). The connection is not accidental or lately foisted on the OT; it is germane to its own messianic consciousness.

10. See Walter C. Kaiser, Jr., *Toward an Old Testament Theology* (Grand Rapids: Zondervan, 1978), pp. 101–3.
11. Homer A. Kent, Jr., "Matthew's Use of the Old Testament," *Bibliotheca Sacra* 121 (1964):37. "It would seem that Matthew found the key ... in ... the expression 'my son'." Also R. C. H. Lenski, *St. Matthew's Gospel* (Minneapolis: Augsburg, 1943), p. 78. R. T. France, "Formula-Quotations," p. 243, n.22 cites R. Pesch, "Der Gottessohn im mattäischen Evangelienprolog (Mt. 1–2)," *Biblica* 48 (1967):397ff.

THE DESTINATION AND DEPARTURE FROM EGYPT

It is interesting to note that Hosea uses "Egypt" in several senses. When he threatens in Hosea 9:3 that "Ephraim shall return to Egypt and shall eat unclean things in Assyria," it is clear that he is calling Assyria Egypt in a figure of speech known as metonymy. Again, in Hosea 11:5, Northern Israel is told plainly that they would "not return to the land of Egypt, but the Assyrian [would] be his king." Clearly, Egypt functioned as a symbol for the place of bondage and oppression, regardless of where it was located.[12] But in Hosea 11:1 it is clear that Egypt is the real geographical place from which Israel was delivered. But it is precisely in that context where it is also stressed that Egypt was the place where God manifested His paternal care and preservation of the nation. That same point is repeated in Hosea 12:13, "By a prophet the Lord brought Israel out of Egypt and by a prophet he was preserved." Thus, "Egypt" also functions as a symbol or type of bondage and oppression in Hosea 8:13; 9:3, 6; 11:3–5; and 12:13. Such paternal relationships between a father and his son are stressed in Hosea 11:3–4, for "I taught Ephraim to walk, taking them by their arms; but they did not know that I healed them. I drew them with gentle cords, with bands of love."

Not much seems to be gained from a discussion as to whether the preposition "out of" is a local ("from Egypt") or a temporal ("since Egypt") usage. Robert Gundry has argued that because the departure from Egypt is not taken up until after Matthew 2:20, we may conclude that Matthew intended a temporal sense here, "Since Egypt I have called my Son."[13] Whereas the suggestion is a possibility, it is doubtful whether either Hosea or Matthew meant to pivot their argument on that point.

Much more interesting is the suggestion made by Barnabas Lindars.[14] Noting that the idea of a star from the east mentioned in Matthew 2 points back to the Balaam prophecies in Numbers 24, he suggests that "out of Egypt" also occurs in these prophecies twice (Num. 23:22; 24:8) and might also have reminded Matthew of Hosea 11:1. Thus he took his text from Hosea 11:1, but the interpretation (or *pesher,* if you please) came from the LXX of Numbers 24:7–8: "There will come a man out of his [i.e., Israel's] seed and he will rule over the nations. . . . God led him [Jacob] out of Egypt." Whereas verse 8 refers

12. Note also that the place where Christ was crucified is "spiritually called Egypt" in Revelation 11:8.
13. Robert H. Gundry, *The Use of the Old Testament,* p. 93. See his citation on p. 93, n.2. Also, Arndt and Gingrich list this as one of the meanings of *ek,* 5a.
14. Barnabas Lindars, *New Testament Apologetic,* pp. 216–17.

to Jacob, it could be interpreted messianically by the same token and thus we have the missing connection between Hosea 11:1 and Matthew 2:15.

Unfortunately for this ingenious suggestion, the Masoretic text has "Water shall flow from his buckets." The Syriac Peshitta reads instead, "a mighty man shall proceed from his sons," and the Targum Onkelos has, "a king shall grow great, who shall be reared from his sons." It is evident that the first part of verse 7 has a poor Masoretic text, but the evidence is too slim at this point to suggest what the original reading was.

Kittel's Hebrew Bible[15] can only make various proposed readings based on the versional evidence we have already mentioned. Should the Septuagintal reading prove to be the correct one, I doubt if Lindars' connection would hold. It would only serve to show that Hosea had a larger base of informed theology of what was involved when he said, "Out of Egypt have I called my son." The antecedent theology of Balaam would have added to his messianic understanding, but surely he had such already when he deliberately chose to use a technical messianic term ("My Son") with its generic connections with the one and many, that is, the Messiah and Israel, as well as with those antecedent contexts of deliverance and love shown to God's son, the seed of the woman, Abraham, and David.

MATTHEW'S POSITIONING OF THE QUOTE

The fact that Matthew introduced this quote at verse 15 and not after verse 20 or even verse 22 clearly points to the fact that the *Exodus*, or *departure*, of the Holy Family from Egypt is *not* his reason for introducing the quotation at this point. Instead, the emphasis falls exactly where it did in the context of Hosea: the preserving love of God for his seed, Israel. The Exodus for Hosea was only one of the numerous acts of God's love while rebellious Israel ran away from Him.

C. H. Dodd rightly emphasized that often a NT citation of an OT text indicated that the whole context of that OT quote was involved.[16] It is precisely this regard for the larger Hosean context that will explain why Matthew placed his text where he did.[17] Both Israel and

---

15. *Biblia Hebraica*, ed. Rudolf Kittel, 7th ed. (Stuttgart: Württembergische Bibelanstalt, 1951), p. 236.
16. See the Introduction for a discussion of this point. C. H. Dodd, *According to the Scriptures*, p. 126.
17. K. Stendahl, "Quis et Unde?" (p. 97) suggested that Matthew did not wait until 2:21 to insert this citation because he wanted to give a different geographic emphasis to the return journey—not a journey from Egypt, but a journey to Nazareth. Raymond E. Brown, *The Birth of Messiah* (p. 220), added he may also have wanted this reference to the Exodus to precede his reference to the exile in Matthew 2:17–18.

the infant Jesus were the objects of God's love and deliverance in the face of an oppressor.

Thus, the NT writer quoted a single verse not as a prooftext, but as a pointer to his source's larger context. Instead of interrupting the flow of his argument with a lengthy digression, he let the words of Hosea 11:1 introduce that whole context in Hosea. Despite Hosea's sharp words of judgment, he nevertheless emphasized God's love in his preservation of his son, Israel—especially during an early stage in her life. Similarly, Matthew stressed the evidence of God's love in the preservation of his son once again during the early years of Messiah's life on earth.

THE FULFILLMENT FORMULA AND SUMMARY

The discussion of the meaning of *plēroō* in Matthew, much less elsewhere in the NT, has occasioned a massive literature[18] with very few agreed-on conclusions by the scholarly community. It would appear that *plēroō*, in this context, signifies the *completion* or *consummation* of what was only partially realized at the time of Genesis 46:4 ("I will go down to Egypt with you and I will also certainly bring you up again") or the time of the Exodus (Ex. 4:22–23).

To appreciate Matthew's use of Hosea 11:1, the following points need to be kept in mind: (1) both Israel and Jesus are intimately related to God in the title "My Son"; (2) both are intimately interrelated in a corporate solidarity in the use of this technical and theological term, "My Son"; and (3) both Hosea and Matthew are emphasizing not so much the departure point, Egypt, as they are stressing the gracious act of God's preservation in a time of great distress, oppression, and opposition.

Did Hosea, you ask finally, intend to give a prophecy when he penned the words "Out of Egypt have I called My Son"? No, it was not a prophecy as was Micah 5:2; but on the other hand, it was not merely a historical reminiscence either. No doubt Hosea understood the technical nature of "My Son" along with its implications for corporate solidarity. Furthermore, Hosea had a wide range of time before his eyes. He began with the time when Israel was a child, continued through the era of Israel's present distress when God was still loving them because they belonged to that elect "Seed," and

---

18. See, for example, Bruce M. Metzger, "The Formulas Introducing Quotations of Scripture in the NT and The Mishnah," *JBL* 70 (1951):297–307; Brevard S. Childs, "Prophecy and Fulfillment: A Study of Contemporary Hermeneutics," *Interpretation* 12 (1958):259–71, esp. 264–68; C. F. D. Moule, "Fulfillment-Words in the New Testament: Use and Abuse," *NTS* 14 (1967–68):293–320; and Gurdon C. Oxtoby, *Prediction and Fulfillment in the Bible* (Philadelphia: Westminster, 1966), pp. 66–68.

ended in the future eschaton when "they shall go after the Lord" (Hos. 11:10) and his sons "shall come trembling from the west,... from Egypt,... and ... from Assyria (Hos. 11:10–11). Hence, his point about the Son's preservation invited future comparisons with what God would do in subsequent history as He again and again delivered that "Son" until the final and ultimate deliverance in the last Man of Promise came. This is biblical typology at its best, for it begins with a clear divine designation, is limited in its sphere of operation to the act of preservation and deliverance, and is circumscribed in its effects: the redemptive action of God in history. There is no distortion or abuse of the context of Hosea by Matthew; nor has he added his own interpretation to the text.

MATTHEW'S USE OF JEREMIAH 31:15

Matthew 2:18 poses almost as great a difficulty for the student of NT citations of the OT as Matthew 2:15. It would appear that Herod's slaughter of the infants at first has little or nothing at all to do with the Genesis account of Rachel, one of the mothers of the twelve-tribe nation, or Jeremiah 31:15, which is cited here. Thus, the question is simply this: Did Matthew use Jeremiah 31:15 in the same way that Jeremiah meant it to be understood, or did Matthew misappropriate Jeremiah's text and shape it for his own purposes?

THE CONTEXT OF JEREMIAH 31:15

Charles A. Briggs[19] divided Jeremiah 30–31 (the first half of the "Book of Comfort," Jer. 30–33) into six strophes, each commencing with the characteristic, "Thus says the Lord," as follows: (1) the time of Jacob's trouble (30:1–11); (2) the healing of the incurable wound (30:12—31:6); (3) Ephraim, God's firstborn (31:7–14); (4) Rachel weeping for her children (31:15–22); (5) the restoration of Israel in Judah and the new covenant (31:23–34); and (6) God's inviolable covenant with the nation Israel (31:35–40). It is the fourth strophe from which Matthew took his citation.

THE LOCATION AND SIGNIFICANCE OF RAMAH

Four sites have been proposed for Ramah including: Ramallah (eight miles north of Jerusalem), Beit Rama (twelve miles northwest of Bethel), Nebi Samwil (immediately to the north of Jerusalem), and

---

19. Charles A. Briggs, *Messianic Prophecy* (New York: Scribner's, 1889), pp. 246–57. Essentially the same outline is given by George H. Cramer, "Messianic Hope in Jeremiah," *Bibliotheca Sacra* (1958):237–46.

Er-Ram, the Ramah of Benjamin, near Bethel.[20] If we are to locate this site in connection with one of the traditional sites of Rachel's grave, then consideration must be given to Genesis 35:16–20; 48:7, which locates it "some distance from Ephrath" (identified with Bethlehem in Gen. 35:19) on the road from Bethel. However, 1 Samuel 10:2 specifies that it was in the territory of Benjamin. The rabbis themselves debated over these two rival traditions for Rachel's grave already in the third century: was it near Bethlehem in Judah or was it in Benjamin?[21] Thus, it still is impossible to determine with any degree of certainty.

However, it is certain that the Judean captives were assembled in chains along with the prophet Jeremiah for their exile to Babylon at Ramah (Jer. 40:1). It may well be as B. Lindars[22] has suggested that the proverb about Rachel's weeping did not begin with Jeremiah. It may already have taken hold of the heart of the people after the Assyrian deportation and the fall of the Northern Kingdom that had preceded this Babylonian menace. If that suggestion were proved to be correct, it would tend to locate the collecting-point for the captives at Ramah of Benjamin on the border of Ephraim. The lament, at any rate, was a traditional one associated with Rachel and perhaps her tomb, whether it was located in Benjamin or Judah. In fact, because of the constant confusion, perhaps there continued to be rival laments offered simultaneously at both sites; hence the appropriateness of connecting it with the collecting-point in the north and with the destruction of the children of Bethlehem by Herod.

RACHEL'S WEEPING AND REFUSING COMFORT

The two verbs used by Jeremiah are key to understanding his message: "Rachel is weeping (*mᵉbakkâh*, a *piel* participle) for her children" and "she refuses (*mēᵃ̓nâh*, a *piel* perfect verb) to be comforted."[23] Because we can rule out the past and future senses of the verb by the context of Jeremiah 31:16, the present tense remains to translate the verb, "she refuses." Moreover, the perfect tense is what we might call a "characteristic perfect," reflecting an ongoing static character of someone or something. The value of this observation

20. James A. Thompson, "Ramah," *New Bible Dictionary* (London: Intervarsity, 1962), pp. 1075–76. See also F. M. Abel, *Géographie de la Palestine* (1933), 2:427.
21. Gen. Rab. 82.10; I owe this reference to R. T. France, "Formula-Quotations," p. 245, n.32.
22. Barnabas Lindars, "Rachel Weeping for Her Children—Jeremiah 31:15–22," *JSOT* 12 (1979):47–62.
23. I am indebted to my student Alan N. Schramm for many of the insights in this section. Alan also credits his teacher and my colleague, Thomas McComiskey, for defining the perfect as a "characteristic perfect" in this text.

can be seen when we realize that the participle can also denote duration. But the really conclusive piece of evidence comes when it is realized that the verb *bākâh*, "to weep," although it is a very common verb, it used only one other time in the *piel* stem—in Ezekiel 8:14. There it is used of women weeping for Tammuz in a ritualistic practice. This would tend to confirm the durative action of the participle and justify calling the perfect a characteristic perfect. Rachel has continued to weep, according to this proverb, for an unspecified length of time, but especially on those occasions when her children were once again visited by the grim hand of death, calamity, and national disruption.

THE END OF THE WEEPING

Even though Jeremiah clearly says that the Babylonian Exile will last for seventy years (Jer. 25:11, 12; 29:10), it is just as clear that he knows that the Exile will not end until the coming of the new David. The whole book of comfort (Jer. 30-33) offers not only the renewal of the ancient covenant with the inhabitants of Judah and Israel, but a new David who will sit on the throne of Israel once again (30:8-9; 33:14-15, 17).

The termination of Rachel's weeping could not come until (1) Israel's fortunes were once more restored (30:3*a*); (2) all Israel was returned to her land (30:3*b;* 31:8-12, 16-17; 32:42-44); (3) their mourning has been turned into joy (31:13); and (4) a permanence to all these good things has arrived (31.40). Clearly, the context of Rachel's weeping lies within the bounds of the ultimate hope of God's final eschatological act.

Thus, Jeremiah's message and intention were not confined to the people of his day. In fact, there are clear eschatological signals in his expressions. "At that time" (Jer. 31:1) is the time indicated in Jeremiah 30:24, "in the latter days" (i.e., "in the end of the days"). It is the era of the "new covenant" (Jer. 31:31-34) and the day when his covenant with David and the Levitical priests comes to fruition (Jer. 33:17-26).

MATTHEW'S USE OF JEREMIAH 31:15

If Jeremiah realized that Rachel wept over her children/nation in the past, and had continued to do so in his day with the unspeakably horrible events of the Babylonian sack of Jerusalem and its Temple, did he not also realize that she would yet have future occasions to weep in the days that lay ahead prior to the eschatological inbreaking of the new David and the restoration of Israel to her land? How many chastisements, when they would appear, and under what circumstances they would come, Jeremiah does not profess to know, much less imagine. But the iterative and durative nature of these days of trouble he does know.

In addition to Rachel's reason for tears, is it not fair to note that the next verse in Jeremiah (31:16) is the divine word that Rachel should "Hold back [her] voice from weeping, and [her] eyes from tears; for [her] work would be rewarded"? There was hope for their future (v. 17) and they would come back from the land of their enemy (v. 16c).

Did Matthew, then, misuse Jeremiah 31:15? Did Jeremiah specifically predict the slaughter of infants in Bethlehem during Jesus' day? No, not specifically, but *generically* he did. A *generic prophecy*, according to Willis J. Beecher, "is one which regards an event as occurring in a series of parts, separated by intervals, and expresses itself in language that may apply indifferently to the nearest part, or to the remoter parts, or to the whole—in other words, a prediction which, in applying to the whole of a complex event, also applies to some of its parts."[24] That is the situation here. The words are indeed proverbial and in that sense are timeless, but once again more must be considered than the mere citation. Again, the whole context of the book of comfort must be brought to bear on the total understanding of this passage. Thus, Rachel must weep yet once more in Herod's time before that grand day of God's new David and new Israel.

Those who see Matthew's purpose strictly as a geographical one[25] cannot handle this text properly because Jeremiah focuses on the action of weeping and not on the place. It is precisely the place that remains unknown and troublesome for the interpreter, whereas the old familiar cries of suffering and the biblical context for this citation are not unknown or troublesome. There is no obvious connection between the place name of Ramah and the narrative; in fact, Matthew 2:16 does not mention Ramah at all, only Bethlehem. Thus, "if there is any significance in the mention of Ramah, it is certainly not on the surface."[26]

Matthew knew that in one sense Jeremiah's Exile and Rachel's weeping was a current phenomena when Jesus was born. Had not Amos predicted that the new David would come *during* the days of the collapse of David's dynasty—in effect, during the Exile? Accordingly, until that day, one had only to name another calamity in Israel and the Rachel factor would once more be involved.

24. Willis J. Beecher, *The Prophets and the Promise* (Grand Rapids: Baker, 1963 [1905]), p. 130.
25. See above, n.5.
26. R. T. France, "Formula-Quotations," p. 244.

CONCLUSION

Matthew 2:15 and 18 are not the easiest OT quotations to explain; admittedly, they are among the most difficult. But we have found no evidence to substantiate the claims that Matthew disregarded the OT context from which those citations were taken. S. L. Edgar is wide of the mark when he judged Matthew 2:18 to be "the most striking case of disregard of context in the N.T."[27] First, he is too certain that Ramah cannot be equated with Bethlehem (the evidence is much more ambivalent). Second, he assumes that the only common element left to both narratives is the expression of great sorrow. But this fails to deal with the distinctive quality of Jeremiah's verbs and the eschatological context of his pericopae on Rachel's weeping. Failure to include the whole canonical context of this section along with the informing theology of the antecedent Scripture leaves one with a flat Bible and the single concern of historical context. Historical context is important, but it must not become so dominant that it swallows up other legitimate exegetical concerns.

Matthew displayed a sensitivity for the whole context of Hosea and Jeremiah—one that involved an awareness of their canonical, theological, and eschatological contexts in addition to their historical context. Therefore, the charge that Matthew was cavalier in his use of OT materials or that he introduced his own interpretations as part of the text do not stand up to any detailed analysis of either the OT or the NT.

27. S. L. Edgar, "Respect for Context in Quotations from the Old Testament," *NTS* 9 (1962–63):58. With this estimate on Matthew 2:18 agreed Richard T. Mead, "A Dissenting Opinion About Respect for Context in Old Testament Quotations," *NTS* 10 (1963–64):281—"... *violation* has occurred when the historical OT situation is thoroughly disregarded (e.g., Matt. ii.18 ...)." He argued that in Jesus' use of OT words we find less disregard for the context!

PART 2

THE PROPHETIC USE
OF THE OLD TESTAMENT
IN THE NEW

Introduction

No question has begged more insistently for an answer than the problem of the Christian interpretation of the OT. One of the issues that strikes at the heart of this question is the concept of prophecy and the allusions in both Testaments to specific fulfillments, for, as Raymond E. Brown counseled, "whether modern scholars like it or not, prediction was the way the New Testament writers themselves related the testaments."[1]

PREDICTION OR PROMISE?

However, is the word *prediction* the best way to speak of the way OT prophetic texts relate to the NT? A prediction is a foretelling or a prognostication. It usually concentrates the listener's or reader's attention on only two items: (1) the word spoken before the event to which it refers; and (2) the fulfilling event itself. Now, much in this method is commendable and appropriate where exegesis legitimizes such claims. But it does have some serious deficiencies. One deficiency is that its focus is too narrow in that it forces a concentration on the two ends of the spectrum, virtually dropping out everything between those two ends.

---

1. Raymond E. Brown, "Hermeneutics," in *Jerome Biblical Commentary* (Englewood Cliffs, N.J.: Prentice-Hall, 1968), 2:615, 651.

The corrective we would suggest for this imbalance is the category of *promise*. The difference between mere prediction and promise is that the latter embraces, as Willis J. Beecher taught us:

> ... the means employed for that purpose. The promise and the means and the result are all in mind at once. ... If the promise involved a series of results we might connect any one of the results with the foretelling clauses as a fulfilled prediction. ... But if we preeminently confined our thought to these items in the fulfilled promise, we should be led to an inadequate and very likely a false idea of the promise and its fulfillment. To understand the predictive element aright we must see it in the light of the other elements. Every fulfilled promise is a fulfilled prediction; but it is exceedingly important to look at it as a promise and not as a prediction.[2]

This one contribution may fairly revolutionize the way most interpreters handle prophetic passages. So much of the OT prophecy often involves not only a series of words, but also a series of results emanating from those words before the climactic fulfillment comes. Therefore, fairness would demand that the exegete handle prophetic materials as promise rather than as mere predictions.

But there is more. Several additional interpretive issues have perennially confronted the church in her use of the prophetic statement in Scripture.

1. There is the concept of "prophetic perspective," which deals with the question of the time relationships between the original predictive word and the future events they signaled. Was the prophet aware of a time lapse between his ultimate hope and his present realization of some of the immediate results of his prophetic word?

2. Did the OT writers have any feeling or understanding of the ultimate hope to which their words pointed in their messianic or eschatological significance?

3. Did those prophetic words receive only a partial fulfillment, double or multiple fulfillment, continuous fulfillment, or a complete fulfillment?

4. Were their predictions cosmopolitan, often embracing the whole world, or were they nationalistic and limited to Israel's geographical sphere and political career? Such are some of the key issues demanding hard, but exegetically faithful answers, if we are to make progress in the hermeneutical analysis of prophetic statements. Accordingly, besides answering whether these are predictions or promises, we must also decide whether the OT prophecies are: (1) separate or

---

2. Willis J. Beecher, *The Prophets and the Promise* (Grand Rapids: Baker, 1963 [1905]), p. 361.

cumulative?; (2) temporal or eternal?; and (3) national or cosmopolitan?

The amazing feature of OT prophecy is that there is a unity and a single plan throughout the testament—not diverse, separate, and scattered predictions. Each new word is invariably added to the ongoing and continuous promise-plan of God that was first announced to Eve, Shem, and the Patriarchs.[3] In turn, those are then enlarged and periodically supplemented throughout the historical process until the postexilic era of Haggai, Zechariah, and Malachi. Yet, it ever remained as God's single, cumulative promise.

Almost all interpreters note, however, that this single plan often occurs with a phenomena known as *prophetic foreshortening.* The perspective of the prophet in certain predictive passages often simultaneously included two or more events that were separated in time at their fulfillment, yet, there often was no indication of a time lapse between these various fulfillments in the predictive word as they were originally given.

DOUBLE OR SINGLE MEANING?

It has been almost a badge of honor among many evangelical interpreters to account for this phenomena by attributing a *double sense* or *double meaning* to such passages. Likewise, when many interpreters use the term *double fulfillment,* they often mean that a prophetic passage possesses a double meaning or double sense.

A double meaning may be defined in this way:

> If we ascribe to any passage of Scripture a literal, obvious, historical sense, and interpret it as conveying the meaning which its words naturally and obviously seem to convey, and yet at the same time ascribe to these same words another meaning which is occult or obscure but still is designed to be conveyed by those same words, we then make out a double sense.[4]

The controversy over the principle of double sense has a long history. As far back as Theodore of Mopsuestia (A.D. 350–428) we find contrary opinions, for Theodore rejected "all interpretations of any prophecy that favored duplicity."

3. For the development of this thesis, see W. C. Kaiser, Jr., *Toward an Old Testament Theology* (Grand Rapids: Zondervan, 1978), pp. 71–99.
4. Moses Stuart, *Hints on the Interpretation of Prophecy* (Andover: Allen, Morrill, and Wardwell, 1842), p. 12. See the programmatic study by David Jeremiah, "The Principle of Double Fulfillment in Interpreting Prophecy," *Grace Journal,* vol. 13 (1972):13–29.

The case for double fulfillment has been summarized most succinctly and used most widely from the pen of J. Dwight Pentecost:
"Few laws are more important to observe in the interpretation of
prophetic Scriptures than the law of double reference. Two events,
widely separated as to the time of their fulfillment, may be brought
together into the scope of prophecy."[5]

But the older work of Thomas Hartwell Horne is even more explicit:

> The same prophecies frequently have a double meaning, and refer to
> different events, the one near, the other remote, the one temporal, the
> other spiritual or perhaps eternal. The prophets thus having several
> events in view, their expressions may be partly applicable to one and
> partly to another, and it is not always easy to make the transitions.
> What has not been fulfilled in the first, we must apply to the second;
> and what has already been fulfilled, may often be considered as typical
> of what remains to be accomplished.[6]

Now there is much that we can commend in Horne's observations,
for we do not deny that the OT prophets often had a plethora of detail
within the compass of a single concept—including near and far
fulfillments with a prophetic foreshortening of the time perspective.
But we cannot agree that this also involved a dual sense or meaning
for the prophecy (e.g., literal and spiritual).

The axiom of interpretation that makes communication possible is
"no passage in any literature has more than one sense" unless that
literature signals us that we are dealing with phrases with double
entendre, enigmas, or the like. The answer many give to this axiom,
of course, is that the Bible is a divine book whose real author is God.
When the human authors of Scripture wrote, they composed their
books under a divine guidance that protected them from error or
mistake. All of this is true. But can we deduce from this anything that
would defend a double meaning theory? Certainly the content and
matter of Scripture transcends the discovery of unaided reasoning
powers, but should the manner of communicating that information
to us, the listening and reading church, differ from what is usual or
normal among them?[7] We strongly deny that the manner is different.
If it should have been so, how would the Bible be what it is: a
revelation from God? Rather than concealing and hiding meanings, a
revelation is intended to be a disclosure, an unveiling, and an exposing

5. J. Dwight Pentecost, *Things to Come* (Findlay, Ohio: Dunham, 1958), p. 56.
6. Thomas Hartwell Horne, *Introduction to the Critical Study and Knowledge of the
   Holy Scriptures* (New York: Robert Carter, 1859), 1:390.
7. See our fuller defense of this line of reasoning in our article, "Legitimate Hermeneutics," in *Inerrancy*, ed. Norman L. Geisler (Grand Rapids: Zondervan, 1979), pp.
   118–24.

of divine thought to mortals. Just as no thoughtful father would attempt to teach his children, and yet use language and principles that go beyond their ability to grasp them, so also, when God spoke in revelation, he intended to be understood.

The implications of this line of arguing are momentous. The situation is exactly what Moses Stuart said it was:

> Indeed, the moment we assume that there is in the Scriptures a substantial departure from the *usus loquendi* (= "spoken current usage"],[8] either in the choice of words, the construction of sentences or the modes of interpretation, that moment we decide that, as far as this departure extends, they are no *revelation*.[9]

We are faced, then, with this choice:

> We must, therefore, either concede that the *usual* laws of language are to be applied to the Bible, or else that it is, and can be, no proper revelation to men, unless they are also to be inspired in order to understand it. For if we suppose words are to be employed, and sentences constructed and interpreted, in a manner entirely new and different from all that has hitherto been known or practiced, then there is no source from which we can derive rules to interpret the Bible, unless it be one which is supernatural and miraculous.[10]

But, if some still insist that a *huponoia* or occult sense exists and that that sense is not deducible from or by the laws of language, then another question must follow: How is this double sense to be ascertained? Surely we will not let fancy or imagination be the judges. And if we choose to delay the interpreting process until the NT writers pass a decision on the matter, how shall we validate those claims of the apostles? If indeed a NT fulfillment has taken place, who is to agree when we are without any knowledge of an OT prediction— seeing such phenomena exceed the laws of language and *usus loquendi?* Furthermore, what boundaries are to be placed on double meaning? It would appear that once a mystical second sense is conceded, every man and woman is likewise extended the liberty of foisting on Scripture such meanings as each may please. Examples of such are all too numerous in the history of the church, much less in present-day practice. Consider the Jesuit who preached seven sermons on the interjection *O!* Why stop at seven? Or smile (if you can) at the eighty-two comparisons between the horses (text: Song of

---

8. For a classical discussion on the meaning of *usus loquendi*, see Milton S. Terry, *Biblical Hermeneutics* (Grand Rapids: Zondervan, n.d.), pp. 181–90.
9. Moses Stuart, *Hints*, p. 16.
10. Ibid., p. 17.

Solomon 1:9: "I will liken you, my beloved, to a mare harnassed to one of the chariots of Pharaoh") and the church—the last of which was that both the steeds and the church move at a steady gait of perseverance over hill and dale through the wilderness of this life![11]

Of course, the abuse of a method is not a good argument against its use, "but if a thing is of such a nature that it is all abuse ... it is a good argument against it."[12] Such a method, of course, would never be used (except in cultic mentalities) to establish any scriptural doctrine or precept; but then, why would we commend such a method for prophecy?

DOUBLE OR GENERIC FULFILLMENT?

Nevertheless, the phenomena of prophetic foreshortening does occur. It is, as we have already said, the situation where two or more events, often separated in time at their fulfillment, are described with no specific indication of the time lapse between them. If this does not call for a double meaning, what does it indicate?

No doubt the most extensive discussion of this issue was offered by Franklin Johnson.[13] In his judgment, "A large part of this controversy might have been avoided had writers on both sides used the term 'double reference' instead of the term 'double sense.'"[14] Franklin Johnson proceeds for approximately 200 pages to give illustration after illustration from secular and sacred literature of the phenomena of double reference. His warning is this: "If we say that every passage

11. Ibid., p. 22; Edwin Penner, "Interpreting Old Testament Prophecy" (*Direction* 6[1977]:44) had argued: "That there was a sense intended by the Holy Spirit which the human author did not intend, or know about, is understandable because God is ... the principal author of Scripture, and man only the instrument. [Therefore, God's] intentions are the criteria by which the meaning of Scripture must be understood.... This 'fuller' sense lies beyond our immediate exegetical control." In reply to that article, Delbert L. Wiens correctly argued ("Response," *Direction* 6[1977]:49), "If exegesis is to remain the discovery of the intention of the author, [who] drops out of the picture, [then] ... a third approach emerges. It is God whose intentions must be divined in the text. But who can discern the hidden intentions of God in a text that God apparently intended to be obscure? The doctrine of the *sensus plenior* tends to undermine all attempts at exegesis despite the claim that God himself will interpret his previous revelations in yet another revelation. The New Testament interprets the Old Testament. But do we now dare to interpret the New? By what principle may we be confident that God's latest revelation contains no *sensus plenior*? The more that this approach seems to succeed, the more it reveals exegesis to be either impossible or arbitrary unless it is the product of yet another special revelation (in which case we have revelation, not exegesis)."
12. Ibid., p. 25.
13. Franklin Johnson, *The Quotations of the New Testament from the Old Considered in the Light of General Literature* (Philadelphia: American Baptist Publication Society, 1896), chapter IX, "Double Reference," pp. 186–335.
14. Ibid., p. 197.

of Hebrew literature must be interpreted as having one reference, and no more, we apply to it an arbitrary rule which we must abandon the moment we begin the study of any other great literature which the world has produced."[15]

This much we will cheerfully allow if by "reference" Johnson refers to the "significance" a passage may have. But Johnson goes on to claim that:

> the secondary references in any literature are not always clear to the reader; they do not always lie on the surface; they often belong to the deeper things, and may perplex the most skillful interpreter, as the manifold references of 'The Second Part of Faust' sometimes caused Bayard Taylor almost to despair. In such cases the author himself is our best guide, if he still lives to be consulted. So when the Holy Spirit in the New Testament explains to us this feature of the Old, of which he himself is the author, we should listen to him with reverence.[16]

It is here that we must part company with our learned guide, Franklin Johnson.

In the area of prophecy, there is a much better way of handling this same phenomena. It is what Willis J. Beecher termed a "generic prediction" or what I would call a *generic promise*. He defined it this way:

> A generic prediction is one which regards an event as occurring in a series of parts, separated by intervals, and expresses itself in language that may apply indifferently to the nearest part, or to the remoter parts, or to the whole—in other words, a prediction which, in applying to the whole of a complex event, also applies to some of its parts.[17]

The fundamental idea here is that many prophecies begin with a word that ushers in not only a climactic fulfillment, but a series of events, all of which participate in and lead up to that climactic or ultimate event in a protracted series that belong together as a unit because of their corporate or collective solidarity.[18] In this way, the whole set of events makes up one collective totality and constitutes

15. Ibid., p. 331.
16. Ibid., pp. 331–32.
17. Beecher, *The Prophets*, p. 130.
18. It is customary to credit the coining and application of this concept in biblical studies (though under the more objectionable phrase of "corporate personality") to H. Wheeler Robinson in his *Corporate Personality in Ancient Israel* (1935) from his 1907 *Century Bible Commentary* on Deuteronomy; yet Willis J. Beecher, *The Prophets*, had used it in 1905 (pp. 265–66; p. 380, n.1), and in 1903 in *The American Journal of Theology* (July 1903), p. 543. See our critique in *Toward Old Testament Ethics* (Grand Rapids: Zondervan, 1983), pp. 67–72.

only one idea, even though the events may be spread over a large segment of history by the deliberate plan of God. The important point to observe, however, is that all of the parts belong to a single whole. They are generically related to each other by some identifiable wholeness.

What is the identifiable element in the OT prophetic context that alerts the interpreter to the fact that we are dealing with a generic promise? For one thing, it is the presence of collective singular nouns whose singular form may take, at one and the same time, a singular and a plural connotation, yet, all within the scope of the *single* meaning of that collective singular noun. Thus a biblical term, such as "Seed," "Branch," and "Holy One" (along with other terms used like collectives: "Son," "Antichrist," "Day of the Lord"), is a generic term that simultaneously may embrace a series of persons (or events), first, as a set of historical antecedents functioning as harbingers, previews, down payments, samplers, or guarantees of the future, and second, as the final or climactic fulfillment of that original word. Accordingly, it may be viewed singularly when seen in any of its separate manifestations or in its final realization in the messianic or eschatological era, or it may be viewed as a plurality when seen as a set or a series of interconnected events that continue to perpetuate that word throughout history, even as each successive birth of the next patriarch or Davidic scion functioned to maintain in history the ancient word and to promise the surety of the final one who embodied everything that the whole series pointed forward to.

Another linguistic clue is the rather frequent shift between the singular and plural pronouns or pronominal suffixes of the Hebrew text. At one and the same time Israel is regarded as an individual and a whole group. Only on the basis of the generic promise can we explain how, for example, the "Servant" can simultaneously be designated as "Israel" (Isa. 44:1) and an individual who ministers to all Israel (Isa. 52:13—53:12). Likewise, the pronoun suffixes in Amos 9:11–12 alternate between the singular and plural, involving the final Davidic ruler, Christ, and the restored and reunited divided kingdoms of northern and southern Israel.

The third, and probably most decisive sign that we are dealing with a generic prophecy and not a dual or multiple meaning prediction, is to be found in the analogy of *antecedent* theology[19] and Scripture to which this new element in the single plan of God belongs. Each prophecy has a canonical setting that cannot be ignored; for if it is treated in abstraction and isolation from all that has *preceded* it in

19. See a fuller discussion in Walter C. Kaiser, Jr., *Toward an Exegetical Theology* (Grand Rapids: Baker, 1981), pp. 131–40.

the history of revelation, it will soon degenerate to being little more than religious soothsaying.

But what is it that triggers appropriate association for the interpreter with biblical material on the same subject that has appeared *prior* to the time of this new addition to that same genera of revelation? Some of the clues to the antecedent theology in a text are:

1. The use of terms that by now have acquired a special use and taken on a technical status in history of salvation such as "seed," "servant," "rest," "kingdom," and "holy one";
2. A *direct quotation* of a portion or the entirety of an earlier word from God;
3. An *allusion* to a phrase, clause, sentence, or formula found in the earlier texts of Scripture;
4. An allusion or direct reference to earlier *events* in the history of Israel that had special significance for that day and all later generations of believers; and
5. A reference to the *contents* of God's numerous promises or covenants that formed the substance of His promise-plan for the created-redeemed order of the universe

The reader will notice that we have deliberately avoided all references to using later texts, such as the NT in order to interpret the OT. When the Reformers announced that *scriptura scripturam interpretatur,* "Scripture interprets scripture," along with *analogia fidei,* the "analogy of faith," they were not erecting an absolute or external standard by which all Scripture itself had to be measured. To do so would only have reversed the hard-fought-for and newly acquired *independent* authority of Scripture and returned it once again to a new set of traditions or a canon within a canon, which would act as the super interpreter and arbitrator of competing views concerning Scripture. Instead, the Reformers had always intended those two standards to be a *relative* expression aimed explicitly at the tyrannical demands and stranglehold that tradition tended to exercise over Scripture. "*Analogia fidei* was intended solely to deny that tradition was the interpreter of the Bible."[20] The clearest statement of this principle was given by John F. Johnson:

> To put it tersely: *analogia* or *regula fidei* is to be understood as "the clear Scripture" itself; and this refers to articles of faith found in those

---

20. Herbert Marsh, *A Course of Lectures, Containing a Description and Systematic Arrangement of the Several Branches of Divinity . . . , seven parts* (Boston: Cummings and Hilliard, 1815), 3:16. See especially John F. Johnson, "*Analogia Fidei* as Hermeneutical Principle," *Springfielder* 36 (1972–73):249–59.

passages which deal with individual doctrines expressly (*sedes doctri-nae*). Individual doctrines are to be drawn from the *sedes doctrinae* and must be judged by them. Any doctrine not drawn from passages which expressly deal with the doctrine under consideration is not to be accepted as Scriptural.[21]

Thus, Johnson correctly limited this principle to teaching us that doctrine must first be identified and explicated on the basis of large blocks of texts where that doctrine was most fully developed or was announced in its "chair" position (which practice, incidentally, would more than restore the falling fortunes of systematic theology if it would be reestablished as the starting point for teaching Christian doctrine in the church and its academies). Therefore, we reject the all-too-prevalent practice of using the NT fulfillment as an "open sesame" for OT predictions. Not only does that practice develop a canon within a canon, but it tends to establish false levels or qualities of revelation, which, in turn, are subject to newer revelations (of a super-exegesis), and thereby binding the Word of God when it was intended to be an open disclosure, unveiling and making naked the truth of God.

B.C. OR A.D. FULFILLMENT?

Must we then choose either an antique, historically bound OT word or a rejuvenated and recently unlocked NT fulfillment of prophecy? Must we choose between an earlier literal meaning and a second, plural meaning that may exceed this earlier literal sense?

It is clear that the one and same message of the OT writers often envisaged two or more audiences separately (and as we now know, widely separately) in time. Moreover, it is also clear the referents intended within that single message were often plural in number, but that plurality (and here is the most critical observation) was such that it shared a unity much like the *parts* of one mechanism belong to the *whole* machine. Thus, there is a "generic" wholeness, as Beecher[22] would say, or a "compenetration" as some Roman Catholics[23] would label it. It is as if the prophet, on receiving the divine oracle, looked out over the future horizon and was divinely enabled prophetically to

21. John F. Johnson, "*Analogia Fidei*," p. 253.
22. Beecher, *The Prophets*, p. 130 (as cited in n.17 above).
23. Sutcliffe, "Prophetical Literature," *A Catholic Commentary on The Holy Scripture*, p. 537 as cited by Bernard Ramm, *Protestant Biblical Interpretation* 3d rev. ed. (Grand Rapids: Baker, 1970), p. 253: "In an Old Testament passage the near meaning and the remote meaning for the New Testament so *compenetrate* that the passage at the same time and in the same words refers to the near and the remote New Testament meaning."

see both one or more near results as well as a distinctive, but more distant climactic fulfillment, with both the near and distant results of that word so generically linked that the words possessed one meaning in a collective whole.

Such a solution is very close to the concept of *theoria* posed by the Antiochian school of interpretation. In the main, this solution to Biblical prophecy (from the Greek word *theorein*, "to look, gaze at," hence a vision of the future) connected three things:

1. The *historia*, literal, historical divine word that came in the prophet's own day;
2. A forthcoming result or fulfillment of that divine oracle that became a means of connecting that divine oracle and a new perpetuation of the ancient promise given by God and pointed to the bigger, better, more definitive and ultimate fulfillment in the remote future;
3. The ultimate conclusion of this series, which was generically and corporately part and parcel of that same word and intervening events that were the means of guaranteeing and keeping this hope alive.

Once again, then, we argue that all three aspects are to be embraced in the one, single sense: (1) the divine word, (2) the near fulfillments that transmitted that word through the events of history; and (3) the climactic realization in the eschaton. If diagrammed, our plea for generic prophecy or Antiochian *theoria* would graphically appear like this.

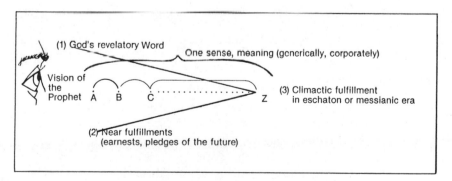

Thus, we would conclude that the truth-intention of the present was always singular and never double or multiple in sense. Yet, by design that same prophetic word often embraced and encompassed an extended period of time by describing protracted events, giving characteristics that belonged to several periods of time, or, in the messianic line it would link a whole string of persons, who in their office, function, or person pointed to the last person in the series who shared those same features specifically prophesied about the Davidic forerunners.

Such a solution, which features only one sense or meaning in a generic wholeness concept, will not square, according to the critics of this theory with Caiaphas's alleged witness to the contrary. The text used here is John 11:49–52:

> And one of them, named Caiaphas, being high priest that same year, said to them, "You know nothing at all, nor consider that it is expedient for us, that one man should die for the people that the whole nation should not perish." This he spoke not of himself, but he, being high priest that year, prophesied that Jesus should die for that nation; and not for that nation alone, but that he should also gather together in one the children of God that were scattered abroad.

Let it immediately be noted that Caiaphas's judgment about his colleagues was accurate: "You know nothing at all!" (John 11:49). But as Rudolph Stier asked, "What better, then [did Caiaphas] know?"[24] His suggestion was purely one of political expediency: it is better to let one man be a sacrificial lamb to save the Jewish cause than to have everyone in the nation implicated and the wrath of Rome falling on the whole body politic.

John's comment on Caiaphas's speech was: "This he spoke not of himself: but he being high priest that year, prophesied." This comment calls for several observations:

1. These words are not to be classed along with later Rabbinic alleged examples of unintentional prophecy, as Strack and Biller-beck have argued in their comments on John 11:51 and 2 Peter 1:20–21 (2:546). Nor is this proof that the earlier prophets belonged to such a category as Rabbi Eleazar (ca. A.D. 270), who argued, "No prophets have known what they prophesied. Only Moses and Elijah knew." Indeed, according to this same line of logic, even "Samuel, the master of the prophets, did not know what he prophesied."[25] On the contrary, Caiaphas illustrates the reverse process. He said what he wanted to say and mean for his own cool, calculated, political good. There was no compulsion or constraint in his speech any more than there was in the super-

---

24. Rudolf Stier, *Words of the Lord Jesus* (Edinburgh: T & T Clark, 1865), 6:56.
25. As quoted by Edwyn C. Hoskyns, *The Fourth Gospel*, 2d ed. (London: Faber and Faber, 1947), p. 412. Charles K. Barrett, *Gospel According to St. John* (London: SPCK, 1960), p. 339.

scription that Pilate put over the cross of Jesus. There was, from John's privileged perspective, however, "a grand irony of a most special Providence"[26] in the words chosen by both Pilate and Caiaphas.

2. The *truth-intention* of Caiaphas (v. 50) is to be sharply contrasted with the *significance* (v. 51) John found in those same words, especially because a person in so high an office as Caiaphas had uttered them—even if he did so as his cynical estimate of the situation. Thus, John introduced a strong contrast (*alla*, "on the contrary") between what Caiaphas had said and meant and the new use when John applies that *same* principle under the inspiration of the Spirit of God.

3. Accordingly, we may properly argue that John *corrected* Caiaphas's provincial statement with its parochial ethnocentricities and thereby turned it into a comprehensive statement of the universal implications of Jesus' death (v. 52). This is most evident in the text, for whereas Caiaphas had used the expression "on behalf of the people" (v. 50), John corrected this posture of political expediency and deliberately expanded it to match the value of Jesus' death; it was now "on behalf of the nation" (v. 51) and on behalf of the "children of God scattered abroad" (v. 52). Caiaphas had only worried about national extinction if Jesus was not made the scapegoat for Rome's wrath. John saw more than national existence on the line; he saw that Jesus must die if any children of God were ever to be united to form the one people of God Jesus had proclaimed in John 10:15–16 and Paul would later describe in Ephesians 2:14.

4. The fact that Caiaphas "did not speak on his own authority" must be carefully understood in the Johannine usage. John uses the expression "on his own authority" in six passages (John 5:19; 7:18; 11:51; 15:4; 16:13; 18:34)—an expression unique to John. In three instances, it clearly means to say something on *one's own* authority: "The son can do nothing on his own authority" (5:19); "a person who speaks on his own authority (7:18); and the Spirit ... will not speak on his own authority" (16:13). If this meaning is also correct for John 11:51—and we believe it is— then John's point was not the method in which Caiaphas spoke (unconscious of involuntary prediction), but what he did had *significance* as a principle that extended beyond his somewhat bitter proverb and his circumscribed reference to the political quandary they found themselves in at the time. Added to that is

26. Stier, *Words of the Lord Jesus*, 6:57.

his high public visibility ("He being high priest that year," vv. 49, 51) and the saying can easily become a byword.

5. When verse 51 commented that Caiaphas was prophesying that (*hoti*) Jesus was about to die, John is not giving to us the contents of Caiaphas's prophecy, but only the fact that the significance of his otherwise witty speech could be found in *reference to the fact that* (*hoti*) Jesus was about to die.

In Caiaphas, then, we do not have the words of a true prophet (such as Balaam's words in Num. 23–24) coming with the authority of God. Instead, we have the jaundiced expression of a wicked priest giving politically sage counsel stated in principial terms that the inspired writer John can easily turn against Caiaphas to make a surprising point that even Caiaphas would need to acknowledge and marvel at its profundity. Thus, God turned back Caiaphas's advice on the head of its speaker to explain the very principle Caiaphas was intent on denying!

Had Caiaphas offered a prophecy in the ordinary sense of the word, there would have been no need for John to have corrected, improved, and added to his prophecy. But when an official with the community stature of a Caiaphas or Pilate could give a verdict that could also take on a proverbial status and significance that accorded with the plan of God, only the God of providence could be praised for turning the wrath of men once more into the glory of God. Had we not had John's corrections and editorial comments on this instance, we might never have attached any other significance to it than the shrewdest of political moves.

But Caiaphas will not support a double-author theory of prophecy or normative revelation. The fact that "he prophesied" is John's playful use of the word against Caiaphas rather than including him as one of the avenues of revelation in the Bible.

Likewise, the text in 2 Peter 1:19–21 offers no consolation to those scholars, like those even of the standing and stature of E. W. Hengstenberg, who argued from this text that the prophets did not always understand nor were they able to interpret their own words. But Peter's point is just the opposite. He said:

> We have also a more sure word of prophecy; whereunto you do well that you take heed, as unto a light that shines in a dark place, until the day dawn, and the day star arise in hearts: Knowing this first, that no prophecy of the Scripture is of any private interpretation. For the prophecy came not in old time by the will of man: but holy men of God spake as they were moved by the Holy Spirit.

Peter had just noted that Christians "have not followed cleverly devised fables" (v. 16), for not only was Peter among those eyewitnesses who saw Jesus' glory on the mount of transfiguration (vv. 16–18), but "we have the stronger [or more secure] prophetic word" found in the OT prophecies (19a). If readers would attentively contemplate what was said in those OT prophecies, they would find the day dawning and the day star rising in their own minds, for they would be instructed, illuminated, and satisfied by means of the light shed from those prophecies (v. 19b).

These OT Scriptures were not a matter of one's own "loosing" (*epiluseōs*, v. 20), "because prophecy came not in old times by the will of man, but holy men of God spoke as they were moved by the Holy Spirit" (v. 21).

To make the word *epiluseōs* mean in this context an "explanation" or "interpretation," as some do, would be to argue that no prophet can interpret his own message and thus the prophet wrote better than he knew. However, that claim is too bold for the following reasons:

1. The substantive *epilusis* in classical usage is a "freeing, loosing" or "destroying"; in other words, it is an unleashing from life. Whereas the NT or LXX exhibits no other example of this form, the verbal form in its original meaning would appear to be "to set at liberty, to let go, to loose," and only secondarily it came to mean "to explain, unfold" or "interpret" as in Mark 4:34.
2. Even if what we have called the secondary meaning were intended by Peter here, would it claim too much? Can it be said, even by these advocates of "wrote better than they knew," that *all* prophetic writings were closed to their writers? We answer no because of the next reason.
3. Peter's readers were urged to give heed to OT prophecies "as unto a light that shines in a dark place," because the Spirit of God had revealed through these prophets what is certain, plain, and intelligible. The "light" offered here came not from the ability of men, deeper insights offered by later prophets, or the like. Rather this "light" came from the "Father of Lights" above who gave it to individual readers such as the readers and listeners of Peter's letter.

Had Peter's logic been, "Give heed to the light shining in a dark place" because no prophet understood or could even explain what he said but he wrote as he was carried along by the Holy Spirit, then that "light" would have been darkness. How could any, including the prophet, then, have given heed to such an enigmatic word? No, because the prophets were enlightened, instructed, and carried along by the Holy Spirit, the Word that was given to us is sure and certain, and it is that Word that the Holy Spirit can and will apply to our hearts to illumine our minds and lives. Had that communicating ability not been the case, we would have been forced to ask for a second miracle—the inspiration of the interpreter.

Accordingly, we approach the prophetic Scriptures of the OT and their use in the NT with confidence. Perhaps the principles we have traced in this introduction can be best illustrated in the analysis of the two passages we have selected: Joel 2:28–32 and Malachi 3–4.

4

Witnessing and Expecting the Arrival of Elijah

Malachi 4:4–5

The NT's interest in the prophet Elijah may be easily assessed from the fact that he is the most frequently mentioned OT figure in the NT after Moses (80 times), Abraham (73), and David (59); Elijah's name appears twenty nine or thirty times.[1]

Even more significant, however, are the six major and explicit references to Elijah in the synoptic gospels. There, some of Jesus' contemporaries identified our Lord—in the second of three opinions— as Elijah (Mark 6:14–16; Luke 9:7–9). Jesus' disciples were also aware of this popular confusion, for they too repeated it (Matt. 16:13–20; Mark 8:27–30; Luke 9:18–21). This connection between Jesus and Elijah continued to hold its grip on many even up to the time of the crucifixion, for those who heard Jesus' fourth word from the cross thought he was calling on Elijah to rescue him (Matt. 27:45–49; Mark 15:33–36). And who should appear on the mount of transfiguration but Moses and Elijah, talking to Jesus (Matt. 17:1–19; Mark 9:2–10; Luke 9:28–36.

But there were two other references in the synoptics that referred to a future coming of Elijah. One came when Jesus' disciples asked why the scribes claimed it was necessary that Elijah had to come first (Matt. 17:10–13; Mark 9:11–13). Jesus responded that "Elijah had come" and said it in such a way that the disciples knew that he meant

---

1. J. Jeremias, "ἡλ(ε)ιας," *TDNT* (1964)2:934. The disparity of twenty-nine or thirty is because of a textual problem in Luke 9:54.

he was John the Baptist. If any doubt remained, Jesus said just that in Matthew 11:14—"he is Elijah, the one who was to come."

However, when one turns from the synoptics to the fourth gospel, none of those six references are present. Instead, we find John categorically denying that he was either Christ, "that [Mosaic] prophet," *or Elijah* (John 1:21, 25)! John's clear disavowal is so stark by way of contrast with the way he is presented in the synoptics that the synoptics and John appear to contradict one another flatly. What explanation can be offered for this phenomenon? And what impact does it have on the question of the NT author's use of OT citations?

THE ISSUES

At stake in this discussion are three critical points of tension: (1) the identity of that coming messenger or future prophet named Elijah; (2) the time of his coming; and (3) the task(s) assigned to him. Each of those three questions raises a number of hermeneutical and theological issues that have left their mark on various traditions of interpretation.

However, even before those three tension points have been joined, perhaps there is a prior question that asks if Elijah's coming is at all connected with the coming of the Messiah. A recent study by Faierstein concludes that:

> Contrary to the accepted scholarly consensus, almost no evidence has been preserved which indicates that the concept of Elijah as forerunner of the Messiah was widely known or accepted in the first century C.E.... The only datum ... is the *baraitha* in *b. Erubin* 43a–b, a text of the early third century C.E.... The further possibility, that the concept of Elijah as forerunner is a *novum* in the NT must also be seriously considered.[2]

Faierstein, while conveniently avoiding the strong evidence of Malachi 3:1; 4:4–5 and the repeated NT allusions, tends to assign either a post-Christian date or to reserve judgment on a whole series of evidences to the contrary from the Jewish community. Certainly the Qumran fragment J. Starcky cited (*lkn 'šlh l'yh qd[m]*, "therefore I will send Elijah befo[re]....") is incomplete;[3] but it should have reminded Faier-

---

2. Morris M. Faierstein, "Why Do the Scribes Say That Elijah Must Come First?" *JBL* 100 (1981):86. John H. Hughes, "John the Baptist: The Forerunner of God Himself," *NovT* 14 (1972):212 is of the same opinion: "There is no reliable pre-Christian evidence for the belief that Elijah was to be the forerunner of the Messiah, and this helps support the suggestion that the conception originated with Jesus."[!]

3. J. Starcky. "Les Quatre Etapes du Messianisme à Qumran," *RB* 70 (1963):489–505. The fragment is 4QarP. See p. 498 as cited in Faierstein, "Elijah Must Come First?" 80, nn. 33–34.

stein to take another look at Malachi 3:1; 4:4–5 [Heb., 3:24–25]. Faierstein also sets aside the same eighteen rabbinic texts L. Ginzberg
analyzes differently: "Now, in no fewer than eighteen passages in the
Talmud, Elijah appears as one who, in his capacity of precursor of the
Messiah, will settle all doubts on matters of ritual and judicial."[4] But
the *locus classicus* of these eighteen, *m. ʿEd.* 8.7, is exceptionally clear.
Elijah would establish legitimate Jewish descent, family harmony, and
resolve differences of opinion and religious controversies. He would
do all this, says *m. ʿEd.* 8.7 " . . . as it is written, *Behold I will send you
Elijah, the prophet . . . and he shall turn the heart of the fathers to the
children and the heart of the children to their fathers.*"[5] Once again,
we are brought back to the Malachi texts if we are to make any
decision on what was normative either for pre-Christian Judaism or
the NT itself. To this day, Judaism continues to reserve for Elijah a
distinguished place and loosely to relate it to their fading expectation
of the coming of the Messiah. This can best be seen in the cup of
Elijah and the seat reserved for him at every Passover meal. The hope
and prayer of every Jew at the conclusion of the Passover—"next year
in Jerusalem"—is one piece of a larger picture of the coming messianic era. And at the heart of it remains the open door for the new
Elijah.

MALACHI 3:1; 4:4–5

THE IDENTITY OF "MY MESSENGER"

God's answer to the impious complaints of the wicked men and
women of Malachi's day who mockingly sneered: "Where is the God
of justice?" was to send *his* messenger to prepare the way for the God
for whom they allegedly searched. He did not promise merely *a*
messenger, but one that was already familiar to them from the
informing theology of Isaiah 40:3, for the words used to describe this
messenger were the same as those used there: he was "to prepare the
way."

No doubt the words "my messenger" (מַלְאָכִי) were intended to be
both a play on the name of the prophet Malachi and prophetic of a
future prophet who would continue his same work. But he was
certainly to be an earthly messenger and not a heavenly being. This

---

4. L. Ginzberg, *An Unknown Jewish Sect* (New York: Jewish Theological Seminary,
1976), p. 212. These eighteen texts all end eighteen talmudic discussions and are
known by the term *teyqu* which came to mean "The Tishbite will resolve difficulties
and problems." Ginzberg lists the location of these eighteen passages in n.14 on
p. 212.
5. Herbert Danby, *The Mishnah* (London: Oxford University, 1958), p. 437 (italics his).

can be demonstrated from three lines of evidence: (1) in Isaiah the voice which called for the preparation of the nation came from someone in the nation itself; (2) this same messenger in Malachi 3:1 is associated with Elijah the prophet in Malachi 4:5; and (3) he is strongly contrasted with "The Lord," "even the messenger of the covenant" in Malachi 3:1.[6]

Thus this messenger cannot be the death angel, as the Jewish commentator Jarchi conjectured,[7] or an angel from heaven as another Jewish commentator Kimchi alleged from Exodus 23:20, a passage that finds its context in a time when Israel was being prepared for a journey into the desert. God's mouthpiece was an earthly proclaimer.

THE IDENTITY OF THE LORD AND THE MESSENGER OF THE COVENANT

"The Lord" (הָאָדוֹן) can only refer to God when used with the article.[8] That he is a divine personage is also evident from these additional facts: he answers to the question of Malachi 2:17, "Where is the *God* of justice?" (2) he comes to "*his* temple" (Mal. 3:1) and, thus, he is the owner of that house in which he promised to dwell; and (3) he is also named the "Messenger of the covenant" (מַלְאַךְ הַבְּרִית). Furthermore, it is clear from passages such as Zechariah 4:14 and 6:5, "אָדוֹן of the whole earth," that אָדוֹן is used interchangeably with Yahweh.[9]

The title "Angel or Messenger of the Covenant," is found nowhere else in the OT. Nevertheless, the title is very reminiscent of the more frequently used, "Angel of the Lord." That was the same "Angel" who had redeemed Israel out of the land of Egypt (Ex. 3:6), had gone before the army as they crossed the Red Sea (Ex. 14:19), led Israel through the wilderness (Ex. 23:20), and filled the Temple with His glory. He was one and the same as Yahweh Himself. This Angel was God's own self-revelation, the preincarnate Christ of the numerous OT Christophanies.[10] He is the same one discussed in Exodus 23:20–23 ("Behold, I send an Angel ... My name is in him"); 33:15 ("My

---

6. These three arguments are substantially those of E. W. Hengstenberg, trans. James Martin, *Christology of the Old Testament* (Edinburgh: T & T Clark, 1875), 4:164.

7. R. Cashdan, ed. A. Cohen, *Soncino Books of the Bible: The Twelve Prophets* (London: Soncino, 1948), p. 349.

8. So argues T. V. Moore (*The Prophets of the Restoration: Haggai, Zechariah and Malachi* [New York: Robert Carter and Bros., 1856], p. 376). He refers to Exodus 23:17; 34:23; Isaiah 1:24; 3:1; 10:16, 33; Malachi 1:12, etc. In Daniel 9:17 הָאָדוֹן seems to refer to the Son.

9. So argues Joyce G. Baldwin (*Haggai, Zechariah and Malachi* [Tyndale Old Testament: 1).

10. See W. C. Kaiser, Jr., *Toward an Old Testament Theology* (Grand Rapids: Zondervan, 1978), pp. 85, 120, 257–58. See references to the "Angel of the Lord" in such texts as Genesis 16:7; 22:11, 15; Judges 2:1; 6:11, 14.

Presence [or face] shall go with you"); and Isaiah 63:9 (The Angel of his Presence or face").

The covenant of which He is the messenger is the same one anciently made with Israel (Ex. 25:8; Lev. 26:11–12; Deut. 4:23; Isa. 33:14) and later *renewed* in Jeremiah 31:31–34 as repeated in Hebrews 8:7–13 and 9:15. Therefore, whereas the covenant was a single plan of God for all ages, this context addressed mainly the Levitical priesthood (Mal. 1:6—2:9) and the nation Israel (Mal. 2:11; 3:5, 8) for violating that covenant relationship.

Still, it must be stressed that there are not two persons represented in "the Lord" and the "Messenger of the Covenant," but only one, as is proved by the singular form of "come" (בָא).[11] Thus, the passage mentions only two persons: "the Lord" and the preparing messenger.

THE CONNECTION BETWEEN THE ANNOUNCER'S TASK AND
THE WORK OF THE LORD

The preparing messenger was "to clear the way before [the Lord]." The striking similarity between this expression (וּפִנָּה דֶרֶךְ לְפָנָה) and that found in Isaiah 40:3, (פַּנּוּ דֶרֶךְ יהוה) 57:14, and 62:10 is too strong to be accidental. The resemblance between Isaiah and Malachi was drawn out even to the omission of the article from דֶרֶךְ, "way"; the only difference is that in Malachi the *messenger* is to prepare the way whereas in Isaiah the *servants* of the Lord are urged to prepare the road.

Under the oriental figure of an epiphany or arrival of the reigning monarch, the text urged for a similar removal of all spiritual, moral, and ethical impediments in preparation for the arrival of the King of glory. Whenever a king would visit a village, the roadway would be straightened, leveled, and all stones and obstacles removed from the road that the king would take as he came to visit the town. The only other instance of this expression is in Psalm 80:9 [Heb., 10]: לְפָנֶיהָ פִּנִּיתָ, "You cleared [the ground] before it [= the vine (or the nation Israel) brought out from the land of Egypt]." Once again, however, it was necessary to do some *clearing away* as a preparation before the nation Israel, here represented as a vine, was to be able to be planted and to take deep root in the land.

This future messenger would likewise clear out the rubbish, obstacles, and impediments "before *me*"—the same one who was identified in the next sentence as *"the Lord,"* "even the *Messenger of the Covenant."* The equation of those three terms can be argued for even more convincingly when it is noticed that the *waw*, "and," which

11. So argues E. W. Hengstenberg, *Christology*, 4:168.

introduces the phrase "and the messenger of the covenant whom you desire" is an epexegetical *waw* used in apposition to the phrase "The Lord whom you are seeking." Therefore, we translate the whole verse:

> Behold, I will send my messenger. He will clear the way ahead of me. Suddenly, the Lord whom you are seeking will come to his temple; even the messenger of the covenant, whom you desire, will come, says the Lord of hosts.

Over against this preparatory work, the Lord and Messenger of the Covenant was to arrive "suddenly" (פִּתְאֹם) at his Temple. The people had longed for the coming of God in judgment as a redress to all wrongs (Mal. 2:17). Indeed, he would come, but it would be "unexpectedly."[12] The ungodly hoped for a temporal deliverer, but Malachi 3:2 warned that most would not be able to stand when that day of judgment came. Not only would the heathen gentiles be judged, but so, too, would the ungodly in Israel. It would appear that the final judgment associated with the second advent has been blended in this passage with the Lord's arrival in his first advent. It was necessary to be prepared for both!

THE IDENTITY OF ELIJAH THE PROPHET

Does Malachi expect the Tishbite to reappear personally on the earth again? It would not appear so, for Malachi 4:5–6 specifically said, "Behold, I will send you Elijah *the*[13] prophet, before the great and terrible day of the Lord comes." Only the LXX reads "Elijah the Tishbite." The reason Elijah was selected is, (1) he was head of the prophetic order in the nation Israel, and (2) many of his successors indirectly received the same spirit and power that divinely was granted to him. There was, as it were, a successive endowment of his gifts, power, and spirit to those who followed in his train.

This phenomenon is known already in the OT, for 2 Chronicles 21:12 mentions "a writing from Elijah the prophet" during the reign of King Jehoram when Elijah had already been in heaven for many years. Furthermore, many of the acts predicted by Elijah were actually

---

12. T. Laetsch, *Bible Commentary: The Minor Prophets* (St. Louis: Concordia [1956], 531): "Suddenly, *pit'om*, is never used to denote immediacy; it always means unexpectedly, regardless of the lapse of time (Joshua 10:9; 11:7; Num. 12:4; Ps. 64:5, 8, A.V. 4, 7; Prov. 3:25; 6:15; Isa. 47:11; Jer. 4:20, etc.)."

13. Jack Willsey ("The Coming of Elijah: An Interpretation of Malachi 4:5," [master's dissertation, San Francisco Conservative Baptist Theological Seminary, 1969], 31) notes that the use of the article with נָבִיא refers "to Elijah: specifically, the Elijah who was known to the readers as *the prophet* (as opposed to any other possible Elijah)."

carried out by Elisha (2 Kings 8:13) and one of the younger prophets (2 Kings 9:13). Indeed, Elisha had asked for a double portion, the portion of the firstborn (בְּרֹחוֹ, 2 Kings 2:9), as his spiritual inheritance from Elijah. Thus, just as the spirit of Moses came on the seventy elders (Num. 11:25) so the "spirit of Elijah"[14] rested on Elisha (2 Kings 2:15).

We are to expect a literal return of Elijah no more than we expect a literal return of David as the future king over Israel. Surely, passages such as Jeremiah 30:19; Hosea 3:5; Ezekiel 34:23, and 37:24 promise a new David. But it is universally held that this new David is none other than the Messiah Himself who comes in the office, line, and promise of David. Consequently, we argue that the new Elijah will be endowed with this same spirit and power without being the actual Elijah who was sent back long after his translation to heaven.

THE CONNECTION BETWEEN ELIJAH AND THE FORERUNNER

There can be little doubt that Elijah the prophet is one and the same as the messenger whom the Lord will send to prepare the way before him. Malachi 4:5 marks the third great "Behold" in this book (3:1; 4:1, and here) and therefore carries our mind and eye back to the other two passages. A second similarity is to be found in the participial phrase, "I am sending." Third, there is a similarity of mission; for both the verbs "to clear the way" (פִּנָּה) and "to restore" (שׁוּב) are based on verbs which also mean "to turn" and hence imply a repentance or turning away from evil and a turning towards God. Fourth, the play on *sending* "my messenger" with Malachi's name in 3:1 is matched in 4:5 by *sending* "Elijah." Finally, both 3:1 and 4:5*a* are followed by references that speak of the awesomeness of the day of the Lord (3:2; 4:5*b*).

THE TIME OF DAY OF THE LORD

This messenger, who is called the prophet Elijah, is to appear "before that great and terrible day of the Lord comes." That day was described in similar terms in Joel 2:11, 31 and Zephaniah 1:14. A number of the OT prophets view that day as *one* day and a *collective* event that entailed this three-way puzzle: (1) though five prophets refer to that day as "near" or "at hand," their prophecies are spread over four centuries (Obad. 15; Joel 1:15; 2:21; Isa. 3:6; Zeph. 1:7, 14; Ezek. 30:3); (2) those prophets also saw different immediate events belonging to

---

14. For a long discussion of the Christian history of interpretation of the NT identity of Elijah, see E. B. Pusey, *The Minor Prophets* (Grand Rapids: Baker, 1950), 2:499–502, and E. W. Hengstenberg, *Christology*, 4:195–200.

their own day as being part of that "day of the Lord," including destruction of Edom, a locust plague, or the pending destruction of Jerusalem in 586 B.C.; and (3) nevertheless, that day was also a future day in which the Lord "destroyed the whole earth" (Isa. 13:5) and reigned as "King over all the earth" (Zech. 14:1, 8–9), a day when "the elements will be dissolved . . . and the earth and the works that are in it will be laid bare" (2 Pet. 3:10), as well as a day of salvation and deliverance (Joel 2:32).

It is just such a day that Malachi 3:2; 4:1, 5 mention. The principle of generic or successive fulfillment is most important if we are adequately to explain and be faithful to all the biblical data. T. V. Moore stated it this way:

> There are a number of statements by the sacred writers that are designed to apply to distinct facts, successively occurring in history. If the words are limited to any one of these facts, they will seem exaggerated, for no one fact can exhaust their significance. They must be spread out over all the facts before their plenary meaning is reached. There is nothing in this principle that is at variance with the ordinary laws of language. The same general use of phrases occurs repeatedly. . . . Every language contains these formulas, which refer not to any one event, but a series of events, all embodying the same principle, or resulting from the same cause.
>
> [Thus] . . . the promise in regard to the "seed of the woman," (Gen. 3:15) refers to one event but runs along the whole stream of history, and includes every successive conquest of the religion of Christ . . . [This] class of predictions . . . is . . . what the old theologians called the *novissima*. . . .[15]

Thus, the Day of Yahweh is a generic or collective event that gathers together all the antecedent historical episodes of God's judgment and salvation along with the future grand finale and climactic event in the whole series. Every divine intervention into history before that final visitation in connection with the second advent of Christ constitutes only a preview, sample, downpayment, or earnest on that climactic conclusion. The prophet did not think of the Day of the Lord as an event that would occur once for all, but one that could "be repeated as the circumstances called for it."[16]

Now, the future Elijah, the prophet, will appear "before that great and terrible day of the Lord comes." Furthermore, as shown in Malachi 3:1 and Isaiah 40:3, he will prepare the way for Yahweh. But which coming of the Messiah is intended by Malachi—the first or

15. T. V. Moore, *Zechariah, Malachi*, pp. 396–99.
16. Willis J. Beecher, *The Prophets and the Promise* (New York: Thomas Y. Crowell, 1905; reprint, Grand Rapids: Baker, 1970), p. 311.

second advent? Because most conclude, along with the NT writers, that the messenger's preparation was for the first advent of our Lord, and because the events included in that day in Malachi 3:2ff. and 4:1ff. involve the purification of the Levites, the judgment on the wicked, and the return of Yahweh to his Temple, it is fair to conclude that that day embraces both advents. This is precisely the situation that Joel 2:28-32 presents. The fulfillment of Joel's words at Pentecost is as much a part of that day as the seismographic and cosmological convolutions connected with the second advent.

The basic concept, then, is that Malachi's prophecy does not merely anticipate that climactic fulfillment of the second advent, but it simultaneously embraces a series of events that all participate in the prophet's single meaning even though the referents embraced in that single meaning are many.[17] In this way, the whole set of events make up *one* collective totality and constitute only *one* idea even though they involve many referents spread over a large portion of history. Perhaps the best way to describe this phenomenon is to call it a generic prediction that Willis J. Beecher defined as:

> ... one which regards an event as occurring in a series of parts, separated by intervals, and expresses itself in language which may apply indifferently to the nearest part, or to the remoter parts, or to the whole—in other words, a prediction which in applying to the whole of a complex event, also applies to some of its parts.[18]

JOHN THE BAPTIST AND NEW TESTAMENT FULFILLMENT

The NT question may now be asked: "Was John the Baptist the fulfillment of Malachi's prophecies or was he not?"

THREE BASIC POSITIONS

Three basic answers have been given to this inquiry: (1) John the Baptist fully fulfilled all that was predicted of the messenger who would prepare the way and Elijah will not come again;[19] (2) Elijah the

---

17. A most helpful distinction can be found in G. B. Caird, *The Language and Imagery of the Bible* (Philadelphia: Westminster, 1980), chap. 2. He distinguishes between meaning^V (= value: "This means more to me than anything else"), meaning^E (= entailment: "This means war"), meaning^R (= referent: identifies person(s) or thing(s) named or involved), meaning^S (= sense: gives qualities of person or thing) and meaning^I (= intention: the truth-commitment of the author).

18. W. J. Beecher, *The Prophets and the Promise*, p. 130.

19. John Calvin, *Commentaries on the Twelve Minor Prophets* (Grand Rapids: Eerdmans, 1950), 5:627; E. W. Hengstenberg, *Christology*, 4:165; Oswald T. Allis, *Prophecy and the Church* (Nutley, N.J.: Presbyterian and Reformed, 1974), p. 49; David Allan George Knight, "John the Baptist and Elijah: A Study of Prophetic Fulfillment" (M.A. thesis; Trinity Evangelical Divinity School, Deerfield, Ill., 1978), pp. 115-16.

Tishbite will personally reappear and minister once again at the end of this age;[20] and (3) John the Baptist did come as a fulfillment of this prophecy, but he came in "the spirit and the power of Elijah" and is thereby only one prophet in a series of forerunners who are appearing throughout history until that final and climactically terrible Day of Yahweh comes when it is announced by the last prophet in this series of forerunners.[21]

A GENERIC FULFILLMENT OF THE ELIJAH PROPHECY

From our examination of Malachi's prophecy it is clear that we should adopt the third alternative. The identity, timing, and tasks of this messenger in Malachi all argue for his appearance in two different individuals, if not a series of them, rather than a single individual such as John the Baptist.

The NT evidence yields a similar construction. Matthew 11:14 quotes Jesus as affirming that "he [John the Baptist] is himself (αὐτός ἐστιν) Elijah, the one who is to come." Again in Matthew 11:10 (= Luke 7:27), "This (οὗτος) is the one of whom it is written, 'Behold I send my messenger before thy face, who shall prepare the way before thee.'" So John was that one—Elijah the prophet!

Yet it is just as clear that John denies that he is Elijah: "I am not [Elijah] (ἐγὼ οὐκ εἰμί, John 1:21, 23); and that Luke assures us that John the Baptist came only in the "spirit and power of Elijah" (ἐν πνεύματι καὶ δυνάμει, Luke 1:17). Even when it is clear that John only denied being Elijah in the popular misconceptions entertained by the people of John's day, John could be identified as Elijah only because the same Spirit and power that had energized Elijah had now fallen on him.

THE NEW ELIJAH'S TASKS

Even the task of this coming prophet had this same two-pronged focus. Mark 9:12 answers the inquiry of Peter, James, and John ("Why do the scribes say the first Elijah must come?") as they were returning from the mount of transfiguration and hearing about the Son of Man suffering and being raised again by saying: "Elijah has come [ἐλθών, past] first and is restoring [ἀποκαθιστάνει, present] all things." Matthew

20. John Paul Tan, The Interpretation of Prophecy (Winona Lake, Ind.: BMH Books, 1974), 185–87; Tertullian, "A Treatise on the Soul," 3:217.
21. Justin Martyr, "Dialogue with Trypho," 1:219–20; Aurelius Augustine, "St. John's Gospel," 7:27; T. T. Perowne, Malachi (The Cambridge Bible for Schools and Colleges; Cambridge: Cambridge U., 1890), p. 39; J. T. Marshall, "The Theology of Malachi," ExpT 7 (1895–96):126; J. Dwight Pentecost, Things to Come (Grand Rapids: Zondervan, 1958), pp. 311–12.

17:11, referring to the identical event, combined the present with the future tense: "Elijah is coming (ἔρχεται, present) and he will restore [ἀποκαταστήσει][22] all things." Because this present is coupled with a future tense, the present must be interpreted as a futuristic present—"Elijah is coming."

Now the term "restoration" is used in the OT both as a technical term for the restoration of Israel to their own land[23] and as a moral restoration of the inner man.[24] We believe that Matthean and Markan uses of this verb are parallel, in part, to the noun form (ἀποκαταστήσεους) used in Acts 3:21. In Acts, Peter states that Jesus now remains in heaven "until the time of the restoration (or 'establishing')[25] of all things that God has spoken by the mouth of his holy prophets." That too is a future work associated with the *parousia.*

Luke has described John's work as one of going before the Lord to prepare his ways, of giving the knowledge of salvation to his people, and giving light to those in darkness (Luke 1:76–79). He would also "turn the hearts of the fathers to the children (ἐπιστρέψαι καρδίας πατέρων ἐπὶ τέκνα, Luke 1:17, which follows the Masoretic text of Malachi 4:6 in the verb ἐπιστρέφω instead of the LXX ἀποκαθίστημι)."

CONCLUSION: HERMENEUTICAL IMPLICATIONS

The emerging picture is clear. How can we disassociate Elijah who is to come from the Day of the Lord? And how can we limit the day of the Lord entirely to the second advent and the *parousia*? Both errors will lead to a result less than what was intended by Malachi. Elijah still must come and "restore all things" (Matt. 17:11) "before the great and terrible day of the Lord comes" (Mal. 4:5).

Nevertheless, let no one say that Elijah has not already in some sense come, for our Lord will affirm the contrary: "Elijah has come." Now, what explanation will adequately answer all of these phenomena? Were it not for the fact that this same kind of phenomenon occurs with so many other similar prophetic passages, we would need to conclude that the text presented us with internal contradictions.

22. Both Matthew and Mark's word for "restoration" is found in the LXX. The Hebrew MT of Malachi 4:6 has הֵשִׁיב. The text of Sirach 48:10 followed the LXX.
23. Jeremiah 15:19; 16:15; 23:8; 24:6; Hosea 11:10.
24. Amos 5:15. I owe these references to David A. G. Knight, "John the Baptist and Elijah," p. 93.
25. Some prefer to link this idea with the fulfillment or establishment of OT prophecy; see K. Lake and H. J. Cadberry, *The Acts of the Apostles, The Beginnings of Christianity* (ed. F. J. Foakes Jackson and K. Lake; 5 vols.; London: Macmillan, 1933), 4:38, as cited by Knight, "John the Baptist and Elijah," p. 94. This is a strange word to express that concept when so many others were available and used by Luke. The OT usage appears to be too fixed to allow this novel meaning—especially in a passage that appeals to the prophets!

But this is not so, for the list of generic prophecies wherein a single prediction embraced a whole series of fulfillments when all those fulfillments shared something that was part and parcel of all of them is a long one.[26]

Some will argue that this is nothing more than what most name "double fulfillment of prophecy." This we deny. The problem with "double fulfillment" is threefold: (1) it restricts the fulfillments to two isolated events and only two; (2) it usually slides easily into a theory of double senses or dual intentionality in which the human author usually is aware of none of these referents or meanings or at most only one (if it is contemporaneous), with the other or both fulfillments left as surprises for the future generation in which they take place; and (3) it focuses only on the predictive word (usually given in abstraction from the times in which that word came) and on the final fulfillment without any attention being given as to how God kept that word alive in the years that intervened between the divine revelation and the climactic fulfillment.

Only generic prophecy can handle all three foci: (1) the revelatory word; (2) the series of intervening historical events that perpetuate that word; and (3) corporate, collective, and generic wholeness of that final fulfillment with whatever aspect of realization that event has had in the interim as God continued to promise by His Word and to act by His power throughout history. The intervening events, then, while being generically linked with that final event, were earnests, down payments, samplers, partial teasers until the total payment came in God's climactic fulfillment.

That exactly is what happened in the case of John the Baptist. He was only a sample of a portion of the work that was to be done in the final day. We can show this by referring to the identities, tasks, and timing given in Malachi and the gospels without adding at this time the further evidence of the work of one of the two witnesses in Revelation 11.

John then was Elijah as an earnest, but we still await the other Elijahs and especially that final Elijah the prophet before the great and terrible Day of our Lord. The meaning[1] is *one;* not two, three, or *sensus plenior.* Only that sense given by revelation of God can be normative, authoritative, and apologetically convincing to a former generation of Jews or to our own generation. We urge Christ's church to adopt the single meaning of the text and a generic meaning for prophecies of the type found in Malachi 3:1 and 4:5-6.

---

26. See chapter 5 for this evidence.

5

Participating In and Expecting the Day of the Lord

Joel 2:28-32

Evangelical students of Scripture have experienced such unusual amounts of rapprochement in recent years that many of the older distinctions made between various theological systems now need heavy qualification or major readjustment. As a parade example one could cite recent writings and the revival of interest in the theology of the land of Israel or the present participation of the church in the new covenant made with a future national Israel. One could only hope that this spirit of earnest Bible study and evangelical collegiality might continue.

Another area where some new work in exegetical and biblical theology could contribute to this new rapprochement is Peter's use of Joel 2:28-32 in his Pentecost speech. Did he mean to say that Pentecost fulfilled Joel's prophecy or merely illustrated it? Did Joel intend that the scope of his prophecy should include Gentiles as well as Jews? At what time did Joel believe that his prophecy would be accomplished? And what would the results of the outpouring of the Spirit be? Were all the events in Joel 2:28-32 to be literally fulfilled, or were some to be realized figuratively? But before those issues can be considered, a word must be said about the interpretation of prophetic literature.

JOEL 2:28-32 (HEB., 3:1-5]

THE SIGNIFICANCE OF THE PASSAGE

Varying estimates have been placed on the meaning of Joel's prophecy of the outpouring of the Holy Spirit and its connection with the event of Pentecost in Acts 2. For a significant number of biblical interpreters the blessings predicted in these five verses of Joel refer in their entirety only to a future millennial kingdom. Thus, Peter's citation of these verses on the Day of Pentecost was merely used as an illustration of his point. They were not, according to this recent popular view, cited in any sense as a fulfillment.[1] Whereas the point is usually granted by this interpretation that there is a "close similarity"[2] between Joel's prophecy and the marvelous outpouring of the Holy Spirit on the Day of Pentecost, the usage of the OT Scriptures at this juncture in Peter's message is "primarily homiletical"[3] and not theological argumentation.

However, the hermeneutical problems encountered in this passage are very similar to those faced in the use of the new covenant passage (Jer. 31:31–34) in the book of Hebrews. For while the address of Jeremiah's word is distinctively to the "house of Israel and the house of Judah" (Jer. 31:31; Heb. 8:8), still it is also found to be a fitting prediction of the NT age and the church.[4] So serious was this problem that many championed the view for a while that there were two new covenants—one for Israel and one for the church. Fortunately, few hold to this view anymore.

Accordingly, the fact that Joel 2:30–31 predicted that there would be world- and cosmic-shaking events in connection with the Day of the Lord need be no more of a detraction from the view that the Day of Pentecost was at least a partial fulfillment to this prophecy than the fact that the new covenant also includes the provision for a future restoration of Israel to her land (Romans 11, esp. v. 27). Meanwhile, it is also affirmed that we already are ministers of the new covenant and that we now participate in some of its benefits.

1. "Clearly Joel's prophecy was not fulfilled at Pentecost.... The events prophesied by Joel simply did not come to pass" (C. C. Ryrie, "The Significance of Pentecost," *BSac* 112 [1955]:334). Likewise, M. F. Unger opined, "It seems quite obvious that Peter did not quote Joel's prophecy in the sense of its fulfillment in the events of Pentecost, but purely as a prophetic illustration of those events.... Peter's phraseology 'this is that' means nothing more than 'this is [an illustration of] that which was spoken by the prophet Joel'" ("The Significance of Pentecost," *BSac* 122 [1965]:176–77). C. L. Feinberg also called it an "illustration" (*Joel, Amos, Obadiah* [New York: American Board of Missions to the Jews, 1948], p. 29). However, a quiet change is underfoot even in this school of interpretation as can be seen in W. K. Price, *The Prophet Joel and the Day of the Lord* (Chicago: Moody, 1976), p. 66: "Pentecost fulfills Joel's prediction about the coming of the Spirit. It does not exhaust it, however." It must also be noted that J. F. Walvoord wrote the introduction for this book.
2. Unger, "Significance," p. 176.
3. Ryrie, "Significance," p. 334.
4. See W. C. Kaiser, Jr., "The Old Promise and the New Covenant," *JETS* 15 (1972):11–23.

Neither may it be argued that the introductory formula[5] of Peter is wrong if he had in mind any kind of fulfillment logic. Why is it that "this is that" cannot mean this Pentecostal event is the fulfillment of that word predicted by Joel? The truth of the matter is that there is no single formula[6] used consistently in Acts or elsewhere in the NT for that matter.

Nor can it be successfully argued that Joel's prophecy cannot be fulfilled "until Israel is restored to her land, converted, and enjoying the presence of the Lord in her midst (Joel 2:26–28) [sic]."[7] To insist on these criteria would logically demand that the new covenant's current benefits to the church likewise be rescinded until Israel is restored to her land. There was no way around it: "This" outpouring of the Holy Spirit on the Day of Pentecost "is that" eschatological outpouring of the Holy Spirit predicted by Joel centuries before.

However, already that "Day of the Lord," which some would deny to Peter, had come as a destruction from the Lord (Joel 1:15; 2:1). The dark clouds of locusts (whose Latin name, incidentally, means "burners of the land") had come as a flame and an invading army (2:2–11). And if that was a preview of the ultimate and final day of the Lord, so also was the repentance of the people a foretaste of the climactic revival and the healing of the land. Why could not Peter's experience of the outpouring of the Holy Spirit on the Day of Pentecost likewise be a foretaste of God's ultimate flood of the Holy Spirit?

THE ORGANIZATION OF THE BOOK OF JOEL

The message of Joel revolves around the pivot verse of Joel 2:18. Prior to that verse Joel had issued two separate calls for Israel to repent (1:13–14; 2:12–17). Only by turning from her sin in repentance could Israel begin to experience the blessing of God again. Only then would her land be healed.

Thus when Joel 2:18 suddenly announced in the past tense[8] that the Lord "was jealous," "had pity," "answered," and "said," we may be sure that the people did repent. That, then, is the reason 2:19–27 gave the immediate and temporal effects of this repentance, whereas 2:28–

---

5. Ryrie, "Significance," p. 334.
6. See W. C. Kaiser, Jr., "The Davidic Promise and the Inclusion of the Gentiles (Amos 9:9–15 and Acts 15:13–18): A Test Passage for Theological Systems," *JETS* 20 (1977):106–7. Also see the references there to additional literature.
7. Ryrie, "Significance," p. 334.
8. Those translations (e.g., KJV, NIV, NASB) that fail to translate the *waw*-conversive with the imperfect tense of the verb as a narrative past tense are in error. Whatever else remains ambiguous about the Hebrew verb, this one form is constant and without any variation.

32 went on to list the distant future and more spiritual results of God's response to the people's repentance.

THE SHAPE OF JOEL 2:28–32 [HEB., 3:1–5]

This portion of Joel's prophecy is divided into three sections, each section beginning with a Hebrew verb form called a converted perfect tense.[9] Thus, the three sections are: verses 28–29, verses 30–31, and verse 32. The first and third sections employ the literary device known as inclusio (i.e., the section is bracketed by a repeated clause or phrase coming at the beginning and the end of the section). Verses 28a and 29b both begin and end the section with "I will pour out my Spirit" whereas verse 32, the third section, begins and ends with the almost identical "who call on the name of the LORD" and "whom the LORD calls."

Such an analysis is sufficient to suggest that there are three distinct movements or parts to the passage. Two of those sections also conclude with a reference to the fact that the events described in them will take place "in those days"[10] (Joel 2:29) or "before[11] the great and terrible day of the LORD comes" (2:31). The exegetical problem would appear to be the temporal relationship between the three parts.

THE TEMPORAL SETTING FOR THE TEXT

But before the internal relationships are established, it is necessary to determine how the entire block of verses 28–32 is related to the preceding and following context. The phrase "after this" in verse 28 [Heb., 3:1] does not appear in and of itself to be an eschatological expression even though the passage clearly does include at least two such formulae—namely, "in those days" (v. 29 [Heb., 3:2]) and "before the great and terrible day of the LORD comes" (v. 31 [Heb., 3:4]). Rather Joel intended to show that the promises of verses 28–32 would come

9. The three verbs are $w^e h \bar{a} y \hat{a}$ (v. 28), $w^e n \bar{a} t a t t \hat{\imath}$ (v. 30) and $w^e h \bar{a} y \hat{a}$ (v. 32). This division is the same as L. C. Allen, *The Books of Joel, Obadiah, Jonah, and Micah* (Grand Rapids: Eerdmans, 1976), p. 97.
10. Whereas the "day of the Lord" is not formally linked with "that day," "those days," or the "latter days," Deuteronomy 31:17–18 does connect God's coming judgment with "that day" to come. See W. C. Kaiser, Jr., *Toward an Old Testament Theology* (Grand Rapids: Zondervan, 1978), pp. 186, 188–91. G. E. Ladd, *A Theology of the New Testament* (Grand Rapids: Eerdmans, 1974), p. 344, has created an unnecessary problem when he has Peter separating the "last days" from the "day of the Lord" and "re-interpreting" them so that they could appear in history rather than the consummation. Ladd misunderstands the OT prophetic perspective we have explained above.
11. A phrase repeated verbatim in Malachi 4:5 [Heb., 3:23].

after those immediate and material blessings promised in verses 19–27.

The key temporal term in verses 19–27 is found in verse 23: "in the first [act of blessing?]" (*bārî'šôn*). The Lord God would send both the autumn and spring rains in this his first act of blessing. Thus, the pastures, the fields, the trees, and the vines would thrive once again as God revived the land that had just been decimated by the locust invasion and the accompanying drought.[12]

Then a second, subsequent act would come "afterward" or "after this": a shower of natural rain. But the text does not say how long after that first act. Thus, the text clearly sets apart two distinct blessings in a clear order of appearance, yet, it refrained from telling us the time that would intervene between the two.

One might fairly conclude that the second blessing (vv. 28–32) was more intimately tied to God's distant future work, because verses 29 and 31 used the formulae of the Day of the Lord and the passage was so closely joined to the eschatological events of the last chapter of Joel where God would regather Judah and judge all the nations of the earth for scattering Israel and partitioning her land (3:1–8 [Heb., 4:1–8]). However, even while making this strong tie with the events of the second coming we must not refuse on basic principles to allow any fulfillments of this word in the Christian era any more than we have for a prophecy like Jeremiah's new covenant with the house of Israel and the house of Judah.

In fact, Peter introduced his famous "this is that" reference to Joel 2:28–32 with a new temporal clause for Joel's "after this": "It shall come to pass in the last days, says God." For the NT writers the church already was in the "last days." Hebrews 1:2 is one good example of this declaration: God had spoken to the NT saints "in these last days" in his Son, Jesus. Thus, the last days had broken in upon the church, but they were only a sample, an "earnest," a foretaste of what the "age to come" would be like in all its fullness when Christ returned a second time. We conclude then that nothing in the temporal formulae

---

12. It is impossible to enter into the question of the translation of *hammôreh lis°dāqâ* of verse 23. The suggested translations are almost unlimited: "rain at the proper time" (H. Ringgren, *Israelite Religion*, p. 83); "rain in abundance" (M. Dahood, *Psalms* 1:146); "the autumn rain in token of covenant harmony" (Allen, *Joel*, p. 86); "rain according to what is fit" (Calvin); "rain moderately" (KJV); "rain in just measure" (RV); "rain in due measure" (NEB); "rain amply" (Moffatt); "teacher for righteousness" (NIV). This last suggestion has much to commend it. See Proverbs 5:13; 2 Chronicles 15:3, 2 Kings 17:28, Job 36:22. Note that the messianic King who brings "righteousness" to his people gives blessings to his country "like rain falling on the mown grass, like showers that drip on the earth" (Ps. 72:6). See C. Roth, "The Teacher of Righteousness and the Prophecy of Joel," *VT* 13 (1963):91–95; J. Weingreen, "The Title *Moreh Ṣedek*," *JSS* 6 (1961):162–74; G. W. Ahlström, *Joel and the Temple Cult of Jerusalem*, VTSup 21 (1971):98–110.

of this passage prejudices us against the use of this passage or finding its partial fulfillment[13] in the early church and that nothing limits this passage to the total fulfillment at Pentecost apart from any second advent realizations. For Peter specifically, the event he experienced inaugurated the last days and was itself part and parcel of the final consummation.

THE OUTPOURING OF GOD'S SPIRIT

Here is the heart of the matter. Three basic items need to be noted here: (1) the distinctiveness of this "outpouring" of the Spirit; (2) the identity of the "all flesh" on whom the Spirit would come; and (3) the results of this outpouring.

Never had an individual in the OT been completely without the aid and work of the Holy Spirit. Certainly, Jesus held that the subjects of the new birth and the special work of the Holy Spirit in the gift of salvation were not new or inaccessible doctrines to OT men and women before the cross. In fact, he marveled that Nicodemus could have been a teacher in Israel and still have been so totally unaware of this fact (John 3:10). Thus, if salvation is not of works so that no man or woman ever could boast but is a gift of God to all who ever believed so that it might always forever be by grace (Eph. 2:8), then OT saints were indeed regenerated by the Holy Spirit.[14]

Likewise, John 14:17 is especially important, for it affirms that our Lord's disciples already had known the "Spirit of truth" because he was living "with" them and he was already "in" them. The prepositions are *para*, "with," the same word used in John 14:23 of the Father and the Son's abiding in the disciples—a nonfluctuating relationship,[15] and *en*, "in," with a present tense verb *estai*, "is" (rather than "will be" as in RSV, NASB,* and NIV).

However, there are a number of NT passages that would seem to suggest that the Holy Spirit had not yet been given to believers even during our Lord's earthly ministry. He must come at Pentecost (John 7:37–39; 14:16; 16:7–11; Acts 1:4–8; 11:15–17; 15:8). We have deliberately

* *New American Standard Bible.*
13. See the fine statement by Price, *Prophet*, pp. 65–66: "Therefore, Joel's prediction has *initial* fulfillment at Pentecost, *continuous* fulfillment during the Church age, and *ultimate* fulfillment at the second coming of Christ" (italics his).
14. G. W. Grogan argues in "The Experience of Salvation in the Old and New Testaments," *Vox Evangelica* 5 (1967):13, that "the same Spirit of faith" in 2 Corinthians 4:13 means that Paul claims that our faith is the product of the same Holy Spirit who was at work in the author of Psalm 116:10 whence he derived the quotation in 2 Corinthians 4:13.
15. See ibid. We have developed this point in our article "The Single Intent of Scripture," *Evangelical Roots* (ed. K. Kantzer; Nashville: Nelson, 1978), pp. 133–34.

deleted from this list John 14:25–26; 15:26–27; 16:12–15, for these promises of the Holy Spirit's coming were solely directed to those disciples whose distinctive work it would be to write the NT. The Spirit would "bring to their remembrance all that [Jesus] had said," and they would be witnesses to Christ because they "had been with [him] from the beginning [of his earthly ministry]." The disciples would teach doctrine ("what is mine"), future events and past deeds. Thus, only these men were promised the Spirit's leading them into revelational truth.[16]

Even allowing for those exemptions, how shall we explain the apparent tension between these two sets of texts on the Holy Spirit? Had the Holy Spirit been given or had he not? Was Pentecost necessary or was it not?

The answer is similar to one given for the necessity of the death of Christ. Men were truly forgiven and made part of the people of God in the OT on the basis of God's promise to send the Suffering Servant. If Christ had not given his life as a ransom and been raised from the dead, then all the OT saints would have believed in vain. Likewise, had the Holy Spirit not come visibly at Pentecost with all its evidential value, then the previous ministry of the Holy Spirit in the lives of individuals would also have been in vain. Just as Passover is linked to the "Feast of Weeks" (Ex. 34:22; Lev. 23:15–21), so the cross is linked to Pentecost. Thus, Goodwin correctly commented. "[The Holy Spirit] must have a coming in state, in solemn and visible manner, accompanied with visible effects as well as Christ had."[17] This we believe to be one of the main reasons for emphasizing the necessity of the Holy Spirit's coming at Pentecost: He must come visibly as an exhibition that all who had previously depended on the ministry of the Holy Spirit were totally vindicated just as those who had depended on the future death of Christ.

Moreover, what had now happened at Pentecost was both climactic and effusive. This new, outward, evidential coming of the Holy Spirit would be a downpour—a word conveying abundance in contrast with the previous scarcity. Thus Joel had carefully selected the verb meaning to "pour out."[18] This verb easily links up with the one Jesus would

16. This should not be viewed as restricting the meaning of "you" too severely as if it would defeat the universal reference of "you" in the great commission of Matthew 28:18–20, for 28:20 clearly has the broader idea in mind when it says, "Lo, I am with you always, even to the end of the world."
17. T. Goodwin, *Works* (Edinburgh: 1861), 6:8, as cited by G. Smeaton, *The Doctrine of the Holy Spirit* (London: 1958), p. 49, and Grogan, "Experience," p. 14.
18. There are five Hebrew verbs for "pouring out": *nātak, nāsak, nābaʿ, yāṣaq,* and the one used here, (*šāpak*). Also note the apocryphal work, Enoch 62:2: "The Spirit of righteousness has been poured out on him [i.e., Messiah]." See also F. F. Bruce, "The Holy Spirit in the Qumran Texts," *ALUOS* (Leiden: Brill, 1969), p. 53.

use: the "rivers of living water" that would come on all who believed (John 7:38–39)—indeed the very baptism of the Holy Spirit (Matt. 3:11; Mark 1:8; Luke 3:16–17; Acts 1:5; 8:15–17; 11:16). If this connection is correct, as we believe it is, then there was something additional and unique about this ministry of the Holy Spirit that first occurred at Pentecost, Samaria, and Caesarea. Now a believer was not only regenerated and indwelt to some degree by the Holy Spirit but, beginning at Pentecost and following, all who believed were simultaneously baptized by the Holy Spirit and made part of the one body (1 Cor. 12:13).[19]

If Joel was written in the ninth century, then his word was the basic teaching passage on the coming advent of the outpouring of the Holy Spirit and the forerunner of those in Isaiah and Ezekiel. The eighth-century prophet Isaiah affirmed the same word: "[Jerusalem would be deserted] until the Spirit is poured on us from on high and the wilderness becomes a fertile field" (32:15). "I will pour out my Spirit on your seed and my blessings on your descendants" (44:3).[20] Likewise, the sixth-century Ezekiel also took up the same theme of the outpouring and linked it with Israel's restoration to the land of promise as had Isaiah: "I will gather them to their own land ... for I will pour out my Spirit on the house of Israel" (39:28–29). Yet in three other passages Ezekiel does not use the verb "to pour" but the verb "to put": "I will give them one heart and I will put a new Spirit in them" (11:18–19); "I will give you a new heart and put a new Spirit in you.... I will put my Spirit in you ... and you shall dwell in the land that I gave to your fathers; and you shall be my people and I will be your God" (36:26–28); "I will bring you back to the land of Israel.... I will put my Spirit in you and you will live" (37:12–14).

Clearly, then, the ultimate and final downpour will still take place in the land in connection with the future restoration of Israel to the land in that complex of events belonging to the second coming of our Lord—a downpour of the Holy Spirit indeed.

But who will the recipients of this downpour be? Joel had it fall on "all flesh." This expression, kol bāśār, appears thirty-two times in the OT outside of Joel. In twenty-three of those occurrences the expression refers to Gentiles alone. For example, in four of those twenty-three instances it is used as a synonym for the "nations" (Deut. 5:26; Isa. 49:26; 66:16; Zech. 2:13). Certainly the preponderance of usage

19. Yet even here there were careful anticipations of the fact that Christ is over his house, the one in which Moses was faithful, the same house we are in if we hold on to our courage and our hope (Heb. 3:2–6).
20. The other Isaianic references to the Spirit and the coming Servant of the Lord are slightly different in that he has the Spirit "put on" him (42:1; 59:21; 61:1).

favors the meaning of "all mankind"[21] without distinction of race, sex, or age. Thus Isaiah 40:5–6 declared that "all flesh" will see the glory of the Lord. The extent of this expression had been set as early as Genesis 6:13. There God had told Noah that he was going to put an end to "all flesh" because of the violence they had done on the earth.

Seldom if ever may "all flesh" be reserved and restricted to all Israel. The two passages cited for this exclusive meaning both turn out to be larger references than what had at first been assumed. Psalm 65:2, "to thee shall all flesh come," refers also to Gentiles because verse 5 claims that this offer is the "hope of all the ends of the earth" (see also Isa. 66:23; cf. 66:20). Likewise, Psalm 136:25, "who gives food to all flesh," is also universal in its scope as can be seen from the identical sentiment in Psalms 104:27; 145:9.

But what about Joel's use of this expression? He explained what he meant by the term by first listing sons, daughters, old men, young men. Then by way of surprise the prophet abruptly declared "and also" or "and even" (w^{e}gam) menservants and maidservants would receive the Spirit of God. It is this epexegetical addition that was marked by the "and even" phrase that forces the interpreter to acknowledge that Joel had "all mankind" in mind here. Even the Gentile slaves[22] in the Jewish households would benefit in this outpouring. Thus the Jews were not the only ones fit to receive this visitation of God's Spirit (as Rabbi Ibn Ezra had claimed) but literally "all mankind."

The NT, therefore, was once again on the mark when it also invited the Gentiles to receive the gift of the Holy Spirit (Acts 2:38). The reason was obvious: the promise was for Israel and for "all who are afar off[23] (pasin tois eis makran; Acts 2:39). To describe someone as belonging to "those who were afar off" was merely a circumlocution for saying "Gentiles." This is plain from Paul's usage in Ephesians 2:13, 17: Christ has abolished the wall of partition between Jew and Gentile and has brought "those who once were afar off" (or "far away") into the commonwealth of Israel and the covenants of promise. And Acts 10:45 is conclusive, showing that God had intended that the gift of the Holy Spirit would also be "poured out even on the Gentiles."

21. For the most recent word study on this expression see A. R. Hulst, *"Kol baśar . . . ,"* *Studies in the Book of Genesis*, OTS 12 (1958):47–49. Many recent commentators, however, unnecessarily restrict this phrase in Joel to Israel.
22. The LXX translators apparently could not believe their eyes, so they deliberately changed the servants of men into servants of God by rendering "my servants" and "my handmaids."
23. For a study of this expression see H. Preisker, *"makran,"* TDNT (1967), 4:373–74. He notes how Ephesians 2:17 sets Isaiah 57:19 in the context of salvation history with a similar phrase for the Gentiles.

Thus, this gift would be given without regard to age (old men, young men), sex (sons, daughters), social rank, or race: It would provide for both the Gentile servants and handmaids of the Jewish employers as well as their owners.

Joel must have startled his audience both by his reference to the Gentiles and to women. Yet, this is not to say that they were totally unprepared for this truth. Had not Moses prayed, "I wish that all the LORD's people were prophets and that the LORD would put his Spirit on [all of] them" (Num. 11:29)? And that was exactly what was to be inaugurated at Pentecost but totally realized in the day of the Lord.

Finally, we may ask, what were the results of this outpouring of the Holy Spirit? Put in the most succinct terms they were these: Everyone would immediately and personally know the Lord. There would no longer be a need for someone to teach each child of God. In this sense Joel explains the means (the outpouring of the Holy Spirit) by which Jeremiah's later revealed fact of the new covenant would be implemented (similarly, Jer. 31:34: "they will all know me, from the least to the greatest"). Heretofore it took the mediation of a prophet to have God revealed to the people (Num. 12:6) or a priest to have the people represented to God (8:15–19). But now everyone, regardless of age, sex, or social status, would be able to prophesy, dream dreams, and see visions.

True, there were OT examples of the Holy Spirit coming on almost everyone of the categories Joel mentions.[24] There were sons (Bezalel, son of Uri; Ex. 31:2–3), daughters (Deborah, Judges 4–5; Huldah, 2 Kings 22:14), old men (Moses was 120 years old when he wrote Deuteronomy), young men (young Jeremiah, Jer. 1:6; young Daniel, Dan. 1), and menservants (perhaps the messengers of Saul, 1 Sam. 19:20–23). But nowhere did any of these receive the Holy Spirit in such profusion as was now promised in this outpouring.

However, some results promised by Joel did not take place at Pentecost, Samaria, Caesarea, or anywhere else as yet. Especially troublesome to many interpreters is that second or middle section of Joel's prophecy, verses 30–31. Even though some interpreters[25] have attempted to show that God did fulfill his promise to put "wonders in the heavens and on the earth" ("blood, fire, billows of smoke, the sun

24. These were pointed out to me by my student Keith Ghormley.
25. M. W. Holmes, "The Interpretation of Joel in the New Testament" (M.A. thesis, Trinity Evangelical Divinity School, 1976), p. 68, n.61, did point to an article by F. Gardiner, "Descriptions of Spiritual Phenomena Under the Figure of Natural Convulsions," *Old and New Testament Student* 9 (1889):162. His argument is that since Pentecost fulfills Joel 2:28–32, therefore there is "inspired authority" that these signs were fulfilled at the same time and accordingly must be interpreted figuratively. Many contemporary interpreters also opt for this explanation. The problem with this logic is its assumption that there is a total fulfillment here.

turned to darkness, the moon to blood") in his first advent, the argument is not very convincing. Hermeneutical talk about figurative language must be stretched to the breaking point (all without any of the requisite textual clues that we are dealing with such figures), or certain phrases must be seized while others are conveniently dropped from the discussion. So, for some, the darkness is easily related to the hours Christ spent on the cross. But what shall we say of the "moon being turned into blood" or the "billows of smoke"?

Likewise, we also find unsatisfactory the conclusion that "what is recorded in Acts 2:19–20 [= Joel 2:30–31] is simply a connecting link between two key points in his argument[26]—between verses 28–29, what "the Spirit was able to do,"[27] and verse 32, the invitation to accept the Messiah. But Hengstenberg[28] had already solved this problem. He pointed to Acts 2:40: "With many other words he warned them.... Save yourselves from this corrupt generation." Accordingly, Hengstenberg correctly concluded that Peter had deliberately used these words from Joel 2:30–31 to bring before his hearers a proper respect for the God who could right then and there deliver them from threatened judgments to come. For that was exactly the connection made by Joel. Thus, whereas there has not yet been any fulfillment of verses 30–31 in that they await our Lord's second advent, nevertheless, Peter used this truth in the same way that Joel used it in his day: It was an incentive to call on the name of the Lord.[29]

The coming wonders would certainly remind mankind of the terrible plagues of Egypt. Such descriptions of future cosmic judgment are similar to numerous other descriptions of the Day of the Lord. Yet, in the midst of such catastrophes God's offer of salvation shone through clearly.

CONCLUSION

We conclude that the promise of the outpouring of the Holy Spirit in the last days has received a preliminary fulfillment in the series of events at Pentecost, Samaria, and Caesarea. But those events and the subsequent baptisms of the Holy Spirit that take place whenever anyone receives Christ as Lord and Savior and is thereby ushered into the family of God are all mere harbingers and samples of that final downpour that will come in that complex of events connected

26. Ryrie, "Significance," p. 335.
27. Ibid.
28. E. W. Hengstenberg, *Christology of the Old Testament* (abridged by T. K. Arnold; Grand Rapids: Kregel, 1970 [1847]), p. 533.
29. Note Paul's use of this verse in Rom. 10:12–13; note also Kaiser, "Davidic," pp. 103–4.

with Christ's second return. However, these events—past, present, and future—make up one generic whole concept, for in the prophet's view there is a wholeness and a totality to what he sees.

Furthermore, Joel specifically intended to announce that this blessing was to fall on the Gentiles as well as the Jews. In its final realization it was always connected by Isaiah and Ezekiel with the restoration of the people of Israel to the land just as it was in the Joel prophecy. Thus, the spiritual benefits may not be abstracted and isolated from the national and political promises made to the patriarchs and David. The plan of God is a single plan that embraces the entirety of soteriology and the historical process. Anything less than this must be attributed to our western tendencies to dualism, docetism, and spiritualizing.

Finally, in no way must this special profusion of the ministry of the Holy Spirit that operates much in accordance with the blessing found in the new covenant be interpreted in such a way as to suggest that the individual OT saints and believers were unaware of any ministry of the Holy Spirit in their lives apart from temporary endowments of the Spirit for special tasks at special times. On the contrary, the Holy Spirit was the author of new life for all who believed in the coming man of promise (= regeneration), and he also indwelt those same OT redeemed men, at least to some degree, even as David testified in Psalm 51:11. There David pleaded with God: "Do not cast me away from your presence, and do not take your Holy Spirit from me." His reference did not seem to be to the Spirit's gift of government and administration but rather to his personal fellowship with God. This judgment is strongly supported by Jesus' pre-cross affirmation in John 13:17: "[The Holy Spirit] lives with you and is [now] in you."

What believers knew only in a seminal and preliminary form was now promised for "those [coming] days" as a veritable downpour. The baptism or incorporation act would not only bring all believers together in one body, but it would also so gift each individual that ultimately, in that last day, everyone would personally and directly know the Lord without being taught. And that would be a most unique outpouring of God's gift.

PART 3

THE TYPOLOGICAL USE
OF THE OLD TESTAMENT
IN THE NEW

Introduction

If exegesis is the science of establishing the true meaning of the original text as the human author received it in revelation from God and intended it to be understood, will that definition embrace all typological interpretation as well? Is typology, strictly speaking, an exegetical science? Or is it more of a theological art reserved for those readers of the Scripture who have already committed themselves to the unity of the Bible and who see in the *whole* canon "something more" than can be observed by the grammatico-historical method in any of its *individual* pericopae? Can the whole exceed its parts?—that is the question. Much of the answer to this question will depend on the definition of a *type* in the Scriptures.

THE DEFINITION OF A TYPE

Francis Foulkes astonishes us with his absolute candor. He concluded that:

> in one way it is true to say that typological interpretation involves a *reading into* the text of a meaning extrinsic to it. It takes more than a literal sense of a passage. The New Testament does this when it sees Christ as the theme and fulfillment of all the Old Testament, without limiting this to what is explicitly Messianic prophecy.... Typology *reads into* Scripture a *meaning which is not there* in that it *reads in* the light of the fulfillment of the history. This is *not* exegesis, drawing out from

a passage what the human author understood and intended as he wrote. Nevertheless it does not read a new principle into the context; it interprets the dealings of God with men from the literal context, and then points to the way in which God has so dealt with men in Christ.[1]

But Foulkes is not alone in making this disclaimer. R. T. France affirmed:

It is not correct to describe typology as a method of exegesis.... If every type were originally intended explicitly to point forward to an antitype, it might be correct to class typology as a style of exegesis. But this is not the case. There is no indication in a type, as such, of any forward reference; it is complete and intelligible in itself.[2]

France argues that Deuteronomy 6–8, for example, gives no indication that the writer had any typological intentions when he recorded that passage—nor must an adequate exegesis indicate such. But in Foulkes's view, Jesus used those passages typologically in the temptation (Matt. 4:1–11; Luke 4:1–13; Deut. 6:13, 16; 8:3). Was His use illegitimate? asked France. Only if it were a question of exegesis; however, typology is application—not exegesis. "It is theological reflection in the light of later events,"[3] he reasoned.

France, however, did insist that strict exegesis was a prerequisite of typology. In spite of the fact that modern scholars warn against divorcing typology in any fundamental way from the process of exegesis, most, if not all, appear to be convinced with Gerhard von Rad that "typological interpretation transcends the self-understanding of the Old Testament text ... [and] frees Old Testament exegesis from the compelling constraint always, in order to be theologically relevant, to bring into the discussion some meaning, some truth beyond that inherent in the event itself."[4] Types, then, are not discovered by means of exegesis even though they "must be consistent with the literal meaning."[5]

One writer did repeatedly refer to typology as "an exegetical method." K. J. Woollcombe defined "typological exegesis [as] ... the search for linkages between events, persons, or things *within the*

1. Francis Foulkes, *The Acts of God: A Study of the Basis of Typology in the Old Testament* (London: Tyndale, 1958), pp. 38–39. Italics are mine.
2. R. T. France, *Jesus and the Old Testament: His Application of Old Testament Passages to Himself and His Mission* (Downers Grove, Ill.: InterVarsity, 1971), p. 41.
3. Ibid., p. 42.
4. Gerhard von Rad, ed. Claus Westermann, "Typological Interpretation of the Old Testament," in *Essays on Old Testament Hermeneutics* (Richmond, Va.: John Knox, 1963), pp. 37–38.
5. D. L. Baker, *Two Testaments, One Bible* (Downers Grove, Ill.: InterVarsity, 1976), p. 258.

historical framework of revelation"[6] (emphasis his). Furthermore, "considered as a method of writing, it may be defined as the description of an event, person or thing in the New Testament in terms borrowed from the description of its prototypal counterpart in the Old Testament."[7] Woollcombe illustrates this search for linkages on the part of the exegete (linkages that in all probability eluded the original writer!) by suggesting that Isaac, who carried the wood for his sacrifice in Genesis, was a type of Simon of Cyrene, who carried the wood of the cross on the exegetical grounds that the names of Simon's children, Rufus and Alexander, had a certain etymological similarity to Isaac's sons, Esau and Israel (Mark 15:21, "father of Alexander [= alexi-anēr, "man who defends himself"] and Rufus [= "red"] paralleled by Jacob-Israel [= "wrestler with God," Gen. 32:28] and Esau-Edom [= "red"]). Note that the linkage belongs solely to the interpreter and not to the text, even though there is a certain amount of historical and literal grounding in the text.

But is Woollcombe actually describing exegetical methodology or is he using his terms loosely to describe convenient employment of the text? Indeed, Leonard Goppelt described typology as a "spiritual perspective" (*pneumatische Betrauchtungsweise*). Unlike allegory, which attempted to attach to the *words* of Scripture a *huponoia* (deeper meaning), typology interpreted the meaning of the present events in salvation history in light of past OT *events*.[8]

But just when we thought we had established that types were not involved in the exegetical process, John Bright reminded us that some types were intended by the writers of Scripture.[9] However, even for Bright,

> typology cannot be used as a tool for the exegesis of the Old Testament texts, nor can it reveal in them levels of meaning not discoverable by normal exegetical procedure.... If types were intended by the author (and sometimes they were), grammatico-historical exegesis will discover them; if not, then they cannot be discovered by [the] exegetical method at all.[10]

6. K. J. Woollcombe, "The Biblical Origins and Patristic Development of Theology," in *Essays on Typology*, ed. G. W. H. Lampe and K. J. Woollcombe (London: SCM, 1957), p. 40.
7. Ibid., pp. 39–40.
8. As reported in E. Earle Ellis, ed., "How the New Testament Uses the Old," in *Prophecy and Hermeneutics in Early Christianity* (Grand Rapids: Eerdmans, 1978), pp. 165, 169.
9. John Bright, *The Authority of the Old Testament* (Nashville: Abingdon, 1967), p. 92.
10. Ibid., p. 92.

THE CHARACTERISTICS OF A TYPE

Our conclusion is that unless the type is intended by the OT writer and is discernible from the normal practice of grammar, syntax, and its related modes of discerning meaning, the rest of what is classified under typology must be categorized as a form of applying and showing significance to some of the patterns in God's salvific activity over the ages. At best then, such nonobjective types are our modern illustrations rather than divine predictions. Typology is, however, a historico-theological reflection on the fact that the God-ordained persons, events, institutions, and things often tended to come in clusters and repeat themselves over and over in the progress of revelation.

It is this repetitive motion that begins to capture the theological sensitivities of the exegete. First, it is essential that the OT type be grounded in a real historical context; for what is being compared is not one word (or words) with another, but one event, person, or ordained institution in the life of Israel with another. The keen exegete, having established the syntactical meaning of the words as used in this context, will begin to observe according to the canons of "informing theology"[11] that there is a theological correspondence to be found in the repeated situation and recurring principle in each of God's new works.

Such a list of candidates for types and antitypes must not be "read into" the text as if *eis*egesis were suddenly given a kosher status in the church. Instead, the beginning reader and exegete of the OT may start by observing the list of *new* things mentioned in the OT. For example, there is the new Moses, the new Elijah, the new covenant, the new David, the new temple, the new heavens and new earth, the new exodus, new cup, and new bread from heaven. Each of those *new* items deliberately invites our theological comparisons of two or more persons, events, things, or institutions in two separated time contexts in some aspect that illustrates the ongoing salvation of God in some act divinely ordained. There is a strong link of continuity between the two historical horizons because both were clearly the work of God in some unique way—a way that always illustrates the same principle or situation.

Yet, there is just as strong evidence of discontinuity in that the new exceeds and outstrips the forerunner in its clarity, implications, or applications of its effects. This aspect of typology is called escalation. The antitype always exceeds the feature that the type and its newest

11. Walter C. Kaiser, Jr., *Toward an Exegetical Theology* (Grand Rapids: Baker, 1981), pp. 134–40, 161–62.

representative share. Had that not been so, the Bible would quickly
be reduced to a flat and level document in which there was no
movement or advance. Accordingly, some of the key characteristics
used to define typology for which there is general agreement may be
summarized.

HISTORICAL CORRESPONDENCE

The first and primary characteristic is historical correspondence.[12]
However, even this agreement is not without its qualifications. Some
modern proponents of typology no longer require the actual facticity
and historicity of both type and antitype. Thus, Gerhard von Rad
expressed great scepticism over the historical facticity of the events
that Israel's theological reflection used in structured analogies to
express her faith.[13] There is also the problem of defining exactly what
the correspondence consists of, as James Barr has reminded us.[14] But
we believe this characteristic is essential if we are to obtain our types
by means of exegesis: a type must be historical.

ESCALATION IN THE ANTITYPE

The second characteristic involves an "escalation," "increase," "intensification," or "heightening" (a *Steigerung*) from the type to the
antitype.[15] But Baker is not impressed by this characteristic, which is
developed mainly in Goppelt. For him such an "increase"

> is simply an aspect of the progression from Old Testament to New
> Testament and not a necessary characteristic of a type. The essence of
> a type is that it is exemplary and it would be theoretically possible for
> something which is more advanced to be typical of something less
> advanced. Moreover, it is possible for one thing to be a type of its
> opposite: for example, the entry of sin into the world by the first Adam
> and the entry of grace by the second.[16]

12. Samuel Amsler, "Où en est la typologie de l'Ancien Testament?" *Etudes théolo-
    giques et religieuses* 27 (1952):79; idem, "La typologie de l'AT chez S. Paul," *Revue
    de théologie et de philosophie*, ser. 2, 37 (1949):118; Patrick Fairbairn, *The Typology
    of Scripture* (Grand Rapids: Zondervan, n.d.), 1:46; Leonard Goppelt, *Typos: The
    Typological Interpretation of the Old Testament in the New*, trans. Donald H.
    Madvig (Grand Rapids: Eerdmans, 1982), p. 18. For others, see David L. Baker,
    Two Testaments, pp. 242–43.
13. Gerhard von Rad, "Typological Interpretation of the Old Testament," p. 36. See
    also von Rad, *Old Testament Theology*, trans. D. M. G. Stalker (Edinburg: Oliver
    and Boyd), 1:106–7. The crossing of the Red Sea " . . . critical historical scholarship
    regards . . . as impossible" and " . . . the picture of Moses . . . as unhistorical."
14. James Barr, *Old and New in Interpretation* (London: SCM, 1966), pp. 103–48.
15. L. Goppelt, *Typos*, pp. 18, 33, 37, 39, 223.
16. David L. Baker, "Typology and the Christian Use of the Old Testament," *SJT* 29
    (1976):152.

We, however, cannot agree with Baker. He appears to miss the point that the correspondence shared is limited to some essential or even metaphysical correspondence. To press beyond the single headship, as witnessed in Adam and then in Christ to discussions about sin and grace, is to overload the type. Not only is the heightening characteristic lost, but so is the *historical* correspondence.

DIVINE INTENT

A third characteristic is divine intent and designation. For Bishop Marsh,

> to constitute a type, something more is requisite than a mere *resemblance* of that which is called its antitype. For one thing may *resemble* another when the things themselves are totally *unconnected*. But it is the very essence of a type to have a necessary connection with its antitype. It must have been *designed* ... from the very beginning to prefigure its antitype ... [having] a pre-ordained and inherent connection between the things themselves.[17] (italics his)

Once again, recent scholars are willing to attribute divine designation in a *general* way to God's activity in salvation history, but this is a far cry from the older insistence of Johannes Cocceius (1603–69), Herbert Marsh[18] (1757–1839), and Patrick Fairbairn (1805–74) that God has ordained and superintended specific persons, events, and institutions and commissioned their recording in Scripture so as to anticipate a larger and greater realization or enactment in future events connected with the first or second coming of Messiah. Whereas it is true that the Cocceian school tended to come close to reviving Origen's view that everything in the OT had a figurative meaning, the same cannot be said for Bishop Marsh and Patrick Fairbairn. So repulsed was Marsh by the excesses and caprice of seventeenth century typology that he argued:

> There is no other rule, therefore, by which we can distinguish a *real* from a *pretended* type, than that of Scripture itself. There are no other

---

17. Herbert Marsh, *A Course of Lectures Containing a Description and Systematic Arrangement of the Several Branches of Divinity.* Part III.B (Boston: Cummings and Hilliard, 1815), Lecture XIX, pp. 1–2.
18. The primary sources of this founder of Federal Theology and his views on typology can be found in his *Summa doctrinae de foedere et testamento Dei* (Leyden: n.p., 1648) and *Summa theologiae ex Scripturis repetita* (Geneva: symptibus I. H. Widerhold, 1662). See Richard M. Davidson, *Typology in Scripture: A Study of Hermeneutical Tupos Structures* (Berrien Springs, Mich.: Andrews U., 1981), p. 33, nn.1–2 for further examples from those belonging to this school of thought.

possible means, by which we can *know* that a previous design and a pre-ordained connexion *existed.* Whatever persons, or things, therefore, recorded in the Old Testament, were expressly declared by Christ or by his Apostles to have been designed as *prefigurations* of persons or things relating to the New Testament, such persons or things so recorded in the *former,* are *types* of the persons or things with which they are compared in the *latter.* But if we assert that a person, or thing, was designated to pre-figure *another* person or thing, where no such pre-figuration has been declared by *divine authority,* we make an assertion for which we neither have, nor *can* have, the slightest foundation.[19] (italics his)

But Patrick Fairbairn refused to restrict the scope of all possible types to those named in the NT as Marsh had done. Instead, types were historical realities explicitly appointed by God and exhibiting the same truths, principles, and relationships in both Testaments.[20] In defense of Fairbairn's stance, it must be noted that nowhere does the NT pretend to be an exhaustive list of types.[21]

The application of this characteristic of divine designation lies at the heart of the struggle in deciding whether or not typology is an exegetical art or a form of eisegesis. Certainly, there is divine designation in the case of the Tabernacle legislation, for God pointedly instructed Moses in Exodus 25:9, 40; 26:30; 27:8; Num. 8:4 to make the Tabernacle and its utensils after the "pattern" (*tabnît;* also of Solomon's "plan" for the Temple in 1 Chronicles 28:11, 12, 19), the "plan" in Exodus 26:30 (*mišpāṭ*), or, the "sight" or "vision" (*her'âh*) in Exodus 27:8. Thus, what Moses was to fabricate was only a model (or "shadow," to use the language of Heb. 10:1) of the real that existed apart from the wilderness representations. Furthermore, this divine designation is enhanced in the OT itself by a "nascent typology"[22] wherein "Egypt" already functions as a symbol of bondage and oppression in Hosea 8:13; 9:3, 6; 11:5 and David is a type of the ideal king who is to come to rule his people again (Hos. 3:5; Jer. 30:9; Ezek. 34:23–24; 37:24). Moreover, Melchizedek of Genesis 14 is connected in Psalm 110:4 with that future divine king and priest whereas Elijah the prophet will appear once again before the great and noteable Day of the Lord (Mal. 4:5; Luke 1:17).

PREFIGURATION

The final and most difficult characteristic to establish is prefiguration. C. T. Fritsch was able to define a type in 1947 as "an institution,

19. Herbert Marsh, *A Course of Lectures,* Part III.A (Cambridge, 1813), Lecture XVIII, p. 107.
20. Patrick Fairbairn, *Typology,* 1:46–47; 141.
21. Charles T. Fritsch, "Biblical Typology," 104 (1947):220.
22. Charles T. Fritsch, "Biblical Typology," p. 91.

historical event or person, ordained by God, which effectively prefigures some truth connected with Christianity."[23] David Baker, on the other hand, flatly denied that there was any prospective direction of movement from the OT to the NT. For him "Typology is not prophecy."[24] Instead, it is retrospective.

Richard Davidson argued that the Bible exhibits a *devoir-etre* ("must-needs-be") prospective/predictive quality to the relationship that exists between the OT types and the corresponding NT realities.[25] Behind the thinking of many modern advocates of typology lies a different understanding from the traditional conservative view of history and revelation. Especially prominent is the current historical-critical emphasis on the primacy of the community's witness to what it believed to be the succession of the great acts of God in their times. Such an emphasis leaves little room for the predictive element.[26] For example, the types Paul cited in 1 Corinthians 10:1–11 were eschatologically structured so that their fulfillment would involve an intensification (*Steigerung*) at the "end of the ages." Thus, the half dozen events cited there were not mere ethical models, nor doctrinal molds in which to categorize certain teachings, but divinely designed prefigurations that involved *devoir-etre* relationships between OT historical persons, events, institutions, and NT eschatological fulfillments.

A direct equation cannot be made between the predictive oracles of the prophets and the prospective nature of types. Types were more like the prophets' use of symbolic actions than their oracles about the future. Nevertheless, when God specially designated events, institutions, and persons, he did so because they had a certain necessity about them that pointed beyond their times to another future time and generation. Even though its future realization would exceed what the designees had experienced, enough would still be shared in common for later generations to know that the repeated situation, recurring office or ritual, or the reiterated principle was the same.

---

23. Ibid., p. 214. So agrees L. Goppelt, *Typology*, pp. 12, 16.
24. David L. Baker, "Typology and the Christian," p. 149.
25. Richard M. Davidson, *Typology*, pp. 74, 265–76, 284–85.
26. See a similar discussion by John H. Stek, "Biblical Typology Yesterday and Today," *Calvin Theological Journal* 5 (1970):133–62.

6

Understanding the Old Testament as "Types of Us"

1 Corinthians 10:1-2

There are five NT passages that can be of great help in illustrating what Scripture signifies when it uses *tupos* structures. These are 1 Corinthians 10:1-13; Romans 5:12-21; 1 Peter 3:18-21; Hebrews 8:5; and Hebrews 9:24.

Generally speaking, the first three (1 Cor. 10, Rom. 5, and 1 Pet. 3) may be classified as "horizontal" or earthly-historical *tupos* structures. The two passages in Hebrews may be labeled "vertical" (earth-heaven) *tupos* structures.[1] This distinction has not always been observed because most studies in biblical typology concentrate on horizontal types and ignore all vertical examples. There is no need to do that, for the Tabernacle legislation and the NT writer of Hebrews placed great emphasis on the vertical aspect. Nor should we imply that the vertical typology has a crypto-pagan background[2] or Platonic roots.[3] Horrace Hummel calls our attention not only to the vertical correspondence

---

1. For brief references to this distinction see Charles T. Fritsch, *"To Antitupon,"* in *Studia Biblica et Semitica: Theodoro Christiano Vriezen dedicata* (Wageningen: H. Veenman and Zoren, 1966):100–107; Charles Hummel, "The Old Testament Basis of Typological Interpretation," *Biblical Research* 9 (1964):19–20; Richard M. Davidson, *Typology,* pp. 99–100; 191.
2. Leonard Goppelt, *"Tupos, antitupos, tupikos, hupotupōsis,"* *Theological Dictionary of the New Testament,* ed. Gerhard Friedrich, trans. Geoffrey W. Bromiley (Grand Rapids: Eerdmans, 1972), 8:258–59.
3. See on this debate in Hebrews, Ronald Williamson, *Philo and the Epistle to the Hebrews* (Leiden: E. J. Brill, 1970), as cited by R. M. Davidson, *Typology,* p. 100, n.1, and pp. 338–42.

between the heavenly and earthly temples but also to the parallelism between the temple and heavenly liturgy in the Psalms, the unity between the wars of Israel and their celestial counterparts already in Exodus 15 and Judges 5 and the setting of the prophetic calls and oracles in Yahweh's council.[4] Ronald Williamson likewise demolishes the alleged Philonic Platonism by noting that there is no room in the heavenly world of ideas, as held by Plato and Philo, for the historical Jesus or the temporal-historical sequence of movement in Hebrews (vis-á-vis the Platonic eternal timeless principles).[5]

If these five major texts exhibit prominent usage of *tupos* vocabulary and illustrations from the OT, would not an exegesis of one or more of those texts aid us in testing our definition of typology and the four characteristics set forth in the above argument against the first century and apostolic practice? No doubt pride of place is to be given to 1 Corinthians 10:1–12 both because of its probable date of A.D. 54–57 (the earliest use of the word *tupos* in the NT) and because of its greater length and the proliferation of its examples from the OT.

PRELIMINARY CONSIDERATIONS

Special attention must be given to *tupos* class of words in 1 Corinthians 10:6, 11 to see if they are used merely as illustrations, examples and ethical models or as hermeneutical indicators. In addition, it will be necessary to note if the correspondences are historical, and if so, how extensive, manifold, or singular are these connections between the two Testaments? The question of the presence of clear divine designation and intent in the OT cannot be passed over anymore than can the question of any kind of *devoir-etre* prescription or prediction.

The setting and structure of this text are fairly straightforward. The apostle has just given an exhortation on exercising self-control in 1 Corinthians 9:24–27 to which he now attaches the word *gar* in 10:1, "For (or because), I want you to know, brethren." Further confirmation of the ethical purpose of Paul in this section in 1 Corinthians 10:1–12 can be seen in that this block of text concludes with a similar admonition in verse 12: "Therefore let anyone who thinks that he stands take heed lest he fall" (RSV). Accordingly, Israel with its most favored nation status, like the apostle and now the believers at Corinth, had better be warned of the danger of their imminent disqualification if they likewise refuse to repent as those Israelites did. The passage

4. Horace Hummel, "The Old Testament Basis," p. 39, n.4.
5. Richard M. Davidson, *Typology in Scripture: A Study of Hermeneutical Tupos Structures* (Berrien Springs, Mich.: Andrews U., 1981), p. 340. Also see Ronald Williamson, "Platonism and Hebrews," *SJT* 16 (1963):418–19.

appears to fall into three parts: verses 1–2; verses 3–4; and verses 5–12.

THE BAPTISM IN THE CLOUD AND IN THE SEA (VV. 1–2)

The Corinthians appear to have held a magical view of the ordinance of baptism and the Lord's Supper. It seems they believed that mere participation in those two ordinances guaranteed their personal salvation. Such a situation brought with it an antinomian spirit in which they thought themselves free—free from all responsibility to act in accordance with what they professed and to behave as they chose.

A strong note of historical correspondence was immediately struck in verses 1–2 by phrases *"our* fathers" and *"into* Moses."[6] Paul included his fellow believers at Corinth, who were mainly of Gentile roots, as participants in the house of Israel and thereby bound together the people of God from both the old and new covenants.

The emphasis falls on "all" (*pantes*), for it is repeated five times in verses 1–4. But the contrast in verse 5 is all the more striking, for whereas all shared God's gracious gifts, most did not retain God's blessing. The Corinthians' participation in baptism and the Lord's Supper, likewise, would not preserve them in any mechanical operation of grace.

With two catch phrases, "under the cloud" (*en tē nephelē*) and "through the sea" (*en te thalasse*), Paul quickly summarized Israel's experience in the Exodus event. All attempts to relate those phrases to Jewish proselyte baptism are wide of the mark because the rabbinic sources connect that rite with the ritual purification at Sinai and not with the Red Sea experience.[7] Moreover, the phrase "into Moses" is without parallel anywhere else except with Paul's analogous phrase of being baptized "into Christ" (Rom. 6:3; Gal. 3:27). Thus, it is Christian baptism that is in view here whereby a believer is incorporated into fellowship with Christ in the same way Israel was inseparably linked with Moses as they underwent the Red Sea experience.

The exact nature and extent of the historical correspondence between Christian baptism and Israel's Exodus must be obtained from those two catch phrases. The focus can hardly be the mode of baptism because the *en*, "in," need not be taken as a locative denoting *place*, which is in line with several rabbinic legends in which the sea formed a vault or tunnel through which Israel passed.[8] In what sense, then,

6. Andrew J. Bandstra, "Interpretation in I Corinthians 10:1–11," *Calvin Theological Journal* 6 (1977):6; Richard M. Davidson, *Typology*, pp. 209, 221.
7. See the literature and argument of Davidson, p. 214.
8. Davidson, pp. 216–17.

was Israel "in the cloud" and "in the sea"? Some have suggested that the cloud is a Holy Spirit baptism and the sea is water baptism, whereas Meredith Kline[9] argued for an instrumental force to the preposition *en* denoting the means by which God's "judgment ordeal" (a secondary technical sense of *baptizō* found in the NT, OT, and ancient Near Eastern parallels) occurred.

The point of similarity, however, is the experience of God's act of deliverance that both Israel and the Corinthian believers had tasted in the grace of God. It is only in light of the magnitude of such grace that the heinousness and treachery of both community's apostasy became clear. In just one short phrase—"into Moses," which immediately suggests "into Christ"—Paul is able to embrace the entire spectrum of redemption in Christ.

What did Moses know of Christian baptism? Goppelt frankly admits:

> It is not the OT texts that are called *tupoi*, but the historical events, which are depicted in loose dependence on the OT. The section of IC.10 did not arise out of scriptural exegesis.... The correspondence ... is to be seen, primarily in the essential similarity in God's acts. Thus baptism is like the crossing of the Red Sea not merely in virtue of the basic passage through water, but beyond that as the basic deliverance.[10]

However, Davidson calls Israel's "baptism" an *"advance presentation of Christian baptism"*[11] because verse 11 ("upon whom the ends of the ages have come") argues that these OT types had a certain necessity (*devoir-etre*).[12] Only if there is this necessary connection between the saving act of God at the Red Sea and what the Corinthians experienced can Paul convince the unruly Corinthians of the necessity of the judgments of God, claims Davidson.[13] Is this so?

Did God not only lead the Exodus but so design it that it contained in event-forms the foundations for future happenings? Yes, when it is remembered that Israel was helpless to deliver herself. Had God not stepped in to fulfill the promise that He had made with Abraham centuries ago in Genesis 15, there would have been no deliverance. However, that did not prevent Israel from choosing to rebel against the same gracious Lord. Thus, the picture for the Corinthians was

9. Meredith Kline, *By Oath Consigned: A Reinterpretation of the Covenant Signs of Circumcision and Baptism* (Grand Rapids: Eerdmans, 1968), p. 70.
10. Leonard Goppelt, *TDNT*, 8:251.
11. Davidson, p. 222.
12. A term coined by Gustave Martele, "Sacrements, figures et exhortation en I C. 10:1–11," *Recherches de science religieuse* 44 (1956):527–31 as cited by Davidson, p. 223.
13. Davidson, p. 223.

complete: God's initiating act of gracious deliverance and Israel's freedom of choice.

This is a type of theological exegesis in which events, rather than words, reflect the works of God and the responses of men. Certainly exegesis is required to appreciate the groundwork that lies behind the OT type, but then the reader is made responsible for noticing the reappearance of the identical pattern when it occurs again in the same connection.

THE SPIRITUAL FOOD AND DRINK FROM THE SPIRITUAL ROCK (vv. 3-4)

The apostle clearly refers to the Lord's Supper in these verses, but what does he mean by the word *spiritual* (*pneumatikos*)? And who or what is the *pneumatikos* Rock that "accompanied" (*akolouthousēs*) them and is called "Christ"?

Frederick Godet observes that the epithet "spiritual" cannot refer to the nature of the food and drink, for they were material in substance.[14] Therefore, it must refer to the source of these gifts (i.e., they were "supernatural" or "miraculous"). Thus, these gifts were the result of God's power and came directly from His hand.

In verse 4*b*, Paul refers to the two events narrated in Exodus 17:6 and Numbers 20:11: water from the rock. But the spiritual Rock, in Paul's usage, cannot refer to where this Rock came from, but instead, to its nature. The causal connection (*gar*, "for") explains how the drink they were enjoying could also be called "spiritual"; it came from that "spiritual Rock which accompanied them and that Rock was Christ."

Paul does not say in an allegorical fashion that Christ *is* (*estin*) that Rock; no, for him Christ "*was*" (*ēn*) that Rock already in the OT. This view is also supported by the strong and early manuscript evidence (e.g., P[46]) pointing to "Christ" in 1 Corinthians 10:9 as being present when Israel put him to the test and were destroyed by serpents.[15]

Many commentators insist that Paul is not working from the OT but from the rabbinic legend of a rocky well that followed Israel during their wilderness wanderings.[16] Amazingly, the only two correspondences between those embellished rabbinic traditions of this rolling well are: (1) both refer to the water which Israel drank; and (2)

14. Frederick L. Godet, *Commentary on the First Epistle of St. Paul to the Corinthians*, 2 vols. (Grand Rapids: Zondervan, 1957), 2:54–55. See the important discussion of *pneumatikos* in Davidson, pp. 225–32, and the literature he cites there.
15. See Bandstra, p. 18; Davidson, pp. 259–60. Nestle-Aland and the United Bible Society (*UBS*, 2d ed.) favored *kurion*, but *UBS* (3d ed.) adopted *Christon* because it was the *lectio difficilior* and the one that best explained the other readings of *theon* and *kurion*.
16. See Earle E. Ellis, "A Note on First Corinthians 10:4," *JBL* 76 (1957):53–56; Davidson, pp. 233–48.

both refer to something "accompanying" or "following" Israel. That is hardly a convincing parallelism! Moreover, the legend of the rock following Israel was not extant in that form in Paul's day.[17]

In Paul's view, the one who stood by Moses on both occasions was none other than Christ Himself. In Exodus 17:6 it was explicitly stated: "I will stand before you there on the rock at Horeb," whereas Numbers 20:1–10 has no such explicit assurance. Nevertheless, the Lord is called the "Rock" (both *ṣûr* and *s*e*lā'*) of Israel in numerous texts in the OT (Deut. 32:4, 15, 18; 2 Sam. 22:2, 3, 32, 47; 23:3; Pss. 18:2, 4, 31; 78:35; Isa. 17:10; 26:4).

Because Philo identified the rock in the wilderness with the wisdom of God, Andrew Bandstra and others have argued that Paul followed Philo, for Paul began his letter to Corinth by also identifying Christ as the true wisdom of God (1 Cor. 1:24, 30).[18] But Paul never makes this Philonic equation of the rock with wisdom. The apostle's background for equating Christ with the Rock may be found in the OT's constant reference to the Angel of the Lord, who accompanied Israel in the wilderness (Ex. 13:21; 14:19, 30; 15:26; 23:20–23; 32:34; 33:2, 14–15; Acts 7:30, 38). God said of this angel that went with Israel in Exodus 23:20: "My name is in him." This can only be a claim for the full deity of that angel that was sent from God to accompany Israel! So agrees Godet:

> The passage forms an analogy to the words of John xii.41, where the apostle applies to Jesus the vision in which Isaiah beholds Adonai, the Lord, in the temple of His glory (ch. vi).... We have the same view here ... the angel *of the Lord*, so often identified in Genesis with the Lord Himself, and yet often distinct from Him, in the Being who is called in Isaiah the *angel of His presence* (lxiii.8), and in Malachi: the *angel of the covenant, Adonai* (iii.1).[19] (italics his)

Therefore, we conclude that the Rock in verse 4 should be capitalized and be viewed as an OT Christophany because: (1) The Lord associated Himself with that rock from which Israel drank in Exodus 17:6 ("I will stand before you there on the rock at Horeb"); (2) the "Rock" is repeatedly used as a divine name in the Song of Moses (Deut. 32:4, 15, 18, 30, 31) and elsewhere in the OT; and (3) the alleged rabbinic legend of an accompanying rock is not known to have existed in Paul's day.

It will do no good to object that all three adjectives (*pneumatikos*) should modify literal substantives; for whereas the spiritual food and

17. Andrew Bandstra, "I Cor 10:1–11," p. 11.
18. Ibid., pp. 12–13.
19. F. Godet, 2:58.

drink was literal, nothing demands that the spiritual Rock must also be a literal rock. Davidson feels there is a type of "synonymous parallelism of the three occurrences,"[20] but such thinking is at home in poetry and not in the prose, which is used here. Moreover, Paul's testimony in 1 Corinthians 10:11 to the fact that all the things that he had been discussing were "written down," that is, "inscripturated,"[21] argues for a reference to that Rock known from the OT that could serve as the source for Israel's food and drink.

What, then, is the *tupos* structure of Christ already supplying Israel with food and drink in the wilderness? Whereas we have argued that *pneumatikos* depicted the heavenly and divine source and not the nature of the material gifts supplied to Israel in the wilderness, it is also clear that they were also types (1 Cor. 10:6).

The same historical correspondence noted in verses 1–2 is also present here, for these were "our fathers" and what happened to them should keep "us from setting our hearts on evil." In addition, "Christ" was present and supplying these gifts. The element of escalation or heightening is not explicitly carried through with a direct mention of the eucharist[22]—but neither would such an inference be out of order because the Corinthian problem may have been an unjustified dependence on a mechanistic and external participation in the ordinances of baptism and the Lord's Supper. The divine resemblance and designation of the food can already be seen in the warning of Deuteronomy 8:3 that Israel was fed with manna to teach them that "man does not live by bread alone but by every word that comes from the mouth of the Lord." Thus, Moses gave a clear signal to Israel that the manna was not an end in itself, in spite of God's gracious and providential care, but rather pointed away from itself to a theological significance. But did it prefigure anything in the Christian era? It made clear that life itself came from the rock on the authority of the word of the One who Himself was the Rock. There does not seem to be any evidence to show that the Rock in the OT was treated messianically, but when the presence of the Angel of the Lord, the one sent by God and the one who had God's name in Him, is taken into account, it is impossible to avoid a Christological interpretation. Therefore, Christ sustained not only physical life in the wilderness on the basis of His word, but He taught Israel to expect to live all of life

20. Davidson, p. 244, n.1.
21. See Davidson, pp. 270–71 for an equation between the *tupoi* of these verses, the *tauta*, "these things" of verses 6 and 11 and their being part of the *graphē*. From Paul's use of the verb *graphein* elsewhere, it is clear that he is referring to events recorded in the OT. See Romans 4:23; 15:4; 1 Corinthians 1:19, 31; 2:9; 3:19; 4:5; 9:9, 10; 15:45, 54.
22. Note however, 1 Corinthians 10:17 "*all* partake of the *one* bread" in a common "communion" (*koinōnia*).

completely on the basis of every word from the mouth of the Lord. Manna and water from the rock are no longer merely literal referents, but they have taken on a quality that points beyond themselves to some nascent expectation or symbolic association of life in its basics and fullness with the provision of God.

WARNINGS FROM FOUR EPISODES IN ISRAEL'S HISTORY (vv. 5-10)

Verse 5 is the transitional statement. The introductory "nevertheless" (*alla*) abruptly introduces Paul's warning that most of "all" those who had received God's gifts perished in the wilderness. Likewise, all who had received Christian baptism and had celebrated the Lord's Supper were in similar danger, for "these things" (*tauta*) had happened as (*tupoi*) "types." Verse 6 has at least three important grammatical signals in the first clause that should help us come to terms with the meaning of Biblical types.[23] The text reads: *tauta de tupoi hēmōn egenēthēsan.* As the plural form of *tauta*, "these things" refers to both the positive events of baptism, food, and drink in verses 1–5 as well as the negative judgments in verses 6–9.[24] Thus, more is implied here than mere paraenesis (i.e., a warning). The second grammatical point underscores the historical nature of Paul's *tupoi.* The verb *egenēthēsan* is in the aorist tense, indicative mood, and is not a substitute for the verb "to be" as in the RSV. The fact that verse 11 has in a parallel statement the verb *sunebainen,* "happened," makes it clear that the verb *ginomai* is used here to denote a past event; they "happened" (NASB); "occurred" (NIV). Paul's types were historical events that really took place in the real setting of the wilderness and included acts of blessing as well as judgment. But the third, and most important, grammatical feature of verse 6 is the translation of *hēmōn.* Is it an objective genitive?—"Now these things happened as types *for* us." Or, is it a subjective genitive?—"Now these things happened as types *of* us." Most translations render it as an objective genitive of reference (i.e., "with reference to us"). However, the same genitival construction occurs in Romans 5:14: "Adam is a type *of* Christ" (not *for* Christ). Thus, the events cited in 1 Corinthians 10:1–5; 6–9 contain "types *of* us."

---

23. I am dependent in this discussion on R. Davidson, *Typology,* pp. 250–54.
24. Davidson, p. 250, n.1, contests Earle Ellis's attempt to establish a parallel between Paul's use of *tauta*, "this," and the *raz* formula, "this is" or "the interpretation is" of Qumran pesher hermeneutics. Earle E. Ellis, "How the New Testament Uses the Old," *Prophecy and Hermeneutics in Early Christianity* (Grand Rapids: Eerdmans, 1978), pp. 159–61. Davidson lists: (1) the plural form; (2) the verb is not *estin*, but *egenēthēsan*, meaning "happened, occurred"; and (3) it is the punctiliar aorist tense in harmony with Pauline, but against Qumranic usage.

The significance of this switch of prepositions has major consequences for the subject of typology. Whereas the translation "for us" allowed for a "loose, optional tie between the *tupoi* and 'us,' [it] simply cannot reproduce the semantic range that Paul intends.... There is "an ineluctable link between the *tupoi* and 'us.'"[25]

Four more OT types follow in verses 6–9. They singled out: (1) the idolatry when Aaron made the golden calf (Ex. 32:4, 6); (2) the sexual immorality precipitated by Balaam (Num. 25:1–9); (3) the testing of Christ when the serpents bit the people (Num. 21:5, 6); and (4) the murmuring of the people because of God's judgment over their rebellion against God's appointed leadership (Num. 16:41).

The climax of the section comes in verse 11 and recapitulates verse 6: "[all][26] these things happened (*sunebainen*) to them *tupikōs*. Does *tupikōs* have a paraenetic or hermeneutic sense? If it meant only a "warning example," it would be redundant, as Davidson has argued,[27] for the next clause adds: "they were written for our warning" (*nouthesian*). To have both words, *tupikos* and *nouthesian*, in both clauses saying the same thing would be tautological. Moreover, the clauses are connected by a *de* (which usually expresses contrast, transition, or development), not by an epexegetical *kai*, "and."

Davidson convincingly demonstrates that the solution to the translation of verse 11 lies in recognizing the differing functions of the two clauses of verse 11. The first clause of both verse 11 and verse 6 describe the *nature* of the events: they are types *of* us in their divine intention, the second clauses of verses 6 and 11 denote the *purpose* of those OT events: they are paraenetic warnings "for us."

Verse 11 also makes a strong case for viewing types as prefigurations that have a *devoir-etre* about them. This eschatological focus can be found in the clause "upon whom the ends of the ages have come, (to arrive, or reach [their] destination, *katantaō*). If the expression *ta telē tōn aiōnōn*, "the end of the ages," is understood to mean roughly the same thing as somewhat similar phrases in Hebrews 9:26 ("at the end of the age," *epi sunteleia tōn aiōnōn*), or 1 Peter 1:20 ("at the end of the times," *ep eschatou tōn chronōn*), then Paul is indicating the eschatological character of the *tupoi* described here. Once again the *tupoi/tupikōs* are linked with the "us" who have appeared in the age that began with the first advent of Christ and will be consummated with the coming of Christ in his second advent. The OT events

25. Davidson, p. 254.
26. The word "all" is present in all the important manuscripts, but because its position varies, coming before or after *tauta*, it is usually regarded as a gloss. Davidson argues for retaining it, pp. 266–67, n.2.
27. Davidson, p. 269.

"are bound up with the eschatological 'us' whether the latter want them to be or not."[28]

HERMENEUTICAL IMPLICATIONS OF TYPOLOGY

If the events of the OT "happened as types *of us* (1 Cor. 10:6) in the Christian era, then there is a unity between the Old and New Testaments. "Typology provides one of the keys for grasping imaginatively the unity of the Bible. The recurrence of the same images and themes throughout the Scripture helps to make intelligible the artistic and theological interrelationship of its various parts and helps in avoiding the fragmentation which is frequently the [sic] fruit of purely histori-cal-grammatical studies."[29]

But in what does that unity consist when applied to the discussion of types? Was it to be restricted only to broad similarities between the Testaments and analogous situations? Or, was there some precise and divinely intended events that anticipated NT events?

John W. Drane is sure that what Paul was referring to in 1 Corinthians 10:1–9 was

> not some O.T. event that had direct and detailed correspondences in the N.T. or in Christian experience. What he was really speaking of was the unchanging character of God himself, and in this he stands in direct line with the "typology" of the O.T. prophets, whose message was: if this is how God acted with his people in the past, this is how we can expect him to deal with us. Thus, "typology" really becomes a statement of theology, affirming the unchanging character of the Biblical God.[30]

Drane's denials do not match the biblical vocabulary already observed in 1 Corinthians 10:6, 11 and his affirmation that typology is theology, affirming the unchanging character of God, is certainly on the mark, but minimalistic in its outlook.

Certainly the essence of typology is that it adds a theological perspective to our interpretation of OT texts and is predicated not on anything mystical or subjective, but on the fact that the same general divine plan runs through both Testaments.[31] A type presupposes a *purpose* in history that unfolded in a self-consistent unity throughout the Testaments.

28. Davidson, p. 274.
29. Robert C. Dentan, "Typology—Its Use and Abuse," *Anglican Theological Review* 34 (1952):215.
30. John W. Drane, "Typology," *Evangelical Quarterly* 50 (1978):201.
31. This last point is made by Addison P. Foster, "The Types of Scripture," 28 pp. (an essay read before the Alumni of Andover Theological Seminary at Andover, 30 June 1875), p. 4.

We conclude, then, that types cannot be "read into" or "read back" into the OT from the NT in some sort of canonized *eisegesis*. Neither can horizontal types be reduced to the status of mere illustrations given for paraenetic warnings for the church, for that is to confuse their actual *purpose* with an adequate definition of their real *nature*.

But "it is indeed essential in a type," as Van Mildert argued in his Bampton Lectures of 1815, "in the Scriptural acceptation of the term, that there should be competent evidence of the Divine *intention* in the correspondence between it and the Antitype"[32] (italics Van Mildert's). Some of the verbal signals of this intention are: (1) the long list of "new" things mentioned in both Testaments (namely, the new Moses, the New Covenant, the new David, the new temple, the new exodus, the new cup and bread, and the new heaven and earth); (2) the acquired technical status of some repeated theological terms such as "seed," "my Son," "firstborn," "rest," "blessing," "Branch," "Holy One," "House of David," and so on; and (3) the pointed reoccurrence of dominant events such as desert wanderings, exiles, exoduses, divinely appointed deliverers, and so on. The linking, or homology, has already begun in the text and in that sense belongs to the textual tradition and not to the interpreter's skill or imaginative powers.

Finally, types necessarily contain a foreshadowing feature "of us" in the Christian era. They are not only written "for us" as warnings and instructive guides, but they are "types of us" and in that sense are predictive. Again, this must not be equated or substituted for the prophetic oracular words, for that would be to compare apples and oranges; types are events and prophecies are words. Nevertheless, that does not mean that these events cannot participate by virtue of their inclusion in the grand design of history overseen by God in such a way that the type and antitype converge as "the ends of the ages" converge in the first advent inaugurating a partial realization of the eschaton and consummate in the *parousia* of Jesus Christ. Seen in this light, these NT events and their OT shadows "must-needs-be," for everything comes to the one great finale as history concludes as designed by God.

32. Page 239 as cited by H. L. Ellison, "Typology," *Evangelical Quarterly* 25 (1953):160.

7

Abolishing the Old Order
and Establishing the New

Psalm 40:6-8

Psalm 40 belongs to that unique group of four psalms (Psalms 40,
50, 51, and 69) that appears to depreciate the sacrifices prescribed
in the Levitical legislation of the Torah. Yet, this was the psalm that
the writer of Hebrews used to authenticate four major points as he
concluded his Christological[1] argument: (1) the law was only a shadow
(*sklu*) of the true reality (*eikōn*) of salvation in Christ; (2) the plurality
of sacrifices demanded by Mosaic law is to be strikingly contrasted
with the single unique sacrifice of Christ; (3) the repeated sacrifices
are admittedly ineffective in and of themselves in forgiving and
removing sin; and (4) the Mosaic ritual law is abolished so that another
order might be established in Christ.[2] In the entire NT, only Hebrews
10:5-7 uses Psalm 40:6-8.[3]

INTRODUCTION

THE ISSUES

It is clear that the NT writer cited this passage to demonstrate that
the psalmist had in some way anticipated both the coming of the

1. The epistle's main Christological section is found in Hebrews 7:1—10:18.
2. I am indebted to Theodore G. Stylianopoulos ("Shadow and Reality: Reflections
   on Hebrews 10:1-18," in *The Greek Orthodox Theological Review* 17[1972]:216) for
   the general formulation of these four points.
3. I am indebted to T. Allan Armstrong, "The Use of Psalm 40 in Hebrews 10" (MA
   thesis, Trinity Evangelical Divinity School, 1975) for this conclusion. He surveyed
   four additional references listed in the second edition of The United Bible Societies'
   Greek text, viz., Luke 7:19 (Psalm 40:7), Ephesians 5:2 (Psalm 40:6), and Revelation
   5:9; 14:3 (Psalm 40:3) but found them unconvincing.

Messiah and the abolition of the Mosaic ceremonial legislation. But such major claims touch on some of the most sensitive issues in the whole curriculum of theology.

It is as if the writer wished to settle once and for all the question of continuity and discontinuity between the Old and New Testaments in one fell swoop. Does the psalmist point directly to the heart of this issue with his contrast between sacrifices and obedience? Did that distinction point to the removal of the first order of things and the establishment of the second in Christ?

And if that problem appears to be too broad in its implications for theology, what are we to say about the writer of Hebrews finding Christ and His perfect sacrifice in Psalm 40:6–8? By what legitimate and reasonable method of exegesis can the psalmist's words be made to bear such heavy freight? Of whom were these verses written originally? Was David their author? What possible meaning could these words have had in their original OT context? How can a Messianic prediction be reconciled with the psalmist's admission of sin in verse 11? In this admission he certainly was not a type or an "earnest" of the Messiah. Furthermore, how important is it to recognize the LXX text, which prefers "body" for the Hebrew Masoretic text of "ears"? Is this a deliberate distortion of the actual text in order to make an otherwise shaky case?

Each of those questions takes us to the heart of evangelical theology and to the hermeneutical debate about the method of NT writers in citing the OT. So difficult are many of these questions, that some have gloomily concluded as did S. R. Driver:

> It must be obvious that the Psalm, in its original intention, has no reference to Christ: it is some Old Testament saint, not Christ, who declares that it is his delight to do God's will; hence 'I am come' in v. 7 cannot refer to the Incarnation: if further proof were needed, it would be found in v. 12, where the Psalmist speaks of his 'iniquities,' which, except by most strained and unnatural exegesis, can be understood only of the iniquities which he has himself committed. It is, of course, perfectly true that parts of the Psalm are appropriate to Christ, and might well have been taken up by Him upon His lips ... [but] a possible *application* of a Psalm is no guide to its *interpretation*, and cannot determine its original intention. Rather, the author of the Epistle to the Hebrews puts vv. 6–8*a* into Christ's mouth, not because the Psalm as a whole refers to Him, but because ... these verses are, in the words of the [then] present Dean of Ely a 'fitting expression of the purpose of His life,' and of His perfect conformity to His Father's will. And so the Psalm is suitably appointed in the Anglican Church as one of the proper Psalms for Good Friday.[4]

4. S. R. Driver, "The Method of Studying the Psalter," *Expositor*, Seventh Series 52(1910):356–57 (italics his).

But can such an "application" have any force, especially in a passage that seeks to establish an argument, when it is not based on a fair interpretation as originally intended by the psalmist? Why cite words which in their original intention have no reference to Christ even if it is only by way of appropriating and applying them? Would such a line of argumentation be convincing to any knowledgeable Jew? It is difficult to understand how this kind of citation could be of any evidential or practical value for a frame of mind that might wish to resist such wholesale supplanting of traditional values and convictions. The situation is as F. S. Sampson has described it:

> This passage presents one of the most vexed questions among interpreters, both as to the propriety of the Apostle's reference to this Psalm to the Messiah and as to his adoption of the erroneous translation of the LXX.[5]

It will be the contention of this essay not only that the logic and argumentation is fair, but also that it is consistent with the original intention of the psalmist.

THE AUTHOR OF PSALM 40

The psalm begins with a heading that we believe to be as original[6] as the body of the psalm: "To the chief musician, a Psalm of David."

Most modern commentators such as Briggs[7] prefer to place this psalm in the postexilic era. Usually their arguments are built around alleged reminiscences of the language of Jeremiah and Isaiah, in that order, because of their own systems of late dating. The psalmist's reference to the "pit of destruction" (*bôr sha 'ôn*) and "miry clay" (*tît hayyāwēn*) in Psalm 40:2 [Heb., v. 3] is usually compared with Jeremiah's experience in the "mire" (*tît*) and "pit" (*bôr*) in Jeremiah 38:6. Yet, such terminology also appears in Psalm 28:1 and 30:3 [Heb., v. 4].

5. F. S. Sampson, *A Critical Commentary on the Epistle to the Hebrews* (New York: Carter, 1866), p. 369. My student Stuart Erdenberg pointed out this reference to me.
6. Sigmund Mowinckel, *The Psalms in Israel's Worship*, trans. D. R. Ap-Thomas (Nashville: Abingdon, 1967), 2:98–101, is one of the most recent studies on the authenticity of the Davidic headings in these psalms. He concludes that these are all late titles, but he notes on p. 99, n.52, that only in a half dozen or so of the seventy-three Davidic psalms do we have no manuscript or contradictory manuscript evidence. We conclude that the case for Davidic authorship in Psalm 40, because it is not in this list, is secure and as old as the text. See also Robert Dick Wilson, "The Headings of the Psalms," *Princeton Theological Review* 24(1926):353–95.
7. Charles Augustus Briggs, *A Critical and Exegetical Commentary on the Book of Psalms*, 2 vols., International Critical Commentary (New York: Scribner's, 1906), 1:351.

Likewise, these same scholars find a dependence on the preexilic prophets for the psalmist's contrast between sacrifice and obedience (see Isa. 1:11ff.; Hos. 6:6; Amos 5:22; Mic. 6:6; and Psalm 40:6–8 [Heb., vv. 7–9]). Yet, once again it could be successfully argued that if the psalmist needed a biblical precedent for this truth, he could easily have appealed to 1 Samuel 15:22. Certainly, the Davidic psalms, Psalms 32 and 51, reflect the same theology, which places a premium on the priority of a right relationship to God as the basis for any successful sacrifice to Him. Even the very Torah that set forth the ceremonial law itself insisted on the primacy of obedience and a personal response of faith and love to God as a condition for pleasing God with one's ritual and worship; a fact that shines with special clarity in Exodus 15:26 and Deuteronomy 10:12, 20.

Even the reference to an inward law of the heart (Psalm 40:8 [Heb., v. 9]) need not point to Jeremiah's new covenant or Ezekiel's new heart and new spirit, for David also used it in his psalm, Psalm 37:31.

Thus, all of the alleged evidences[8] fail to show direct dependence; instead, they build a case for a shared informing theology in which many of the writers show an obvious awareness of the others' contributions. Seldom can it be demonstrated, however, that that literary and religious heritage appeared *after* the Davidic period. Consequently, from this standpoint, no case can be made against a Davidic authorship. Too many biblical scholars, from all theological persuasions, are far too skeptical about what a divinely inspired penman could or could not have known at any given period in the OT.

Thus, judged both on internal grounds and external circumstances, it is best to accept the ancient witness in the title of this psalm as the best clue to its authorship, at least until sufficient evidence is forthcoming to the contrary—in the event that some may still be unpersuaded that the psalm titles are an authentic part of the text, as we have argued for here.

THE UNITY OF PSALM 40

Usually Psalm 40 is understood as consisting of two parts which differ widely in tone, character, and type. The first part (vv. 1–11 [Heb., 12]) is epitomized by thanksgiving and gratitude for deliverance; the second part (vv. 12–17 [Heb., vv. 13–18]) ends with a lament in which the psalmist prays for a speedy deliverance from his foes. Many

8. Briggs also lists Isaiah 41:5 (v. 4), Isaiah 55:8, 9 (v. 6) and Psalm 22:26 (vv. 10–11), *Psalms*, 1:351. The old commentator Ewald believed that the prominence given to the roll of the book in verse 7 was enough to link this psalm with the time of Josiah's reformation, but the Mosaic Deuteronomy 17:14–20 could serve just as well as a source for this idea if need be.

interpreters find this association of grand success (1–11) with great disaster (12–17) so troublesome that they believe it only fair to hold that the psalm is a composite of two earlier pieces.[9]

Such tension is not an unresolvable dilemma. As both Wieser[10] and Mowinckel[11] have argued, thanksgiving for past deliverance is the basis for the expected deliverance from the psalmist's present difficulty.

Of course, it is true that the second division appears with very slight textual variations as a separate psalm: Psalm 70. As Carl B. Moll has argued:

> ... this does not prove that two songs originally different have been subsequently united ..., or that the unity can be maintained only by the supposition that the poet speaks in the name of Israel ..., or the pious members of the people.... Still less can it be shown, that Ps. lxx. was the original, and that it is here imitated and attached as a prayer to a Psalm of thanksgiving.... There are rather in Ps. lxx. many signs of its being a fragment. This portion of Ps. xl. moreover might very easily and properly, owing to its character, have been separated for the special use of the congregation....[12]

Thus we think it almost certain that Psalm 40 in its entirety is the original and that the lament was subsequently isolated and given an independent form in Psalm 70. Perowne[13] adds three additional reasons for maintaining the unity of this psalm. (1) The two parts are found together in all manuscripts and ancient versions. (2) It is easier to explain the textual variations in Psalm 70 on the supposition that it was detached from Psalm 40 than on the reverse hypothesis. (3) There is a play in the second half of Psalm 40 on the words appearing in the first half (e.g., "be pleased" [v. 13] with "thy pleasure," omitted in Psalm 70 [v. 8]; "let them be struck" [v. 15] is weakened in Psalm 70:3 to "let them return"). Most significant of all, however, is the fact that "vs. 12 is not a natural ending to the Psalm, and [it] seems to require a prayer to follow it."[14] So we conclude that there are sufficient reasons for maintaining the unity and the originality of this psalm.

9. See Mitchell Dahood, *The Psalms: Introduction, Translation, and Notes*, 3 vols., The Anchor Bible (Garden City: Doubleday, 1966) 1:245; and Thomas Kelly Cheyne, *The Christian Use of the Psalms* (London: Isbister, 1899), p. 125. I owe this last reference to Terry Armstrong.

10. Artur Weiser, *The Psalms: A Commentary*, The Old Testament Library, trans. Herbert Hartwell (Philadelphia: Westminster, n.d.), p. 334.

11. Mowinckel, 2:74.

12. Carl Bernhard Moll, *The Psalms*, Lange's Commentary (New York: Scribner, Armstrong & Co., 1872), pp. 270–71.

13. J. J. Stewart Perowne, *The Book of Psalms*, 2 vols., reprint of 4th ed. (Grand Rapids: Zondervan, 1966), 1:332.

14. Driver, p. 355.

No one can say for sure what the circumstances were when David composed this psalm. Some have suggested that it was written at the time of his flight from his son Absalom. Nevertheless, as is the case with so many psalms, the contents of the psalm are so clear that "if we did know [the historical background], we should hardly understand the Psalm better."[15]

The psalmist began Psalm 40 by describing a past[16] danger[17] he had experienced and God's rescuing him after he had patiently waited on the Lord (v. 1 [Heb., v. 2]). So grave had been the situation that he was like a person sinking into a miry pit. But he had been rescued and placed on a solid rock (v. 2 [Heb., v. 3]). This evidence of God's grace elicited from the psalmist a "new song"[18] of gratitude and praise for the encouragement of all who trust in the Lord (v. 3 [Heb., v. 4]). Such a people the psalmist pronounced happy (v. 4 [Heb., v. 5]). This forms the transition to his mention of the incalculable multiplicity of the Lord's miraculous works and his incomparable plans for the believing community (v. 5 [Heb., v. 6]).

What adequate response can the psalmist then make for such unbounded goodness from God? Surely, God can best be thanked, not by external ritual offerings (v. 6 [Heb., v. 7]), but instead by voluntary obedience to do that will of God, which is written in the roll of the book. This the psalmist will do; he is ready and delighted to do what is written for him (vv. 7–8 [Heb., vv. 8–9]). Thus, he openly proclaimed God's goodness toward him in the great congregation (vv. 9–10).

But then the psalmist prayed for the continuance of this divine protection (v. 11 [Heb., v. 12]). Additional causes of danger had arisen, some as a result of his own transgressions (v. 12 [Heb., v. 13]). Therefore, he prayed that God would once again hasten to his aid (v. 13

15. Driver, p. 348. Franz Delitzsch, *Commentary on the Epistle to the Hebrews*, vol. 2, reprint (Minneapolis: Klock & Klock, 1978), p. 150, places Psalm 40 in the time of Saul's persecution of David. This appears to be too early.
16. Driver, p. 355, has a fine note: "Vv. 2–3 cannot synchronize with V. 12: if the unity of the Psalm is to be preserved, v. 2f. must describe the danger from which the Psalmist was delivered in the past, and v. 12 the fresh troubles which have fallen upon him since. Observe how a single word in P.B.V., A.V., R.V. obscures this. 'Hath put' in v. 3 suggests what has just occurred, and so is in contradiction with v. 12: we require aorists throughout vv. 1–3: what is described in these verses is then thrown entirely into the past: v. 12 describes what is happening in the present; and the two parts of the Psalm become perfectly consistent."
17. The danger could have been a sickness, persecution, exile, bodily harm, or a threatened political revolution.
18. On the theology of a "new song," see Psalms 33:3; 96:1; 98:1; 144:9; 149:1; and Isaiah 42:10.

[Heb., v. 14]) and put his foes to shame (v. 14 [Heb., v. 15]) for all of the scorn they had heaped on him (v. 15 [Heb., v. 16]). Consequently, all who love the Lord are to rejoice and praise Him (v. 16 [Heb., v. 17]) even though at the time the psalmist was poor and needy; yet he believed and prayed that God's assistance would come very shortly (v. 17 [Heb., v. 18]).

INTERPRETATION OF PSALM 40:6-8 [HEB., VV. 7-9]

Very few commentators on this psalm have addressed its main point and purpose as well as C. von Orelli. His key assertion is worth repeating here:

> ['Then I said, "Behold, I come ..."' etc.] applies to the writer's resolve to place himself, his own person, completely at God's disposal. As the servant, when his lord calls him, says *hinnēni* (1 Sam. iii.4), so here the delivered saint: 'Lo, I am come to do what Thou wishest.' How he knows the Lord's wish the further sentence tells: 'In the book-roll it is written concerning me; there it is prescribed to me what I have to do' (2 Kings xxii.13). For the rest, this sentence gives the impression that it is an eminent personage who speaks thus (which is already evident from ver. 3), nay, one of whom the book of the divine law specifically treats. It is a king, so we must conclude, one whose conduct was there specially described, not merely in 'the law of the king' (Deut. xvii.14ff.), but in all that is said in the Torah respecting government and judgment Ps li 17 would naturally suggest David himself, where the latter has spoken in similar terms of the value of sacrifice, in exact correspondence with the great principle ... [of] 1 Sam. xv.22f....[19]

But such a view, no matter how accurate, raises a most important and preliminary question: what are the principles for interpreting messianic psalms?

PRINCIPLES FOR INTERPRETING MESSIANIC PSALMS

In 1852, John Brown[20] set forth two principles for the correct interpretation of messianic passages in the Psalms. His first principle was "that passages in the Psalms, which in the NT are expressly represented as predictions of the Messiah, are to be considered as having been originally intended to be so, and are to be interpreted accordingly."[21] In his development of this principle, he expanded it to

19. C. von Orelli, *The O.T. Prophecy of the Consummation of God's Kingdom Traced in Its Historical Development* (Edinburgh: T. & T. Clark, 1889), p. 178.
20. John Brown, *The Sufferings and Glories of the Messiah*, reprint (Byron Center, Mich.: Sovereign Grace, 1970), pp. 26-30.
21. Ibid., p. 26.

also include what he could have called another principle: "If the *speaker* in a psalm, or if the *subject* of a psalm, is obviously the same from the beginning to the end, and if a portion of such a psalm is, in the New Testament expressly referred to the Messiah, the whole is to be considered as applicable to him."[22]

Brown's second principle is "that when, in the Psalms we meet with descriptions of a perfection of character and conduct—a depth and complication of suffering—a suddenness and completeness of deliverance—a height of dignity, and an extent of dominion, to which we can find no adequate correspondence in David, or in any of the great and good men commemorated in the Jewish history,—we are warranted to hold that they refer to the Messiah."[23]

Helpful as these interpretive principles may be for a Christian audience living in the post-OT era, they are not satisfying as precise *exegetical* principles, that is, those principles which are *drawn from the Old Testament text itself.* Instead, to be very precise, Brown's first principle smacks of eisegesis in that it lays over the text a meaning subsequently derived from a later text; thus, technically it can be faulted.[24] It certainly runs into trouble when it is expanded so as to embrace the entire psalm—witness verse 12 of Psalm 40. An interpreter must resort to enormous hermeneutical gymnastics to avoid saying that Messiah confesses his own iniquities in verse 12. Furthermore, the second principle is too ambiguous to be of any real help. Must every sudden deliverance of any type be interpreted to be a deliverance of Messiah? No, Brown should have stated it differently.

W. M. MacKay[25] initially gains a much better perspective by asking whether the psalms rank as historical or prophetical writings; that is, to appropriate the question of the Ethiopian eunuch in Acts 8, "Of whom does the psalmist speak, of himself, or some other man?" MacKay decides that the psalmist speaks of someone other than himself, since approximately one hundred psalms employ the first person singular, which should not be arbitrarily assigned to two or more different persons in different parts of the same discourse. Moreover, the Holy Spirit has already applied several of these first

---

22. Ibid., p. 27. Italics mine.
23. Ibid., p. 27.
24. See our recent discussions on the proper and improper use of "The Analogy of Faith," especially as an *exegetical* tool in W. C. Kaiser, Jr., "The Single Intent of Scripture," *Evangelical Roots*, ed. Kenneth Kantzer (Nashville: Nelson, 1978), pp. 139–40; idem, "Meanings from God's Message: Matters for Interpretation," *Christianity Today* 22 (5 October 1979):30–33.
25. W. M. MacKay, "Messiah in the Psalms," *Evangelical Quarterly* 11(1939):153–64.

person singular references to Christ in the NT;[26] therefore, the speaker may be presumed to be the same in all of these psalms. MacKay also lays down as a rule that whenever "a passage in a psalm is not completely true regarding David, then it does not apply to David."[27]

But both these interpreters miss exactly what Willis J. Beecher pointed out: "Most of [the psalmist's predictions] should not be regarded as disconnected predictions, but as shoots from a common stem—the common stem being the body of connected messianic promise-history."[28] Beecher went on in the same place to acknowledge that many of these psalms have a "certain quality of universalness" that can be understood as "direct forecasts of a coming personal Messiah." Thus the original setting of the psalm occasionally could be left out of the account without seriously jeopardizing the basic meaning. Yet, he correctly argued that a more satisfactory and consistent meaning could be obtained if it were linked with the designated men and accumulating doctrine of promise. The psalmists, like the prophets, usually employed promise phraseology that had already accompanied the original statement of the promise in the preceeding eras. Thus, they frequently used amplification of existing promises as the basis for disclosing additional revelation (e.g., Ps. 89 expands on 2 Sam. 7).

In some of these psalms, however, there is something new. It is the idea that some suffering may not only be for the benefit of others; some calamities that the current representative of the coming man of promise or that the whole nation as the people of promise suffer are connected with their mission as the channel of blessing for all the nations of the earth. Prominent among such psalms are Psalm 22 and the psalm under investigation here, Psalm 40.

What then are the internal clues in Psalm 40 that indicate that the psalmist as the vehicle of revelation is aware that what he now says and does relates more to his office and function as the current

26. MacKay, pp. 160–61, goes on to find "seven unchallengeable references covering ten psalms which Christ takes authoritatively to Himself," viz., Psalm 41 (= John 13:18); Psalm 82 (= John 10:35); Psalm 118:22 (= Matt. 21:42; Acts 4:11; Eph. 2:20); Psalm 118:26 (= Matt. 21:9); Psalm 31:5 (= Luke 23:46) (a Psalm that is parallel to passages in Psalm 18, 25, 69, and 102); and Psalm 2 (= Rev. 2:26; 12:5; 19:15; Acts 4:25, 13:33; Heb. 1:5; 5:5). J. Barton Payne, *Encyclopedia of Biblical Prophecy* (New York: Harper & Row, 1973), pp. 258–60 finds "13 definitely Messianic psalms": Psalms 8:3–8; 72:6–17; 89:3–4, 26, 28–29, 34–37; 109:6–19; 132:12*b*; 45:6–7; 102:25–27; 110:1–7; 2:1–12; 16:10; 22:1–31; 40:6–8; and 69:25. He has grouped them according to third person, second person, or first person pronoun usage respectively.
27. MacKay, p. 162.
28. Willis J. Beecher, *The Prophets and the Promise*, reprint (Grand Rapids: Baker, 1963), p. 244.

representative in a long series of fulfillments of that coming man of promise? There are seven words[29] in Psalm 40 located strategically both before and after verses 6–8 so as to tie these key words into the context. But more than that, they also signal David's awareness that the present inspired words elicited by a past deliverance are of more than personal or passing interest.

In verse 5 [Heb., v. 6], David praised God not only for his numerous wonderful miraculous deeds, but more important for our purposes here, for "your plans" (*maḥsh*ᵉ*bōtèka*) towards him and all Israel (*ēlênû*, "to us"). It is interesting that Psalm 33:10–11, which likewise called for a "new song" (Psalm 33:3—40:3 [Heb., v. 4]), had highlighted the eternal plan of God[30] for all peoples and times against the backdrop of the frustrated plans of the nations. This word is also used later of the divine plan for specific nations in Jeremiah 29:11 and 51:29 and is expanded by other synonyms elsewhere. It must be concluded that when David praised God for "his plans" towards *all Israel*, especially when only he, David, had been rescued, he was deliberately showing his cognizance of his own place in that promise-plan.

Such an understanding is strengthened by his employment of six more words in verses 9–11 [Heb., vv. 10–12]. The words of verses 6–8 David proclaimed more accurately, "heralded as good news" (*biśśartî*, v. 10) in the great congregation. This term is the exact equivalent of the NT *kerussō* and *euangelizō*, to herald the good news of the gospel. David's good news was basically about God's maintenance of His covenant promises in His acts of deliverance (*ṣidqātkā*, v. 11), His reliability ('*ĕmûnātkā*, v. 11), His work of delivering the nation (*t*ᵉ*shûʿātkā*, v. 11), and most impressive of all God's lovingkindness or grace and love as evidenced by His covenant (*ḥasd*ᵉ*kā*, and '*ămitt*ᵉ*kā*, v. 12). This final combination of "grace and truth" was a strong reminder of the very character of God as first announced in His "name" (Ex. 34:6) when He forgave Israel for the golden calf fiasco. These were catchwords that signaled that more was underfoot in this public praise than a testimony to God for a rather private and personal escape. Instead it had communal, indeed, worldwide implications; it was another link in God's promise-plan.

If we have heard David properly, as he and the Spirit of God indeed intended to be understood, then we are now ready to tackle verses 6–8, which had brought such an "evangelical" delight to David as he announced them "in the great congregation."[31]

---

29. As pointed out by my student Wayne Werner.
30. See Walter C. Kaiser, Jr., *Toward an Old Testament Theology* (Grand Rapids: Zondervan, 1978), pp. 29–32, for further discussion on a single cosmopolitan plan of God.
31. Also in Psalms 22:25; 35:18.

SACRIFICE AND OBEDIENCE

First Samuel 15:22 is the first passage that had formally set forth the principle that sacrifices in and of themselves were worthless unless they were offered out of a heart right with God. Yet, this truth was already implicit in the contrast between Cain's and Abel's sacrifices in Genesis 4. Moreover, the same requirement was explicitly laid down in Leviticus 16:29, 31; that is, that each Israelite who expected to be forgiven of "all" his sins had to truly repent, "afflict [his] soul." Only then could one of the most persistent phrases in the Levitical sacrificial instructions be pronounced over such individuals: "And he shall be forgiven" (Lev. 1:4; 4:20, 26, 31, 35; 5:10, 16; 16:20-22).[32]

Thus, the psalmist was not rejecting sacrifices as such any more than were the prophets who followed him (Isa. 1:11-18; 66:3; Jer. 7:21-23; Hos. 6:6; Amos 5:21; Mic. 6:6-8). These same sentiments appear elsewhere in the Psalms (50:8, 14; 51:16 [Heb., v. 18]; 69:30-31 [Heb., vv. 31-32]) and Proverbs (15:8; 21:3) not to mention Exodus 15:26; Deuteronomy 10:12, 20; and 1 Samuel 15:22. Sabourin labels the form of the psalmist's statement "dialectical negation,"[33] that is, the ceremonial practice is held in tension until the ethical and spiritual preparation for the performance of that practice is met. The effect is to speak in a proverbial form: "I do not desire this so much as I desire that," or "without this there is no that." It is the language of priorities. What is the use of having this (sacrifices) without that (a prior heart of obedience)?[34]

Neither does there appear that any special emphasis is placed on the four words for sacrifice. It may be indeed, as many commentators suggest, that the offerings are named in respect to: (1) their material, zebah, animal offering, and minhah, cereal offering including perhaps mesek, wine, and (2) their purpose, 'ōlâ, to obtain the divine favor, and hattā't, to turn away the divine wrath.[35]

32. The old, but false, definitions for "witting" and "unwitting" sins must now be reexamined, for "all" sins were pardonable, except high rebellion or blasphemy against God and His Word (Num. 15:27-36). See W. C. Kaiser, Toward an Old Testament Theology, pp. 117-19.

33. Leopold Sabourin, The Psalms: Their Origin and Meaning, 2 vols. (New York: Society of St. Paul, 1969), 2:48.

34. Terry Armstrong found an older commentator, Benjamin Weiss, New Translation, Exposition and Chronological Arrangement of the Book of Psalms (Edinburgh: Oliphant, 1858), p. 429, who tried to solve this tension by contrasting hāpas with rāṣôn. But the exercise is both unnecessary and unconvincing—as if one word meant God's chief desire and the other just His wish apart from ranking it primary or secondary. Furthermore, the other parallel word used here is shā'al, "to require."

35. So Moll, p. 272; A. F. Kirkpatrick, The Book of Psalms (Cambridge: U. Press, 1906), p. 210.

Between these two pairs of sacrificial terms in parallel stichs is the middle clause: "ears you have dug for me." Initially, this unique biblical phrase suggests the well-known custom of boring a slave's right ear to denote the slave's voluntary dedication of himself in perpetual service to his master (Ex. 21:6 and Deut. 15:17). But this otherwise suggestive explanation has two serious drawbacks: (1) the technical word for bore is not *kārâ*, "to dig," but *rāṣaʿ*, "to bore" (Ex. 21:6), and (2) only one ear was bored, not both[36] "ears" (*ʾoznayim*), as in this verse.[37]

In addition to Psalm 40:6, *kārâ* is used fourteen times in the OT. These may be tabulated as follows:

"to dig" a pit (eight usages)—Exodus 21:33; Psalms 7:16; 57:7; 94:13; 119:85; Proverbs 26:27; Jeremiah 18:20; 18:22

"to dig" a well (two usages)—Genesis 26:25; Numbers 21:18

"to dig" a grave or tomb (two usages)—Genesis 50:5; 2 Chronicles 16:14

"to dig up" evil (one usage)—Proverbs 16:27

"to prepare" a feast (one usage)—2 Kings 6:23

Thus, the meaning "to dig" is well established, even though the LXX *katērtizō* "to prepare," may be explained by the 2 Kings 6:23 usage. The phrase then refers to the fact that the instruments for obedience, the ears, were made by God (cf. Psalm 94:9: "He who planted the ear . . ."). Thus the ability to obey has been given by God. Perhaps the phrase may be compared with a later development of a similar concept in the prophets, "to *open* the ear" (Isa. 48:8; 50:4–5) or the earlier form "to *uncover* the ear" (1 Sam. 9:15; 20:2, 12, 13; 22:8, 17; Job 33:16; 36:10, 15). Thus, in effect, one part of the body (the one that receives the command and word of God) is put for the whole body in a *pars pro toto* [part for the whole][38] argument. Significantly, the prophet Jeremiah complains, "Lo, [Israel's] ears are closed (*ʿărēlâ*) so they cannot hear, the word of the Lord is offensive to them; they find no pleasure (*ḥāpēṣ*) in it" (Jer. 6:10). But David in Psalm 40 instead "delights" to do God's will (v. 8 [Heb., v. 9]).

36. Ancient interpreters are most arbitrary when they apply the plural of ears to the *active* and *passive* obedience of Christ or that Christ offered himself for a congregation composed of two parts: Jews and Gentiles. So reports Moll, p. 272.
37. Note the NIV has opted for this translation: "my ears you have pierced."
38. The writer to the Hebrews following the LXX will just reverse this same process and express it by a *totum pro parte* argument by using "body" instead of ears.

THE PRESCRIPTIONS OF THE BOOK AND THE WORK OF THE MAN OF PROMISE

Instead of connecting verse 7 [Heb., v. 8] in a temporal sequence, the psalmist emphasized the internal connection between the declaration of the preceeding verse and this one. "Then," verse 7, marks the consequence of the announced obedience which he had contrasted with mere ritualistic offering of sacrifices.

But what form was that expression of obedience to take? David now placed himself at God's service: "Behold, I come [or] have come." His very first words were those of a servant who presented himself at the beck and call of his master (cf. Num. 22:38; 2 Sam. 19:21; or Isa. 6:9).

What he came to do, however, is that which was written of (or concerning, for, about) him in the roll of the book (v. 7 [Heb., v. 8]). Certainly, this clause is not to be regarded as a parenthetical remark, since the infinitive "to do your will" in verse 8 [Heb., v. 9] cannot serve as the object of "I come" because it has its own verb. Accordingly, the function of the *bet*, ("in, with," etc.) before *megillat sēper*, "roll of the book," becomes as crucial for exegesis as the *ʿālāy* "of, concerning, about, or for me"—all in verse 7 [Heb., v. 8].

The phrase *ʿālāy* "for, upon, concerning, about me" is not to be taken as meaning "*upon* me" as if it were parallel to the clause in verse 8 [Heb., v. 9], "and your law is my (inmost) heart," for the heart hardly has "a roll of the book" written on it. Therefore, the preposition points to the one respecting whom the Word of God was written. It was a word written for David. The combination of this verb and preposition (*kātûb*) occurs also in 2 Kings 22:13, except that there the words of the book prescribed Israel's duty: "because our fathers did not listen to the words of this book to do according to all which is written for [or concerning] us" (*kekol-hakkātûb ʿālênû*). The preposition, *ʿal* in Psalm 40:8 [Heb., v. 9] denotes the object of the contents: David. Similarly *ʿal* functions as the object of prophecy in 1 Kings 22:8 *yitnabbēʾ ʿālay* and Isaiah 1:1, *ḥāzâ ʿal*.[39]

Where then did David find a word *concerning* himself? "In a roll of a book." The absence of the Hebrew article appears to emphasize the

---

39. E. W. Hengstenberg, *Commentary on the Psalms*, trans. P. Fairbairn and J. Thomson, 3 vols. (Edinburgh: T. & T. Clark, 1846), 2:72 decides against the messianic view of this passage (which he had held to earlier, see E. W. Hengstenberg, *Christology of the Old Testament*, abridged by T. K. Arnold, reprint (Grand Rapids: Kregel, 1970), pp. 90–93, because of this expression which he translated "to write *over* me" in the sense of prescribing. He pointed to Joshua 1:7 and 1 Kings 2:3 as convincing reasons. But this is strange, because the terminology used there is nothing like that used in Psalm 40. He should have retained his earlier view and substantiated it with better exegesis than appears in his earlier *Christology*.

fact that it was written.[40] The preposition *Bet* with verbs of motion like "come" usually carry the sense of accompaniment, "with";[41] yet the usage here appears to be more elliptical[42] in that the verb of motion is less intimately tied to this clause than is usually the case. Therefore, we believe it is the preposition of location, "in."

What book then was this? The exact phrase "roll of a book" appears in Jeremiah 36:2, 4 and Ezekiel 2:9, whereas "roll" alone appears in Jeremiah 36:6; Ezekiel 3:1–3; Zechariah 5:1–2; Ezra 6:2 (Aramaic). Some would wish to restrict David's reference to the *lex regia*, the law of the king found in Deuteronomy 17:14–20. But it is better to understand the reference to be all of the written will of God to the extent that it was available to David in his day: the Torah (*i.e.*, the five books of Moses) and perhaps part of Samuel's composition or some of the earlier prophets such as Joshua, Judges, Ruth (just then released?) and parts of 1 Samuel.[43]

It would be extremely helpful to be able to decide if this psalm were written before or after Nathan's disclosure that Yahweh would make David's line the continuation of the patriarchal promise (2 Sam. 7). Unfortunately, we know of no way to determine this. But we can show that David in Psalm 40 shows awareness that he was a man about whom the Scriptures were written (v. 7) and that he employed catch phrases that were becoming household terms for the promise. Individually the arguments are not terribly moving, but collectively they force us to conclude that the obedience mentioned by David has to do with a new office and function he had as the current installment in God's coming man of promise.

Verse 8 [Heb., v. 9] completes the psalmist's statement. He delights (*ḥāpēṣ*, see v. 6 [Heb., v. 7]) to do God's "will," in this passage (*rāṣôn*), similar to the word for God's "plan," although it stresses the aspect of pleasure and favor connected with that plan. In fact, the law of God is in the "innermost parts" of his being (*bᵉtôk mēʿāy*), (cf. Isa. 16:11; Jer. 31:20). That God's Torah should be written on the heart was already indicated in Deuteronomy 6:6; Psalm 37:31, and later on in Proverbs 3:3; 7:3. According to Jeremiah 31:33, the law of God would

40. Kirkpatrick, p. 211. He compares Hosea 8:12.
41. E. Kautzsch, *Gesenius' Hebrew Grammar*, ed., A. E. Cowley, 2d ed. (Oxford: Clarendon, 1910), p. 380.
42. Note the NIV rendering: "Here I am, I have come—it is written about me in the scroll."
43. David L. Cooper, *Messiah: His First Coming Scheduled* (Los Angeles, Biblical Research Society, 1939), p. 187, felt David quoted from the "Roll of the Book." Thus Cooper concluded, "Evidently there was a primitive revelation given originally by the Lord for a definite and specific purpose.... When it had served its purpose, the Lord caused it to pass out of circulation." There is no need to create an Old Testament "Q source," however, for the reference is not a citation that is no longer in existence.

be implanted in the heart of all God's people as a characteristic of the era of the new covenant; however, already in the OT era this was true at least to some degree: "A people in whose heart is my law" (*'am tôrātî be libbām*, Isa. 51:7).

We conclude that in Psalm 40 the psalmist presents to God an obedient spirit, willing to go and do all that is written about himself. He carries in his person and in each favored descendant all that God is going to do for all the nations of the earth. What had been written thus far in Scripture about the coming Messiah and His work was written, in effect, about David, so far as he and his generation were concerned. He, David, delighted to do every bit of what he found written therein, for God had also dug out his ears, as it were, and had given him a willing heart and mind. Such a spirit was more to be desired than all the false religiosity of compounded ritual upon ritual. Such also, especially in light of David's most recent deliverance from danger and in light of all of God's past acts and His all-encompassing plan with so many aspects of His thought, was the substance of the good news that he would herald forth in the midst of God's gathered congregation.

HEBREWS 10:5-10 AND CONCLUSION

THE GREEK TEXT

The variants from the Hebrew Masoretic text in the Greek LXX (= Psalm 39:7–9*a*) are: (1) the appearance of *sōma*, "body," instead of the expected *ōtia*, "ears," for Hebrew *'oznayim;* (2) the Hebrew, Vaticanus, and Sinaiticus LXX have singular "burnt offering," Alexandrinus LXX and Hebrews 10:6 uses the plural "burnt offerings"; (3) the Hebrew *shā'al* "to require" is accurately rendered by Vaticanus *ēitē-sas*, and nearly so in a variant *ezētēsas* in Sinaiticus and Alexandrinus, but Hebrews 10:6 has *eudokēsas*, "take pleasure in";[44] (4) by omitting *eboulēthēn*, the writer to the Hebrews is able to connect "I come" directly to the phrase "to do your will" (a fact further emphasized by placing "your will" at the end of the quotation).[45]

None of these variants is harmful to the truth-intention of the psalmist. The use of "body" for "ear" is, as we have already argued, a case of the whole being used for the part.[46] In this case the translator

44. A word paralleled in Psalm 50:18 and found in LXX[2013] Bohairic Sahidic. See Kenneth J. Thomas, "The Old Testament Citations in Hebrews," *New Testament Studies* 11(1964–65):314.
45. So Thomas, p. 314.
46. This common figure of speech is known as synecdoche. According to T. Armstrong, John DeWitt (*The Psalms: A New Translation with Introductory Essay and Notes* [New York: A. D. F. Randolph, 1891], p. 108) was the first to make this suggestion in recent times. Many have followed him since then.

opted for the culturally meaningful dynamic equivalent. The use of the plural "burnt offerings" is hardly worth noticing except as it sheds light on the lines of textual dependence. Again, in the third variant, the writer might have been pressed into using a different verb than "require" since he had just argued in Hebrews 9:12–19 that God had commanded the sacrifices of goats and bulls. The final variant developed when the writer to the Hebrews stopped short of *eboulēthen* (LXX, Ps. 39:9) and thus the infinitive became the object of "Behold, I come." Since this textual change did not affect the overall meaning of the psalmist, the writer to the Hebrews adopted this shorter quotation, even though from twentieth-century rules on style and procedures for citing quotes it could be faulted.

THE ARGUMENT OF THE WRITER TO THE HEBREWS

Because Psalm 40 is quoted only once in the NT, it certainly does not lend credence to Rendel Harris's hypothesis[47] that the NT writers tended to draw from a list of proof texts known as *testimonia* rather than drawing directly from the OT and its context. More important than that discussion is the one concerning the exegetical practices of the writer to the Hebrews.

Was this writer guilty of using homiletical midrash[48] in Psalm 40 where the original setting was either forgotten or considered irrelevant and thus was blithely applied to Jesus? Or, as Kistemaker suggested, did he use a *pesher* type of exegesis,[49] according to which the psalmist delivered a mystery (a *raz*) for which he had no explanation, but which only a much later *pesher* could unlock?

Frankly, neither suggestion offers any satisfaction or textual demonstration. Instead of finding that the scriptural exegesis of Hebrews was fantastic, Alexandrian, or even Philonic, G. B. Caird opined that it was "one of the earliest and most successful attempts to define the relation between the Old and New Testaments, and that a large part of the value of the book is to be found in the method of exegesis which was formerly dismissed with contempt."[50] This, we believe, is closer to the real facts as we have seen them in these two passages.

47. For a criticism of Harris's view, see C. H. Dodd, *According to the Scriptures* (London: Nisbet, 1952), p. 26, and Simon Kistemaker, *The Psalm Citations in the Epistle to the Hebrews* (Amsterdam: Wed. G. Van Soest N.V., 1961), p. 9.
48. The idea belongs to George Wesley Buchanan, *To the Hebrews*, Anchor Bible (Garden City: Doubleday, 1972), p. xxi.
49. Kistemaker, *Psalm Citations*, 88. Cf. Richard N. Longenecker, *Biblical Exegesis in the Apostolic Period* (Grand Rapids: Eerdmans, 1975), pp. 70–75.
50. G. B. Caird, "The Exegetical Method of the Epistle to the Hebrews," *Canadian Journal of Theology* 5(1959):45, as cited by Longenecker, p. 172.

If our understanding of the psalmist's words is even close to what he had intended to say under the inspiration of the Holy Spirit, then it will come as very little surprise to read the argument of Hebrews 10:5-10. What had been a shadow and a type under David became a complete reality finally in Christ's incarnation and substitutionary atonement. David was a true model of the final reality because of the gracious calling and appointment of God. History could reflect this kind of scheme (shadow and reality) solely because of the all-embracing divine plan and divine designation to the office and function of promise, and not because of a Platonic (?) tradition that tended to bifurcate reality into earthly and heavenly divisions.

When we turn to the question of sacrifices, it must be noticed immediately that nowhere in the OT was it ever claimed that the blood of bulls and goats could or ever did take away anyone's sin. What part, then, did those sacrifices play? Did they have any kind of efficacy?

The answer is that if sacrifices were offered out of a heart of contrition and obedience to God, then on the basis of the word of a faithful God these sacrifices were *subjectively* efficacious. Invariably, the word pronounced with such an offering was "And he shall be forgiven." Thus, the offerer did receive relief from the penalty and memory of his sins.

Nevertheless, this sin had not yet been cared for *objectively*.[51] Certainly the principle of substitution was clear by now, but these sacrificial victims were animals, not people. Moreover, the matter was never settled, for sacrifice followed upon sacrifice. Something was missing. Therefore, there was a "passing over" (*paresis*, Rom. 3:25) the sins of the OT on the basis of God's declared word until He himself could provide His own final substitute as a true, but sinless, man.

How then does the writer to the Hebrews employ Psalm 40 in Hebrews 10:8-10? His argument falls into two parts: (1) verse 8, the "above" *anōteron* with the quote from Psalm 40:6 [Heb., v. 7] being repeated; and (2) verse 9 "then he said" with the quote of Psalm 40:7 [Heb., v. 8], deleting, however, the clause "in the volume of the book it is written concerning me." Simply put, he sees in the first quotation the abolishment of the old order and in the second the establishment of the new.

Has he played fair with the text of Psalms? We believe he has. The permanency of obedience of the man (whether it begins with his hearing [ears] or results in the use of his whole body) is correctly set

51. This distinction between subjective and objective efficacy I owe to Hobart Freeman, "The Problem of Efficacy of Old Testament Sacrifices," *Bulletin of the Evangelical Theological Society* 5(1962):73-79, 90.

off against sacrifices that at best could only mirror or symbolize that prerequisite obedience. Thus, the one act (that is, obedience) had to be enduring and permanent while the other exuded forms of obsolescence and temporary usefulness. Clearly, God desired one as being more basic and foundational than the other.

The new order would focus on that man of promise who would always delight to do the will of God. Even though David's obedience and especially his office and person pointed to one who was to come, only Christ fulfilled every aspect of this future hope. Furthermore, if the writer of Hebrews was himself aware and thought his readers might also recall the whole quotation from Psalm 40 with its additional clause about the law of God being in man's innermost being, then he also thereby called for the new covenant era when God's law would be unmistakenly engraved on all His people's hearts.

What then was removed in the first order? The OT? No, it was the ceremonial law that was removed. But that same law carried a warning from the day it had been given to Israel that it was only the model, a copy (e.g., Ex. 25:9, 40; 26:30, "pattern"); the real was yet to come. Hence, no one should have been alarmed at this word of abolishment.

Most important, the writer to the Hebrews does not build his argument on the *sōma* clause of the LXX. In fact, he simply ignores it when he restates and comments on Psalm 40:6 [Heb., v. 7]. True, Hebrews 10:10 does almost incidentally introduce "the offering of the *body* of Jesus Christ once for all," but he does not refer this usage back to the psalmist. Thus, those interpreters are mistaken who make the *sōma*, "body," clause the key to the writer's use of this psalm. Those who focus on the clause about the "roll of the book" being written concerning him are also mistaken. Neither clause is used in his exposition. While the second (i.e., "roll of the book") may have been a reason that the psalmist initially went to this passage to make the connection he did, it cannot be used as a part of his main contention and argument since he made no direct use of it. Instead of the contrast[52] in Hebrews 10 between the Levitical system (10:1–4) and the free surrender of the body of Christ (10:5–10), it is a contrast between the death of an animal, which has no way of entering into the meaning of what is happening (10:1–4), and the perfect obedience of Jesus for which act He specifically came into this world (10:5–10): "I have come to do thy will."

---

52. See the very penetrating and thoughtful presentation of the views of Calvin, Barnes, Westcott, Nairne, Bruce, Montefiore, Morris, Moffatt, and V. Taylor in T. Allan Armstrong, pp. 59–67.

Psalm 40:6–8 contains fewer messianic clues and less promise phraseology than other messianic passages (e.g., Psalms 2, 22, 72, 89, or 110), but patient attendance on the text will reveal that the writer to the Hebrews was on strong exegetical grounds. Meanwhile, it is not necessary to make David's confession of his iniquities (v. 12) somehow fit the Messiah without impugning his sinlessness. But most important of all, Psalm 40 teaches us that the advent of the man of promise was deliberately designed by God to supplement, and in the case of the sacrificial order, to supersede it.

PART 4

THE THEOLOGICAL USE OF THE OLD TESTAMENT IN THE NEW

Introduction

The OT cannot be dispensed with in formulating Christian theology or doctrine. To treat the older Testament merely as a vessel that has little or no content until the interpreter imports Christian meaning from NT texts is demeaning to both the older revelation of God and to those who first heard what they thought was the abiding word of God.

In this connection, the stern words of John Bright must be underscored:

> Let it be repeated: No hermeneutic can be accounted satisfactory that does not allow the preacher to operate with any and all Old Testament texts and to bring them to word in their Christian significance, yet without in any way twisting or departing from their plain sense. A hermeneutic that silences parts of the Old Testament, or enables us to hear only the 'easy' parts, or arbitrarily imposes meaning upon the text, or uses it as the vehicle for a sermon, the content of which is really drawn from the New Testament, will not do. Equally, an uncritical procedure that betrays the preacher into imposing Old Testament institutions, directives, and attitudes directly on the Christian will not do.... We must be prepared to hear each text in its plain intention, yet in its Christian significance.[1]

1. John Bright, *The Authority of the Old Testament* (Nashville: Abingdon, 1967), pp. 209–10.

Too frequently Christians either assume that the OT text no longer has anything to say to us or they prematurely impart NT values and substitute them for OT concepts and words in an attempt to achieve an instant theology with practical relevance.

But all of this only introduces the most fundamental question that has faced theology and the church in every age and which still demands an answer today: Is the OT an essential part of the Christian Bible? Does it contain a valid and authoritative theology for the church? Or, is the OT obsolete? A classic treasured only by scholars and used by Christians only as a supplement to the main message of the NT.

The significance and importance of this key question was expressed by Bernhard W. Anderson in a 1963 introduction of a symposium on the significance of the OT for Christian faith. Anderson said:

> No problem more urgently needs to be brought to a focus than [this] one: ... the relation of the Old Testament to the New.... It is a question which confronts every Christian in the Church, whether he be a professional theologian, a pastor of a congregation, or a layman. It is no exaggeration to say that on this question hangs the meaning of the Christian faith.[2]

And at the heart of this problem is the issue of the amount of continuity and discontinuity between the OT and NT, between Israel and the church, between the Old Covenant and the New Covenant. Clearly everyone senses that there is a tension between the desire to read lines of continuities between the poles mentioned here and the need to honestly observe that there are also real discontinuities. On the one hand, there are a number of common perspectives, themes, patterns, and concerns between the two Testaments. On the other hand, there are some real differences, economies, institutions, and practices between them. Which of those two perspectives should triumph in our attempt to relate these two portions of Scripture?

It would be best, then, to try to describe the areas in which continuities reign and those in which discontinuities take the lead. To take the latter first, all will agree that those institutions representing the theocracy of Israel and the civil and ceremonial legislation of the Mosaic eras are definitely time-bound. In fact, when each was originally given in the OT, a built-in obsolescence was noted. Instead of laying down perpetual statutes or principles, many of the laws such as the ceremonial legislation stretching from Exodus 25 through Leviticus 17 were given expiration notices from the beginning. For

---

2. Bernhard W. Anderson, ed., *The Old Testament and Christian Faith: A Theological Discussion* (New York: Harper & Row, 1963), p. 1.

was not Moses warned that he was not given the real, but only a "pattern" (Ex. 25:40) or a model and shadow of the real?—presumably until the time that the authentic had come! This will account for much, if not all, of the discontinuity between the two Testaments.

There is, however, a plan of God that runs like a thread through history. The best place to anchor this teaching is in the grand passage of Jeremiah 31:31–34: the new covenant.³ In fact, this *locus classicus* was the passage that originally stimulated Origen to be the first to name the last twenty-seven books of the Bible the "New Testament."⁴

This text from Jeremiah 31:31–34 also happens to be the largest piece of text quoted *in extenso* in the NT. It appears complete in Hebrews 8:8–12 and in part in Hebrews 10:16–17. But it also is the subject of nine other NT texts: from dealing with the Last Supper (Luke 22:20; 1 Cor. 11:25; Matt. 26:28; Mark 14:24), three additional references in Hebrews (Heb. 9:15; 10:13; 12:24) and two more in Paul's writings dealing with "ministers of the new covenant (2 Cor. 3:6) and the future forgiveness of national Israel's sins" (Rom. 11:27). Certainly this is an integrating theme between the Testaments if there ever was one!

However, does not the very name of this covenant make the point that there is a deep cleavage between what used to be and the *newness* of the present covenant? But to complicate matters more, the persons addressed in the new covenant were not the Gentiles or the church, but the "house of Israel and the house of Judah."

Here then is a new footing for an old stalemate between those who tended to stress more discontinuity than continuity (dispensationalists) and those who tended to stress more continuity than discontinuity (covenantal theologians). The basis for this new footing is twofold: (1) the word "new" actually is better translated the "renewed covenant"; and (2) the addressees of this new covenant are indeed national Israel; but that did not limit its inclusion of the believing Gentiles and the church any more than did the fact that the Abrahamic and Davidic covenants were also directed to the Jewish nation.

Both Hebrew *ḥādāš* and Greek *kainos* frequently were translated to mean "renew" or "restore" as in the "new" moon (obviously the same old moon renewed), the "new commandment" (which actually was the old one to love one another—renewed, John 13:34; 1 John 2:7; 2 John 5); the "new" heart, the "new" creature in Christ, or the "new" heavens and earth (but the same earth and heaven that would remain,

3. See Walter C. Kaiser, Jr. "The Promise and the New Covenant: Jeremiah 31:31–34," in *The Bible in Its Literary Milieu: Contemporary Essays*, ed. Vincent L. Tollers and John R. Maier (Grand Rapids: Eerdmans, 1979), pp. 106–20.
4. So stated Geerhardus Vos, *Biblical Theology* (Grand Rapids: Eerdmans, 1954), p. 321.

Pss. 104:5; 148:3–6; 89:34–36; Jer. 31:35–36).[5] Whereas Greek, English, and most Indo-European languages have two separate words for "new" and "renew," Hebrew has only one and thus the same word *ḥādāš* must serve both ideas: new in time and renewed in nature. From the context and content of the covenant defined in Jeremiah 31:31–34 and the NT vocabulary distinction (*kainos*, not *neos*), we conclude that this was a "Renewed Covenant."

It is true, of course, that Jeremiah 31:32 explicitly contrasts this renewed covenant with the old covenant made at the Exodus from Egypt. Nevertheless, both Jeremiah and the writer of Hebrews are most insistent that the problem with the old covenant did not lie with the covenant maker (God) or with the covenant itself: it was with the people that God found fault. Jeremiah 31:32 specifically says: "which covenant of mine *they* broke." That is where Hebrews 8:8–9 places the blame as well: " . . . finding fault with *them*" (italics added).

Almost all of the items mentioned in the renewed covenant are but a repetition of some aspect of the promise doctrine already known in the covenants with Abraham, Moses, or David. The items of continuity were: (1) the same covenant-making God; (2) the same law; (3) the same divine fellowship; (4) the same people of God; and (5) the same divine forgiveness. But when the seventeen other passages are included, which used alternate names for this same renewed covenant (including "everlasting covenant", Jer. 32:40; 50:5; Ezek. 16:60; 37:26; Isa. 24:5; 55:3; 61:8; "a new heart and a new spirit," Ezek. 11:19; 18:31; 36:26; and LXX Jer. 32:39; "covenant of peace", Isa. 54:10; Ezek. 34:25; 37:26; and "my covenant," Isa. 42:6; 49:8; Hos. 2:18–20; Isa. 59:21), there are new items added to this long list of renewed features: (1) universal knowledge of God (Jer. 31:34); (2) universal peace in nature and military (Isa. 2:4; Ezek. 34:25; 37:26; Hos. 2:18); (3) a universal material prosperity (Isa. 61:8; Jer. 32:41; Ezek. 34:26–27; Hos. 2:22); (4) an age dominated by the Holy Spirit; and (5) a sanctuary standing in the midst of Israel forever (Ezek. 37:26, 28).

The "new" began with the "old" promise made to Abraham and David. Its renewal perpetuated all those promises originally made to Abraham and David and more. Our conclusion must be that

5. Johannes Beham, "Kainos," in *Theological Dictionary of the New Testament*, ed. Gerhard Kittel, trans. Geoffrey W. Bromiley (Grand Rapids: Eerdmans, 1965), 3:447 suggested that the etymology for *neos* was the Indo-European word for the adverb *nu*, "now, of the moment!" *Kainos* was probably from the root *ken*, "freshly come, or begun." Brevard S. Childs in *Myth and Reality in the Old Testament*, 2d ed. (Naperville: SCM, 1962), p. 77 observed that *ḥādāš* was cognate to semitic roots like akkadian *edēšu*, "to restore" ruined cities or altars.

it would appear that Hebrews does not warrant a radical break between the "old" and the "new".... The Old Testament saints already participate in the New Age in anticipation even though in time they still belong to the old order.... The "new" is only different from the old in the sense of completion.[6]

Accordingly, we may draw lines of continuity where the OT itself did. Thus, there is strong continuity between the Testaments amidst admitted evidence of planned discontinuity, in the people of God (which includes several aspects such as believing national Israelites and believing Gentiles in the church) and in the program of God (which is his redemptive promise-plan that eventuates in a progressive development and then a sudden in-breaking of the kingdom of God, which incorporates spiritual, ethnic, political, economic, ecological, and military aspects).

But some will still hesitate to turn to the OT as a source of theology. After all, they say, will not the Holy Spirit "teach [us] all things" (John 14:26)? Their appeal, of course, is to those three passages from our Lord's Upper Room discourse:

> He will teach you all things, and bring to your remembrance all that I have said to you when I was with you. (John 14:26, RSV)
>
> You also are witnesses, because you have been with me from the beginning [of my earthly ministry]. (John 15:27)
>
> I have yet many things to say to you, but you cannot bear them now [while I am still on earth with you men]. When the Spirit of truth comes, He will guide you into all truth. (John 16:12–13)

As any serious student of the Bible will recognize those passages were not directed to believers at large, but to those disciples who had been with Jesus during His earthly pilgrimage. The promise was for additional revelation and thus we are given some hints as to how the NT canon was shaped.

Almost every cult and aberration from the historic Christian faith has appealed at one time or another to these three texts as the grounds for adding to or bypassing the inscripturated Word of God. But all fail to meet the tests given in these texts because they never personally walked with our Lord on this earth. They never heard instruction from His lips, so how could they recall what they never once heard? Neither were they witnesses from the start of his three-year ministry. But the apostles were! Therefore, they were the ones who would record the life, words, and works of Christ in the gospels with the

---

6. Jacob Jocz, *The Covenant: A Theology of Human Destiny* (Grand Rapids: Eerdmans, 1968), p. 244.

Holy Spirit's aid of recollection (John 14:26); they were the ones who would teach doctrine ("what is mine," John 16:14, 15); and they were the ones who would predict the future (John 16:12), for they had been eyewitnesses and auditors of all that had happened to and was spoken by Christ (John 15:26, 27).

If believers complain that this principle, which restricts the "you" to the apostles appointed by Jesus, would signal the ruin of the great commission of Matthew 28:18–20, and if a similar "you" ("Go ye into all the world") were applied consistently only to the disciples, we will reject the parallelism. For this is precisely the problem William Carey faced when he launched the modern impetus for missions. Believers resisted the appeal to "go and make disciples" by arguing that the command was restricted to the disciples alone. But Carey wisely answered that the summons was issued to all believers, for that same Matthean text also said: "And lo, I am with you always, even to the end of the age." Therefore, our Lord either meant it to be a perpetual call to action or the apostles have lived extremely long lives! Such then is our solution to the use of these Johannine texts: where the extension is limited, we must observe it.

In conclusion, there is no instant "open sesame" for approaching the OT. Neither can we avoid it by relegating it to either an appendix of terms on the NT or an antique with which we can now dispense. Even those who try to stigmatize the OT by connecting it to "the letter that kills" (2 Cor. 3:6) or the "oldness of the letter" (Rom. 2:29; 7:6) have likewise set up a false dichotomy.

The Pauline word for "letter" in these verses is *gramma*, not *graphē*. What Paul was attacking is not the OT; instead he was assailing the outward, fleshly, uncommitted "letterism," that is, that perfunctory, external observance of the law that has no antecedent commitment of life by faith in the one who was to come as promised in the law and the OT. Such a ceremonialism was merely a "serving in the oldness of the letter." But the *graphē* ("the written word") was always sacred to Paul; it was the very Word of God.

Paul's complaint was not about the inadequacy of what was written or about what the words of the OT text meant grammatically and syntactically as used by the individual writers. Rather, his complaint was with those who *by means of* observing the outward "letter" (*gramma*) of the law and *by means of* (instrumental use of *dia* in Rom. 2:20) circumcision itself, were actually breaking the law, for they had not first received the circumcision of the heart *by means of* the spirit (whether in OT or NT times)! They were only letter-keepers; not observers of the Word of God.

Scripture is abused if such contrasts as "the letter kills, but the Spirit makes alive" is turned into a slogan to allow so-called Spirit-led interpreters to bypass the authorial verbal meanings in OT texts in favor of what is fancied to be some more practical, personal, relational, spiritual, or sensational meaning allegedly derived from the Holy Spirit. The OT has a valid and strong contribution to make to the ongoing theology found in the NT. Without diminishing the reality of real discontinuities known in the OT text from the beginning of their inscripturation, we can honestly point to a strong line of continuity between the Testaments in the themes, concepts, issues, and the divine program and beneficiaries of that everlasting plan.

This line of continuity has a center (German, *mitte*) that unashamedly embraces both spiritual and physical realities (e.g., the "Rest" of God, or the "Israel" of God). It also was without parochialism from the start and envisaged the inclusion of the Gentiles as participants and real beneficiaries of those same graces—even though at first they were not *totally equal* sharers in the same promises, inheritance, and people. Such coheirship and comembership waited for the Pauline revelation of the mystery wherein every remnant of dividing walls was to be destroyed (Eph. 2–3). But let us turn in the two following chapters to the passages to analyze how the NT made use of the OT and grounded its case in the original meaning of the OT texts.

8

Experiencing the Old Testament "Rest" of God

Hebrews 3:1–4

In 1933 Gerhard Von Rad aptly observed that "among the many benefits of redemption offered to man by Holy Scripture, that of 'rest' has been almost overlooked in biblical theology...."[1] Fifty years have not substantially changed that assessment of the situation. In fact, except for the brief and conflicting opinions delivered in commentaries on Hebrews 3 and 4, only a few major articles in the journals and fewer graduate theses have been devoted to the concept of "God's Rest" in the last century. Most biblical theologies of the OT and NT biblical encyclopedias, theological wordbooks, Festschriften, and systematic theologies are ominously silent on the topic. The question is, Why?

Whereas reasons may vary, the overriding cause lies in the sheer difficulty of the concept. Added to this obstacle are the problems of one's hermeneutical posture and his solution to the authoritative boundaries placed by the biblical writers on the lines of continuity and discontinuity found between the two Testaments. But it is for precisely this reason that expositors of Scripture should be willing to reexamine once again this neglected biblical concept, for it promises to provide another clue to contemporary readers as to how the two Testaments are related to each other.

1. Gerhard Von Rad, "There Remains Still a Rest for the People of God," *The Problem of the Hexateuch and Other Essays*, trans. E. W. Trueman Dicken (New York, 1966), p. 94.

THE PROMISE THEME

PROMISE THEOLOGY IN GENESIS

No other theme provides such a comprehensive insight into the plan and program of our Lord in both Testaments as the "promise."[2] Beginning with the promise of a victorious "seed" in Genesis 3:15, the content of this single, all encompassing theme builds. A constellation of terms is used in the OT to teach that the promise is God's "word," "blessing," and "oath"[3] to his chosen "seed," whereas the NT focuses the now enlarged picture by limiting the terminology to that of God's "promise," *epangelia*.[4] Both Testaments can also depict the promise doctrine under one of the most ubiquitous formulas in the canon: "I will be your God, you shall be my people, and I will dwell in the midst of you."[5]

Basically, the promise consists of three elements: first, a "seed" or a line of heirs culminating in a chief *heir par excellence*, which is promised to Eve, Abraham, Isaac, and Jacob (Gen. 3:15; 12:3, 7; 13:14–16; 15:4, 5, 13, 18; 16:10; 17:2, 7, 9, 19; 21:12; 22:17; 26:24; 27:28, 29; 28:14); second, the land of Canaan, which is given to the Patriarchs and their descendants forever as an *inheritance* (Gen. 12:1, 7; 13:15, 17; 15:7, 18; 17:8; 24:7; 26:2, 3; 28:13; 49:8–12); and third, the climactic element: that the Patriarchs are the recipients of these favors so that "all the families of the earth might be blessed" by this *heritage* (Gen. 12:3; 18:18; 22:18; 26:4; 28:14). This last item Paul clearly calls the "gospel" in Galatians 3:8.

There were additional items in Genesis that elaborated on these basic three elements: (1) Abraham's seed through Isaac would be countless as the stars and sand of the seashore; (2) they would be a great nation; (3) that kings would come from Abraham, Sarah, and Jacob; and (4) Abraham's name would be great.

2. See the writer's articles: "The Eschatological Hermeneutics of 'Epangelicalism': Promise Theology," *JETS*, XIII (Spring 1970):91–99 (henceforth "Hermeneutics"); "The Old Promise and the New Covenant: Jeremiah 31:31–34," *JETS*, XV (Winter 1972), 11–23 (henceforth "New Covenant"); and see chapter 9 of this book, "Including the Gentiles in the Plan of God—Amos 9:9–15."
3. Cf. Kaiser, "New Covenant," XV, 12 nn.4–8.
4. Luke 24:29; Acts 1:4; 2:33, 39; 7:17; 13:23, 32; 26:6; Rom. 4:13, 14, 16, 20; 9:4, 8, 9; 15:8; 2 Cor. 1:20; 7:1; Gal. 3:14, 16, 17, 18, 21, 22, 29; 4:23, 28; Eph. 1:13; 2:12; 3:6; 6:2; 1 Tim. 4:8; 2 Tim. 1:1; Heb. 4:1; 6:12, 15, 17; 7:6; 8:6; 9:15; 10:36; 11:9 (*bis*), 13, 17, 33, 39; 2 Peter 1:4; 3:4, 9, 13. The verbal form appears in Rom. 1:2; 4:21; Gal. 3:19; Heb. 6:13; 10:23; 11:11; 12:26; James 1:12; 2:15; 1 John 2:25–26. Cf. the fine article by Julius Schniewind and Gerhard Friedrich, "ἐπαγγέλλω," *TDNT*, ed. Gerhard Kittel and trans. Geoffrey W. Bromiley (Grand Rapids, 1964), 2:576–86.
5. Cf. Kaiser, "New Covenant," XV, 12–13, n.10.

PROMISE THEOLOGY IN EXODUS, LEVITICUS, AND NUMBERS

The Exodus narratives do not interrupt the promise; instead they perpetuate the same announcements already given to the patriarchs (Ex. 2:24; 3:13, 15, 16, 17; 4:5; 6:2–5; 13:5; 32:13; 33:1; Lev. 26:42, 45; Num. 10:29; 14:23; 32:11). But the new addition to the promise is this: "I will take you for my people" (Ex. 6:7). Already in Genesis 17:7–8 and 28:21 the first part of the tripartite formula had been promised, namely, "I will be your God." Now the emphasis will fall on the fact that Israel will be Yahweh's "son," his "firstborn son," a people for his possession.[6] Herein lies the heart of the theological development of the promise in these three pentateuchal books (Ex. 29:45–46; Lev. 11:45; 22:33; 25:38; 26:12, 45; Num. 15:41). Of course, the provision of the Tabernacle introduces the third aspect of the tripartite formula: "I will tabernacle, dwell (*šākan*) in the midst of you" (especially Ex. 29:45–46; but also in Ex. 24:16; 25:8; 40:35; Num. 5:3, 35:34). With this word one of the greatest formulas for the promise theme is completed.

Here began the heart of the Bible's own story of progress. God promises to be something and to do something for a select people so as to bring blessing to all mankind and creation. Therefore, this article has as one of its foundations that the key category for understanding biblical revelation is the Bible's own foundational concept, namely, the "promise." If some object saying that the theme of covenant is more prominent, the response is simple: there were *many* formal covenants, but the content of these covenants of redemption was at once *single*, continuous, and eternal; hence, the word to Eve, Abraham, Isaac, Jacob, David, and Jeremiah (31:31–34) is a united plan, but exhibiting many expanding and interlocking specifications in the progress of redemption. One such addition to the promise is the theme of "rest."

The exciting potential offered in the theology of rest is that the Bible deliberately takes a word that is intimately involved in the physical inheritance of the land of Canaan, which had been part of God's promise to Abraham, and uses it to include both a physical concept and a deeply spiritual meaning. The rest that God gives is at once historical (Canaan), soteriological (salvation), and eschatological

6. The word describing the people as God's "distinctive," "peculiar," or "moveable treasure" is *sᵉgullāh*. The word has shown up in Akkadian as *sikiltum* (cf. Moshe Greenberg, "*Hebrew*, sᵉgullā: *Akkadian*, sikiltu," *Journal of the American Oriental Society*, LXXI [July–September 1951], 172–74). At Alalah, King abba-El is the *sikiltum* of the goddess, while a Ugaritic vassal is the *sglt* of his suzerain (Ch. Virolleaud, *Le Palais royal d' Ugarit*, V [Paris, 1965], 84; text: 18.38; 11.7–12). Therefore, the root means basically "to set aside" a property for a good purpose; the root being *sakalu*. See M. Weinfeld, "The Covenant of Grant in the Old Testament and in the Ancient Near East," *Journal of the American Oriental Society*, XC (April–June 1970):195, n.103.

(the kingdom and our reign with Christ). This is another beautiful illustration of the corporate solidarity of some of these themes in Scripture. Each step in the onward movement of such themes as the promise with its subthemes such as the rest from God, the Messiah, and the Seed, points back to the beginning and to the ultimate goal intended by God. Each successive historical step harmoniously combines the beginning step in which the totality was programmatically announced with the end in which that totality shall be unfolded. Therefore, things combined in the promise stage were often disjoined in their actual historical fulfillment, but never in their ideological or theological connection. Each part implied the whole doctrine and the whole stood for each of successive participating steps as they were (and are) being enacted. This can be seen in an Isaac or a Solomon who epitomized the promised heir at that point in history, but then it was always with the tension expressed in Hebrews: "not yet" was the full realization accomplished.

THE THEOLOGY OF REST

One of the new provisions added to the expanding revelation of the promise theme was the provision of "rest" for Israel. So special was this rest that Yahweh would call it *His rest* (Ps. 95:11; Isa. 66:1). It is precisely this aspect of the promise theme that provides that key link between the end of the book of Numbers and the time of David: the corresponding texts for this period of time being Deuteronomy 12:9–10 and 2 Samuel 7:1, 11.

But before the reader quickly assumes that the former is the promise of "the rest" and "the inheritance" of Canaan while the latter is the historical fulfillment of that "rest" under David, he must come to terms with the historical midpoint in Joshua 21:44–45:

> The LORD gave them rest on every side just as he had sworn to their fathers; not one of all their enemies had withstood them, for the LORD had given all their enemies into their power. Not one of all the good promises which the LORD had made to the house of Israel failed; all came to pass.

But this only yields a conundrum. If Joshua fulfilled the promised rest, what is 2 Samuel 7:1 claiming? How often was this state of rest fulfilled? Not only must we work with Joshua and David as the fulfillers of the promise but even Solomon was included, for he was named the "man of rest" (1 Kings 8:56; 1 Chron. 22:9). Even later this same divine rest appears after periods of bloodshed and trouble in the reigns of King Asa (2 Chron. 14:5, 6; 15:15) and King Jehoshaphat (2 Chron. 20:30).

Even the repeated notices of "rest" in Judges (3:1, 30; 5:31; 8:28) reflect *šāqaṭ* periods which were not the permanent rest promised in the *ñuah* group of words. The same *šāqaṭ* type is observed in Joshua 11:23 and 14:15 where the land is given this type of "rest" from war. It is a temporary lull in the continuous surge of the restless sea, Isaiah 57:20, a "respite" from days of trouble, Psalm 94:13. This type of rest must be separated from what God calls "My Rest."

Nevertheless, there still are a number of *ñuah* types offered at different times.

No wonder the Psalmist says the invitation to enter into God's Rest is still open (Ps. 95:11). And that was where the writer of Hebrews boldly announced that the "today" of the ancient promise was still open even in his day. Therefore, that ancient aspect of the promise doctrine can be ours by faith even now in these "last days."

THE REST VOCABULARY

The Hebrew root *ñuah*, "to rest" supplies the majority of the words for this concept.[7] Whenever the *hiphil* stem of this root is followed by the preposition *lᵉ* plus a person or group, it usually assumes a technical status. The resulting form in some twenty instances is *heniah lᵉ*. This rest is a place granted by the Lord (Ex. 33:14; Deut. 3:20; Josh. 1:13, 15; 22:4; 2 Chron. 14:5), a peace and security from all enemies (Deut. 12:10; 25:19; Josh. 21:44; 23:1; 2 Sam. 7:1, 11; 1 Kings 5:18 [5:4]; 1 Chron. 22:9, 18; 23:25; 2 Chron. 14:6; 15:15; 20:30; 32:22— probable reading?) or the cessation of sorrow and labor in the future (Isa. 14:3; 28:12).[8]

The noun is *mᵉnûhāh*, "resting-place," "rest." Here again this form also assumes a technical usage. Perhaps the earliest instance was in Jacob's blessing Issachar with a land which would be a good resting-place (Gen. 49:15). The geographical, material, and spatial association of this rest are strong in Deuteronomy 12:9; 1 Kings 8:56; 1 Chronicles 22:9; Isaiah 28:12; Micah 2:10; consequently, there is the frequent association of the *māqôm* theme. It is "a place" where Yahweh would "plant" His people Israel so that they could dwell in their own place

---

7. A proper name reflecting this verb is that of Noah, Genesis 5:29.
8. Notice the other *hiphil* usages of this root use other prepositions, for example, *bᵉ* in Ezekiel 5:13; 16:42; 21:22; 24:13, or are followed by such accusatives as "his hand" in Exodus 17:11; or "my spirit" in Zechariah 6:8. Also when the *hiphil* form is followed by an accusative of a thing with a place name, the meaning is "to deposit," "lay or set down" or "let lie."

without being disturbed any more, for example, Deuteronomy 1:33; 2 Samuel 7:10.⁹

In spite of all the emphasis on the Promised Land as the rest of God for Israel, the spiritual element also is prominent in this noun form. This finds expression whenever this rest is connected with the themes of the Ark of God or the Temple. Rest is where the presence of God stops (as in the wilderness wanderings, Num. 10:33) or dwells (as in Palestine, Ps. 132:8, 14; Isa. 66:1; 1 Chron. 28:2). It was for this reason, no doubt, that David stressed the aspects of belief and trust for this rest in Psalm 95:11. As with the verb, so here again this rest is associated with Israel's return to the land, Isaiah 11:15.¹⁰

A related noun form is *mānôaḥ*. Out of its seven appearances, four should be included as part of our technical vocabulary: Deuteronomy 28:65 (a disobedient Israel would find no rest while being dispersed among the nations), Lamentations 1:3 (Judah did not find rest in Babylon), Psalm 116:7 (the psalmist will return to God's rest after his resurrection from the dead!), and 1 Chronicles 6:16 [Heb., 6:31] (a resting place for the Ark).¹¹

The case built up from all the technical uses of the root *nûaḥ*, is inescapable: God's rest is the gracious gift of the land promised to the patriarchs with its attendant blessings such as the cessation of all hostile enemy action. It is also the place where the presence of the Lord dwells whether with the traveling Ark or in the Temple.

REST AS THE INHERITANCE OF THE LAND

One of the great ideas dominating the theology of Deuteronomy is that future moment when God will cause Israel to possess the land of Canaan. Possession, inheritance, and rest function almost as synonymous ideas here. Because the gift is as sure as the word of the promising God, everything waits on this one "until"; "until the Lord has given rest ... and until they also possess the land" (Deut. 3:20).

Repeatedly, the emphasis is on the fact that Yahweh has promised the patriarchs this gift of the land (Deut. 1:8, 21, 35, 38 and sixty-five

9. See the suggestive discussion in R. A. Carlson, *David, the Chosen King: A Traditio-Historical Approach to the Second Book of Samuel* (Stockholm, 1964), pp. 99–121.
10. There are six other passages where this noun is used of quietness (Jer. 51:59; Ps. 23:2), security (Ruth 1:9), the abiding judgment of the Word of the Lord (Zech. 9:1), ease (2 Sam. 14:17), and the textual problem of Judges 20:43. Though related to the idea discussed, they are applied to distinct situations from that under consideration. Note the appearance of this form in the Judean place name Manahath, 1 Chronicles 8:6; 2:54; and the Edomite site, Genesis 36:23 = 1 Chronicles 1:40.
11. The other three references include two spoken of birds not resting (Gen. 8:9; Isa. 34:14) and of security for Ruth (Ruth 3:1). A proper name reflecting this noun is Manoah, the father of Samson, Judges 13:2.

other times in Deut.).[12] But with this same promise to Abraham, Isaac, and Jacob, the Lord spoke simultaneously to Moses' generation in the wilderness (Deut. 2:29, and passim). Canaan was to be Israel's inheritance and resting place.

But this rest was also *God's* rest. If one misses this point, he will have the same problem that G. Von Rad had: "It is now quite clear that this notion that the land belongs to Yahweh as stated in Leviticus 25:23; Joshua 22:19 is of a totally different order from that of the promise of the land to the early patriarchs."[13]

On the contrary, the land of Canaan was the (*nahᵃlāh*) "the inheritance of the LORD" (Ex. 15:17; 1 Sam. 26:19; 2 Sam. 21:3; 1 Kings 8:36), therefore, it was His to give away. It was His "possession" (*yᵉruššᵃh* in 2 Chronicles 20:11 and *ahuzzah* in Joshua 22:19). Even more significantly, the people of Israel themselves were the "possession" of the LORD (Ex. 19:5; Deut. 4:20; 9:26, 29; 32:8, 9; 1 Sam. 10:1; 2 Sam. 14:16; 20:19).[14] This latter concept is never tied directly into the concept of God's rest, though the idea is relevant when the discussion turns to "heirs" and "joint heirs" in the "inheritance to come." At that point, suddenly the complex of ideas moves from a geographical fixation to again include a spiritual reality as well. This would tie in with the emphasis on the presence of the Lord in the *nûah* words discussed above.

In the whole of the Hebrew Bible (OT) there are few issues that are as important as that of the promise of the land to the patriarchs and the nation Israel. In fact, '*ereṣ*, "land," is the fourth most frequent substantive in the Hebrew Bible.[15] Were it not for the larger and more comprehensive theme of the total promise,[16] with all its multifaceted provisions, the theme of Israel and her land could well serve as the central idea or the organizing rubric for the entire canon. However, it

---

12. See Johannes Hermann, "κλῆρος," *TDNT*, ed. Gerhard Kittel; trans. Geoffrey W. Bromiley, III (Grand Rapids, 1966): 771 for the listing. Also the lists in J. Plöger, *Literarkritische formgeschichtliche und stilkritische Untersuchungen zum Deuteronomium*, vol. XXVI of *Bonner biblische Berträge* (Bonn, 1967), pp. 124–26; 65–79 as cited by Patrick D. Miller, Jr., "The Gift of God: The Deuteronomic Theology of the Land," *Interpretation*, XXII (October 1969):451–61.

13. Gerhard Von Rad, "The Promised Land and Yahweh's Land in the Hexateuch," *The Problem of the Hexateuch and Other Essays*, trans. E. W. Trueman Dicken (New York, 1966), p. 86.

14. Hermann, III, 772. Also see the discussion on *sᵉgullāh* above in n.6.

15. H. H. Schmid, "ארץ," *Theologisches Handwörterbuch zum Alten Testament* I, (Ernst Jenni and Claus Westermann, eds.) München: Chr. Kaiser Verlag, 1971, pp. 227ff., especially 234 and אדמה, pp. 58ff., as quoted by Elmer Martens, *Motivations for the Promise of Israel's Restoration to the Land in Jeremiah and Ezekiel.* (doctoral dissertation, Claremont, 1972), p. 2.

16. For a discussion which organizes the total message of the Bible around the promise, see Walter C. Kaiser, Jr., *Toward an Old Testament Theology* (Grand Rapids: Zondervan, 1978).

does clearly hold a dominant place in the divine gifts of blessing to Israel.

Yet, there is more to the promise of the land than religious significance and theological meaning; there is an essential interrelationship between the political and empirical reality of the land as a Jewish state and all statements about its spiritual or theological functions. The land of Israel cannot be reduced to a sort of mystical land defined as a new spiritual reality that transcends the old geographic and political designations if we wish to continue to represent the single truth-intentions[17] of the writers of the biblical text.

Instead, the biblical data is most insistent on the fact that the land was promised to the patriarchs as a gift where their descendants would reside and rule as a nation.

The land as promise. The priority of the divine word and divine oath as the basis for any discussion of the land is of first importance if we are to represent matters as they were presented in the biblical text of Genesis. From the inception of his call in Ur of the Chaldees, God had marked out a specific geographical destination for the patriarch Abraham (Gen. 12:1). This territorial bequest was immediately reaffirmed and extended to his descendants as soon as Abraham reached Shechem (Gen. 12:7).

Certainly Albrecht Alt was wrong in rejecting the land as a part of the original promise. Martin Noth[18] was closer to the mark when he declared both the land and the seed promise to be part of the original covenant to the fathers.

So solemn was this covenant with its gift of the land[19] that Genesis 15:7-21 depicted God alone moving between the halves of the sacrificial animals after sunset as "a smoking furnace and a flaming torch." Thus He obligated Himself and only Himself to fulfill the terms of this oath. Abraham was not asked or required to likewise obligate himself. The total burden for the delivery of the gift of the land would fall on the divine provider but not on the devotion of the patriarch. As if to underscore the permanence of this arrangement, Genesis 17:7, 13, 19 stressed that this was to be a *berît 'ôlām*, "everlasting covenant."

Boundaries of the land. The borders of this land promised to Abraham were to run "from the River Egypt (*minne har mizraim*) to the Great River, the River Euphrates" (*hannāhār haggādol ne har perāt,*

---

17. The hermeneutic claimed here is that which was eloquently set forth by E. D. Hirsch, *Validity in Interpretation* (New Haven: Yale U., 1967). See especially chapter 1. For our further comments, see Walter C. Kaiser, Jr., "The Current Crisis in Exegesis and the Apostolic Use of Deuteronomy 25:4 in I Corinthians 9:8–10," *Journal of the Evangelical Theological Society* 21 (1978):3–18.
18. See W. C. Kaiser, Jr., *Toward an Old Testament Theology*, pp. 89–91; 58–59.
19. Note also Genesis 13:15, 17; 24:7; 26:3–5; 28:13–14; 35:12; 48:4; 50:24.

Gen. 15:18). Or, in the later words of the oft-repeated pairs of cities, the land included everything "from Dan to Beersheba" (Judg. 20:1; 1 Sam. 3:20; 2 Sam. 3:10; 17:11; 24:2, 15; 1 Kings 4:25 [Heb., 5:5]; and in reverse order 2 Chron. 30:5). Those two cities marked the northern-most and southernmost administrative centers; not sharply defined boundary lines.

Even though a fair number of evangelical scholars have wrongly judged the southern boundary of the "River Egypt" to be the Nile River,[20] it is more accurately placed at the Wady el-'Arish, which reaches the Mediterranean Sea at the town of El-'Arish, some ninety miles east of the Suez Canal and almost fifty miles southwest of Gaza (cf. Num. 34:2, 5; Ezek. 47:14, 19; 48:28).

Amos 6:14, likewise, pointed to the same limits for the southern boundary: the "brook of the Arabah" (nahal hā'ªrābāh), which flows into the southern tip of the Dead Sea. Other marks on the same southern boundary are the end of the Dead Sea (Num. 34:3–5), Mount Halak (Josh. 11:17), the Wilderness of Zin (Num. 13:21; 34:3), and Arabah (Deut. 1:7) and Negeb (Deut. 34:1–3) and "Shihor opposite Egypt" (Josh. 13:3–5; 1 Chron. 13:5).[21]

The western boundary of the land was "the Sea of the Philistines," that is, the "Great Sea" (Num. 34:6; Josh. 1:4; Ezek. 47:20; 48:28) or Mediterranean Sea, whereas the eastern boundary was the eastern shore of the Sea of Kinnereth, the Jordan River, and the Dead Sea (Num. 34:7–12).

Only the northern boundary presented a serious problem. The river that bordered off the northernmost reaches of the Promised Land was called "the Great River," which was later glossed, according to some, "the River Euphrates" in Genesis 15:18, Deuteronomy 1:7, and Joshua 1:4. In Exodus 23:31 and Isaiah 27:12 it is simply "the River."

But is the River Euphrates to be equated with the Great River as if it were in apposition to it? Could it not be that these are the two

---

20. The argument is usually based on the fact that the Hebrew word nāhār is consistently restricted to large rivers. However the Hebrew is more frequently nahal = Arabic wady instead of the nahar of Genesis 15:18 which may have been influenced by the second nahar in the text. (So J. Simons, The Geographical and Topographical Texts of the Old Testament [Leiden: E. J. Brill, 1959], p. 96, Section 272.) In the Akkadian texts of Sargon II (716 B.C.E.) it appears as nahal muṣar (ANET, 286; cf. also Esar haddon's Arza(ni) or Arsa = Arish(?) in ANET, 290). See Bruce Waltke, "River of Egypt," Zondervan Pictorial Encyclopedia of the Bible (Grand Rapids: Zondervan, 1975), 5:121. J. Dwight Pentecost, Prophecy for Today (Grand Rapids: Zondervan, 1961), p. 65. Also see the interesting case for the Nile made by H. BarDeroma, "The River of Egypt (Nahal Mizraim)," Palestinian Exploration Quarterly 92 (1960):37–56.

21. J. Simons, op. cit., p. 104 argues that Shihor is not a branch of the Nile, the old Pelusiac or easternmost branch of the Nile (which is never a nahal according to K. A. Kitchen, "Egypt, Brook of," Zondervan Pictorial Encyclopedia, 2:224–25), but is the Wady el-'Arish.

extremities of the northern boundary? This suggestion proves to be of some weight in that the other topographical notices given along with those two river names would appear to be more ideally located in the valley north of the Lebanon mountains that currently serves as the boundary between Lebanon and Syria. The river running through this valley is called *Nahr el-Kebir* in modern Arabic, "The Great River."

One of the most difficult topographical features to isolate is the "Plain of Labwah [or "towards, in the coming to"] Hamath" (*r*ᵉ*hob lᵉbo̓ hᵃmāt*, Num. 13:21) or, simply, Labwah Hamath (Num. 34:8; Josh. 13:3–5; 1 Kings 8:65; 2 Kings 14:25; 1 Chron. 13:5; Amos 6:18; Ezek. 47:15; 48:1–28). B. Mazar (Maisler) has identified "Labwah Hamath" or "Towards Hamath" as modern city of Labwah in Lebanon. This city, in a forest just to the south of Kadesh and northeast of Baalbek, was of sufficient stature to be mentioned in Amenhotep II's stele, as Rameses II's favorite hunting grounds (*rwby, r3b3*)[22] and in Tiglath Pileser III's text along with Hamath. Numbers 13:21 seems to point to the same "Plain" (*r*ᵉ*hob*), a district further defined by 2 Samuel 10:6, 8 and Judges 18:28.

Added to this site are Mount Hor, which may be Mount Akkar, just south of the "Great River" in Lebanon; and the towns of Zedad, Ziphron, Hazer Ainon (all found in Num. 34:3–9; cf. Ezek. 47:15–19; 48:1–2, 28) and Riblah (Ezek. 6:14). Each of those towns may be bearers of names similar to some Arabic village names today, for example: Riblah, Sadad, Qousseir (= Hazer), or Qaryatein (Hazer Spring).[23]

Whereas the precise details on the northern border remain extremely tentative, the evidence favors some line far to the north of Dan which would include such old Canaanite settlements as Sidon (Gen. 10:15) and indeed the whole Phoenician coastal section from Sidon to the Philistine Gaza (Gen. 10:19).

Meanwhile, the settlement of transjordania by the two-and-a-half tribes seems to be clearly outside that territory originally promised to Israel. In Joshua 22:24–25 the implication is clear, Gilead was outside the borders of Canaan and the portion allotted by promise. The same

22. B. Mazar, "Canaan and the Canaanites," *Bulletin of the American Schools of Oriental Research* 102 (1946):9. See the excellent discussion in J. Simons, *Geographical and Topographical Texts*, pp. 99–102; George W. Buchanan, *The Consequences of the Covenant*, Leiden: E. J. Brill, 1970, pp. 91–109; Yohanan Aharoni, *The Land of the Bible*, trans. Anson F. Rainey (Philadelphia: Westminster, 1967), pp. 65–67; and Yehezkel Kaufmann, *The Biblical Account of the Conquest of Palestine* (Jerusalem: Magnes, 1953), pp. 48–56. Is the *'ad lᵉbo̓ miṣraim* of 2 Chronicles 26:8 of sufficient weight to offset this interpretation, or is it merely an imitation of the older *'ad lᵉbo̓ Hᵃmāt* as Simons (see the bibliography on Kurt Galling there) argues (p. 101)?
23. See Buchanan, pp. 99–101.

implication is sustained in Lot's removal to transjordan's Sodom (Gen. 13:12) and in the instructions Moses gave to Reuben and Gad: "We will cross over . . . into the land of Canaan and the possession of our inheritance shall remain with us on the other side of the Jordan" (Num. 32:32). Even when three of the six cities of refuge were assigned to transjordania, they were distinguished from the three that were "in the land of Canaan" (Num. 35:14). Thus, the most that could be said for Israel's occupation of these lands on the eastern bank of the Jordan is that it was a temporary occupation, but they did not belong to the land of promise. Likewise, the Negeb in the south was also outside of the parameters of the promise.

THE LATER DEVELOPMENT OF THE THEOLOGY OF REST

In spite of all the insights afforded the researcher into the preceding definitions and distinctions, the climaxing statements on any theology of rest are to be found in Psalm 95 and Hebrews 3:7—4:13.

PSALM 95

This psalm is one of a series of Psalms (93–100) variously designated as "Apocalyptic Psalms" or "Theocratic Psalms" (Delitzsch), "Millennial Anthems" (Tholuck),[24] "Songs of the Millennium" (Binnie), "Group of Millennial Psalms" (Herder), "Second Advent Psalms" (Rawlinson), "Enthronement Psalms" (Mowinckel) and "Royal Psalms" (Perowne). Whatever title is used, there can be no mistaking that the theme is eschatological and that it depicts a time when the Lord alone is King reigning over all peoples and lands (93:1; 96:10; 97:1; 99:1). Not only in the grand symphonic conclusion to these millennial psalms is there a song (Ps. 100) but the theme of a "new song" appears in 96:1 and 98:1[25] which, if it is not messianic by its very name, it is certainly such by content in Psalms 96 and 98. Indeed, the Lord comes to rule (cf. Ugaritic usage of *šapat*) the earth, the world, and the people in it with righteousness and His truth (Pss. 96:13; 97:9).

Therefore, each of these psalms alike tells the story of a divine kingdom which is yet to be set up on the earth. It anticipates the universal outburst of joy that shall greet this future event. To accomplish this result, the psalms seem to group themselves in pairs, that is, Psalm 93 goes with 94; 95 with 96; 97 with 98, and 99 with 100. The pattern thus established is the announcement of the Lord's reign in the first of the pairs (especially in 93, 97, 99, and perhaps in 95's

24. Nathaniel West, *The Thousand Years: Studies in the Eschatology in Both Testaments* (New York, 1880), pp. 74–75.
25. Cf. Psalms 33:3; 40:3; 144:9; 149:1; Isaiah 42:10; Revelation 5:9.

special order) followed by the outburst of praise to the Lord with that "new Song" (esp. 96, 98, and climactically 100).[26]

Now the interesting point to be made in connection with our study is that the divine rest is set in the context of these psalms celebrating the second advent of our Lord. Participation in this kingdom of God, this rest of God, is to be made now on the basis of a decision in the present moment before those events connected with the second coming overtake anyone.

Therefore, in this pair of psalms, a warning and exhortation to enter this rest appears between a triple invitation to praise the Lord based on the fact that He is the only King, Creator, and Shepherd (95:1–7a), and the contents of the new song (96:1–13). The connection then between 95 and 96 is just the inverse pattern found in Isaiah 2:2–5. There the exhortation of verse 5 follows the glorious announcement of the kingdom of God in verses 2–4, but our Psalm (95:7b–11) warns before it breaks into the triumphant strains of Psalm 96 with its announcement in song of the final, universal reign of the Lord.

Once these connections are observed in Psalms 93–100, it follows that the psalmist's understanding of "rest" is tied up with the events of the second advent. It also follows that the generation of the wilderness could have participated in this future kingdom or rest of God to some extent, but they refused to do so in unbelief; therefore they were twice the losers: temporally and spiritually, in that historic moment and in the second advent!

The picture that begins to emerge is one where this eschatological rest (the "inheritance" or land of Israel that figures in a central role in the kingdom of God) is entered into by faith in the historic present. As a token of His ability and willingness to finally do all that He has promised concerning this promise of the land made to the patriarchs, the Lord gave to Israel in the historic past the land of Canaan to Joshua. This was an "earnest" or "down payment" on God's final complete rest yet to come.

THE REST GIVEN TO JOSHUA

The problem arises if the Lord "swore in (his) anger" (Ps. 95:11) that not one of the evil generation should enter in the good land He

---

26. Psalm 94 is a prayer of request and thanks to God for being our "rock." This prepares us for the theme in Psalm 95:1, "The rock of our salvation."

planned to give to the patriarchs (except Joshua and Caleb),[27] how then did anyone arrive there in Joshua's day?

Scripture responds that it was "because Caleb wholly followed the Lord" (Deut. 1:36) as did Joshua, therefore, they went in by faith. As Numbers 14:7–9 teaches, they set a proper value on God's promised inheritance (it was "exceeding good"), they had a proper confidence in God ("If Jehovah delight in us, then He will bring us into the land"), and they feared the sin of rebellion[28] ("only rebel not against Jehovah"). It also notes that the little children whom the older generation feared would become statistics and disaster victims, would instead receive the land by grace as a gift (Deut. 1:39).

But how is it possible to have this "rest" under Joshua (1:13, 15; 11:23; 21:44; 22:4; 23:1) and yet not have it if it is to be connected with some everlasting kingdom-rest as argued from the millennial Psalm 95? Was not Joshua living in the promised "rest home" (Ex. 33:14) and "inheritance" or "rest" (Deut. 12:9)? Why did God seemingly go back on His eternal word and resort to placing this rest safely out of everyone's reach in the millennium?

The solution is along the same lines as observed in the case of the patriarchs themselves. Even though they were already living in Canaan, it still was as yet just a promised land to them. It is repeatedly called "the land of their sojourning" (Gen. 17:8; 28:4; 36:7; 37:1; 47:1; Ex. 6:4) and not their "possession." That is how Stephen put it in his speech in Acts 7:4–5: "God removed him from there into this land ... yet he gave him no inheritance in it ... but promised to give it to him in possession and to his descendants...." Indeed, they did possess a small parcel of that land, their burial grounds, and this was simply an "earnest" or "down payment" on the whole land. In a similar way, Joshua, Caleb, and the new generation received the land. The emphasis in Joshua 21:43–45 is still on the promised word that has not failed Israel, nor will it.

But on the matter of whether Israel will retain its privilege of remaining in the land, that is another matter. Israel had set before her the alternatives of "life and good, death and evil." It was all to be decided on how she responded to one command: Love the Lord your

27. An "oriental negative." For additional examples of this literary device, cf. Joshua 11:22; Exodus 9:3, 6; Galatians 2:20; 1 Chronicles 7:10; 1:14, 16, etc. The passages on which this oath is based are Numbers 14:21–23; 32:10–12; Deuteronomy 1:34–36. Notice that in Numbers 14:21–23, the oath is that they should not see the *land* God promised to the patriarchs whereas in Psalm 95 it is the *rest of God* they shall not enter into. This is another confirmation of the geographical aspect of the rest of God.

28. As pointed out by G. H. Lang, *The Epistle to the Hebrews* (London, 1951), p. 78.

God. The proof that she was doing just that would be seen by how she kept the Lord's commandments (Deut. 30:15-20).

There was to be the crux of the matter—would Israel choose life? Would she live? Really live? Even live on the land which the Lord swore to give to their fathers Abraham, Isaac, and Jacob?

This conditional "if" did not "pave the way for a declension from grace into law" as Von Rad[29] suggests any more than the conditional aspect found in connection with the Davidic promise lowered it into a works salvation. On the contrary, the Davidic promise remains externally valid and immutable as the One who gave it (2 Sam. 7:13, 16; Ps. 89:27, 28, 35, 36; 2 Sam. 23:5; Isa. 55:3).

The "if" in the Davidic covenant (Ps. 132:12; 89:29-32; 2 Sam. 7:14b-15; 1 Kings 2:4; 8:25; 9:4-5) can only refer in those contexts to *individual* and *personal* invalidation of the benefits of the covenant, but they can never affect the certainty of God's eternal oath.

Therefore, the promise of the inheritance of God's rest is protected even in the case of subsequent sins by the recipient's descendants. It would not be a case of "slipping into Law" or even of "slipping from grace." Neither the days of Joshua nor of David were any kind of blank check for their descendants to rest on their father's laurels. The word of promise could also be theirs, if they would appropriate it by faith. If not, they were the losers. However, the promise was not revoked, withdrawn, or nullified for any succeeding generation: rather that word was eternal!

As for the eschatological aspects of the rest theme in the millennial psalms of the Davidic period,[30] the answer is that the promise of God is a single, eternal plan encompassing the end, beginning, and all the points of history in between. Certainly the final triumph of the promised "Seed" and outreach of that salvation in its completed fulfillment awaits the second advent of the Messiah. Why then, should not this rest likewise participate? Was it not a part of the promise doctrine?

Loss of the land. The history and theology of the land divides right at this point. In the succinct vocabulary of Walter Brueggemann,[31] the Jordan is "the juncture between two histories." In the one "history is one of *landlessness on the way to the land*" and in the other it is *"landed Israel in the process of losing the land."* Thus, the *sine qua*

---

29. Von Rad, "Promised Land," p. 91. The passages where he finds this conditionality are Deuteronomy 4:25-26; 6:18; 8:1; 11:8-9; 16:20; 18:21.
30. The LXX calls Psalm 95 a psalm of David. Hebrews 4:7 says, "in (or) through David," which may just be equivalent to "The Psalms." However, Psalm 96, the twin psalm of 95, is ascribed to David and repeated with very little change in 1 Chronicles 16:23-33.
31. Walter Brueggemann, *The Land* (Philadelphia: Fortress, 1977), pp. 71-72. See also the mammoth tome by W. D. Davies, *The Gospel and the Land* (Berkeley: U. of California, 1974), esp., pp. 36-48.

non for continued enjoyment of life in the land is obedience that springs from a genuine love and fear of God. Failure to obey could lead to war, calamity, loss of the land, and even death itself (Deut. 4:26).

Many of the laws were tied directly to the land and Israel's existence on it as indicated by many of the motive clauses or introductory words found in many of them.[32] In fact, when evil was left unchecked, it compounded and caused the land to be defiled and guilty before God (Deut. 21:23; 24:4). This point could not have been made more forcefully than it is in Leviticus 26 and Deuteronomy 28. Naturally, no nation or individual has the right to interpret any single or isolated reverse or major calamity in life as an evidence of divine love that is seeking the normalization of relationships between God and man. Yet, Israel's prophets were bold to declare with the aid of divine revelation that certain events, especially those in related series, were indeed from the hand of God (e.g., Amos 4:6–12 and Hag. 1:4–7).

The most painful of all the tragedies would be the loss of the land (Lev. 26:34–39). But such a separation could never be a permanent situation; how could God deny Himself and fail to fulfill His covenant with Abraham, Isaac, and Jacob? (Lev. 26:42; as surely as the judgments might "overtake" [*hiśśîg*, Deut. 28:15, 45; cf. Zech. 1:6] future generations, just as surely as would every promised blessing likewise "overtake" [*hiśśîg*, Deut. 28:2] them the moment "repentance" [*šub*][33] began [Zech. 1:6]). Forsaking the covenant the Lord made with the fathers would lead to an uprooted existence (Deut. 30:24–28) until God once more restored the fortunes of Israel.

The prophets and the promise of a return. The "headwaters" of the "return" promises, as Elmer A. Martens[34] assures us in one of the first studies of land theology in the prophets, are in Jeremiah and Ezekiel. Both of those men had experienced firsthand the loss of land, yet, between them Elmer Martens was able to exegete twenty-five explicit statements of return to the land[35] and five texts with indirect announcements of return.[36]

32. This fine point is made by P. J. Miller, "Gift," pp. 459–60. The instances from Deuteronomy he lists are 15:1ff.; 16:18–20; 17:14ff.; 18:9ff.; 19:1ff.; 19:14; 21:1ff.; 21:22ff.; 24:1–4; 25:13–16.
33. Deuteronomy 30:2, 6, 8, 10; cf. Walter C. Kaiser, Jr., *Toward an Old Testament Theology*, 137–39, 198, 223.
34. Elmer A. Martens, "Motivations for the Promise of Israel's Restoration," 12 (see n.1). See also the earlier study by Hans-Ruedi Weber, "The Promise of the Land: Biblical Interpretation and the Present Situation in the Middle East," *Study Encounter* 7 (1971):7–10. (= "La Promesse De La Terre," *Foi et Vie*, 71 (1972):19–46
35. He listed the explicit ones as: Jeremiah 3:11–20; 12:14–17; 16:10–18; 23:1–8; 24; 28:1–4; 29:1–14; 30:1–3, 10–11; 31:2–14, 15–20; 32:1–44; 42:1–22; 50:17–20; Ezekiel 11:14–21; 20:39–44; 34:1–16; 35:1—36:15; 36:16–36; 37:1–14; 37:15–28; 39:21–29.
36. The indirect were: Jeremiah 30:17*b*–22; 31:23–25; 33:1–18; Ezekiel 28:20–26; 34:17–31.

The formula for the restoration of Israel to the land that is most characteristic of Jeremiah is "restore the fortunes or captivity" (šabtî 'et šᵉbût). Twelve of its twenty-six occurrences in the whole canon are found in Jeremiah.[37] Ezekiel, on the other hand, usually casts his message in a three-member formula:[38]

1. "I will bring [*Hiphil* of *yāṣa*] you from the people."
2. "I will gather [*Piel* of *qābaṣ*] you from the lands."
3. "I will bring [*Hiphil* of *bô'*] you into the land of Israel."

In one of the most striking passages in the prophets, Yahweh pledges that his promise to restore Israel's fortunes (Jer. 33:26) will be as dependable and as certain as His covenant with day and night (Jer. 33:20, 25).

Whereas the sheer multiplicity of texts from almost every one of the prophets is staggering, a few evangelicals insist that this pledge to restore Israel to their land was fulfilled when Zerubbabel, Ezra, and Nehemiah led their respective returns from the Babylonian Exile. But a strong word of protest must be registered from a significant and increasing number of evangelicals. That protest can be simply put this way: If the postexilic returns to the land fulfilled this promised restoration predicted by the prophets, why then did Zechariah in 518 B.C. continue to announce a still future return (Zech. 10:8–12) in words that were peppered with the phrases and formulae of such prophecies as Isaiah 11:11 and Jeremiah 50:19?

No, such a return of the land to the nation Israel could only come from a literal worldwide assemblage of Jews from "the four corners of the earth" (Isa. 11:12). The God who had promised to bring spiritual and immaterial blessings would also fulfill the material, secular, and political blessings as well to demonstrate that He was indeed God of gods and Lord of the whole earth and all that was in it.

The question as to whether the return follows a national spiritual awakening and turning to the Lord or vice versa is difficult. Sometimes the prophets seem to favor the first, as in Deuteronomy 30, and sometimes it would appear the return precedes any general repentance as in Ezekiel 36:1—37:14 and perhaps in Isaiah 11. But there can be no question about a future return in any of the prophets.

REST IN HEBREWS 3:7—4:13

The synthesis of this study lies in the concluding word of divine revelation concerning the rest of God located in Hebrews 3:7—4:13.

---

37. See E. Marten's discussion of the meaning of this term, pp. 172–96. For scriptural examples see Jeremiah 29:14; 30:3; 32:44.
38. E. Marten, pp. 164–72. For examples see Ezekiel 11:17; 20:41–42; 36:24; 37:21.

The scope of this subject is now almost breathtaking, for as Patrick Fairbairn observed,

> Not only does he [the writer to the Hebrews] thus connect believers under the Gospel with believers under the law in respect to the promised rest, but the promise itself he connects with the very commencement of the world's history—with that rest of God which He is said to have taken, when He ceased from all His works.[39]

There is, however, the prior question of the writer of Hebrews' hermeneutical approach. Is he guilty of a forced exegesis in which he is merely accommodating the old threats and promises formerly addressed to Israel for Christian readers? Is this piece of text in Hebrews a sample of the writer's fanciful misapplication of OT texts for Christian ears and eyes? Or has he just plain allegorized the Canaan rest into some spiritual dimension or into a symbol of heaven?

Each of these charges fails to sustain its case in light of the OT context of Psalm 95, the OT usage of "rest," and the total message of Hebrews. Any one of the above suggested exegetical moves would have destroyed his message totally. This promise which was left to us concerning the divine rest (Heb. 4:1) is part of the promise that he argues is immutable (Heb. 6.7) and better than those of the Sinaitic Covenant (Heb. 8:6).[40] Indeed, he is still looking forward to receiving the fulfillment of the promise of the eternal inheritance (Heb. 9:15) made to Abraham.

If that inheritance was to be the firm possession of the land as Hebrews 11:9 most assuredly asserts, then the joint-heirs of this promise with Abraham are not only Isaac and Jacob, but all who have received the same promise with him (Heb. 11:9; Gal. 4:28; 3:29; Matt. 5:5).[41] Therefore, the writer has no more intention of severing the physical and spiritual aspects of this rest than he has of isolating the promise of the geographical land of Canaan from the spiritual and material aspects of the kingdom of God. Both are germane to his argument.

---

39. Patrick Fairbairn, *The Typology of Scripture* (New York and London, 1900), Appendix E: "The Relation of Canaan to the State of Final Rest," p. 418.
40. Cf. Kaiser, "New Covenant," XV, 11–23. Also see E. W. Hengstenberg, "The New Covenant," *Classical Evangelical Essays in Old Testament Interpretation*, ed. Walter C. Kaiser, Jr. (Grand Rapids, 1972), pp. 237–51.
41. Cf. Werner Foerster, "κληρονόμος," *TDNT*, ed. Gerhard Kittel, trans. Geoffrey W. Bromiley III (Grand Rapids, 1966), pp. 781–85 for some thought-provoking comments.

The number of divine rests. It is common to observe in some commentaries[42] on this passage that there are three or four rests mentioned in Hebrews 3:7—4:11. The list generally highlights three or four of the following:

1. The divine rest (4:1-3, 10-11) or rest of faith
2. The creation rest (4:4)
3. The Sabbath rest (4:4, 9) or the rest that remains (6-9)
4. The Canaan rest (4:8)
5. The redemptive rest (4:10)
6. The eternal rest (4:9)

While it is true that the writer does use the noun *katapausis* in 3:11, 18; 4:1, 3 (*bis*), 5, 10, 11, and the verb *katapauomai* in 4:4, 8 along with the unique appearance of *sabbatismos*[43] in 4:10 to describe this rest, there is every indication that he conceives of a single rest from God. Indeed, there may be aspects of this divine rest that are more obvious at one period than another, but it would be unfair to the writer's point to subdivide this rest. In fact, everyone is startled at first when he suddenly introduces the "sabbath rest" into his argument. But even here he directly connects it with the "rest" under discussion.

It is not that the Sabbath is a type of the eschaton or of heaven, but it was the commencement of the divine rest that the Creator entered into after his six days of creative work. He had intended that man should also share this Sabbath with Him, but then came the Fall. Now the way back to this Sabbath rest is made available in promise form and finally in the actual inheritance of all that was promised. Therefore, the rest is distinctively God's single rest.

The present offer of the divine rest. Modern man can share in the ancient word made to Israel, for the promise "being left" (4:1) "remains for some to enter it" (4:6). Put another way, the "sabbath rest" "remains" (4:9), so "let's labor to enter that rest" (4:11). Four times the text emphasizes that this offer is still current and unfulfilled.

The way all men, past and present, can enter in is by believing the promise also called the "gospel" in 4:2. The text explicitly notes that this "good news" was preached in the wilderness even as it is preached to us, but because they did not exercise "faith" in that announced word of promise, they never entered this rest (4:2).

42. Cf. H. Orton Wiley, *The Epistle to Hebrews* (Kansas City, Mo, 1959), pp. 140-44; Edgar Ainslie, *Christ the Anchor* (Orange, Calif.: n.d.), p. 83; Walter Wright, *Hebrews* (Chicago, 1952), pp. 42-51; Clarence S. Roddy, *The Epistle to the Hebrews* (Grand Rapids, 1962), pp. 46-48.
43. See F. F. Bruce, *The Epistle to the Hebrews* (Grand Rapids, 1964), p. 72, n.13, for earliest attested extrabiblical occurrences of this word.

However, believers can and do enter that rest. They have believed
and obeyed that promise (4:3, 7; cf. on "believe" and "obey" John 3:36).

The nature of the divine rest. This special rest God called "my rest"
is an important aspect of the emerging promise theme (*epangelias*,
4:1) in both Testaments. Because Paul is bold to equate this promise
with the gospel, especially the phrase "In thy seed all the nations of
the earth shall be blessed" (Gal. 3:8), it is no wonder that our writer is
also bold to proclaim that the wilderness generation also had the
same basic gospel proclaimed to them (4:2; cf. 3:17 for the antecedent
of "as well as unto them"). Thus, the correlation of some aspects of
"my rest," promise, and gospel are explicit.

Added to this base is another correlation: the rest into which God
entered at the close of creation is linked with the rest into which all
creatures must enter before they can be perfected. But again, the
entrance to this rest is gained once again by faith, thereby making
the same point made in the promise, gospel, rest correlation made
above.

Another question still insists on projecting itself into our thoughts,
and it is the one that Franz Delitzsch posed and then answered.

> But it may be asked, although the elder generation that came out of
> Egypt perished in the wilderness, did not the younger generation, under
> Joshua, actually enter into the promised rest? To this question the
> author has now to reply; for it is a mistake to maintain, as most
> commentators do, that he at once identifies the entrance into God's rest
> promised by Moses, with that which is the true counterpart of the
> divine Sabbath after the works of creation. The entrance into rest
> which Moses promised was (as is expressed in a hundred passages, and
> as our author himself well knew) simply the taking possession of the
> land of Canaan. *But things combined in the promise were disjoined in
> the fulfilment. It became manifest that the taking possession of Canaan
> did not cover the whole extent of the promise and did not exhaust it.*[44]
> (Italics added)

Therefore there was more to that rest than simply occupying the
land of Canaan. It was that, indeed; but it was also combined with the
whole extent of the spiritual aspects of the promise.

One can hardly do better than to view this "rest of God" in a way
that involves a corporate solidarity of the whole rest with all its parts
or as a collective single program which purposely embraces several
related aspects realized in marked and progressive *stages.* From the
initial divine rest inaugurated at creation to its final realization once

44. Franz Delitzsch, *Commentary on the Epistle to the Hebrews,* trans. Thomas L.
Kingsbury (Edinburgh, 1886), 1:195.

again in that millennial reign of the world's new sabbath with the intervening periods of proleptical entrance by faith and the momentary inheritance of Canaan by Israel, it is all one piece; a single divine rest with related aspects. This is the thesis championed by George N. H. Peters:

> The land of Canaan is called *"rest,"* and it is God's *"rest."* ... It is not typical of something else, for that would overthrow the covenant and its promises. ... After a res[urrection] from the dead, an entrance into this "rest" is to be obtained. Thus e.g. Ps. 116 has *"return unto thy rest, O my soul; for the Lord dealt bountifully with thee*. ... I will walk before the Lord in *the land of the living."* The identical "rest" promised is the one obtained after a res. The Jews thus understood the "rest" to denote the land, and the making of this rest glorious, etc., to mean that under the Messiah it would be renewed and beautified. Paul in writing to Jews[45] does not contradict, but positively confirms this idea of the future inheritance, for instead of calling this rest the third heaven (as many unwarrantedly add), he (Heb. 3 and 4) quotes Ps. 95, and designates the same "rest" the Psalmist does into which certain ones could not enter, but fell in the wilderness. He argues that through unbelief we too shall be cut off, but through faith in Christ, and by the power of Jesus, we too shall enter in *"His rest"* according to the promise. ... *The unity* of the Spirit and Divine Plan required, employs the reasoning *best calculated* to establish them in *the only true idea* of the inheritance promised to the Patriarchs and to all God's people.[46]

THE APOSTLE PAUL AND THE PROMISE OF THE LAND

Likewise for Paul, none of the previous promises have changed— not even the promise of the land. Because an overwhelming majority of evangelicals maintain that the Hebrew Bible has an authority equal to that of the OT, the permanency and directness of the promise of the land to Israel cannot be controvened by anything allegedly taught in the NT. Surely Uriel Tal[47] is very wide of mark for most evangelicals when he summarizes the view that the Hebrew Bible can be set aside now that the NT era has dawned. As he explained the matter, all geopolitical rights promised in the Old Covenant have been cancelled and

---

45. Peters will later refer to such works as Barnabas *Epistle* xv; Irenaeus *Adversus Haereses* v; Justin Martyr *Questions and Answers* 71; *Dialogue with Trypho;* Papias as seen in Eusebius *Ecclesiastical History* iii. 39; Tertullian *Adversus Marcionem* iii. 24.
46. Geo. N. H. Peters, *The Theocratic Kingdom* (New York and London, 1884), 2:441–42; see also pp. 448–60, 463, 467, 469, 470–71.
47. Uriel Tal, "Jewish Self Understanding and the Land and State of Israel," *Union Seminary Quarterly Review* 26 (1970):353–54.

the best that Israel can hope for now is to be a part of the new people of God, the church—but without nationality, land, or statehood.

But this evangelical cannot square such a view with his exegesis of either Old or New Covenant! Whereas there always has been a segment of evangelicals, found mainly in what we call covenant theology, who transferred somewhat arbitrarily and in a cavalier manner the geo-political aspects of the promise with Israel over to the church for their fulfillment, even this segment of evangelicals has begun to show some signs of a willingness to take another hard look at the text. Hendrikus Berkhof found the very events of history itself forcing him back to a more exact exegesis of the texts dealing with Israel and the land. He concluded that

> With the surprising geographical and political fact of the establishment of the state of Israel, the moment has come for us to begin to watch for political and geographical elements in God's activities, which we have not wanted to do in our Western dualism, docetism, and spiritualism.[48]

But this was not a novel statement. At the turn of the century Willis J. Beecher in the Stone Lectures at Princeton Seminary chided:

> But if the Christian interpreter persists in excluding the ethnical Israel from his conception of the fulfillment, or in regarding Israel's part in the matter as merely preparatory and not eternal, then he comes into conflict with the plain witness of both Testaments. His interpretation is even less consistent with the text than is the exclusive Jewish conception. Rightly interpreted, the biblical statements include in the fulfillment both Israel the race, with whom the covenant is eternal and also the personal Christ and his mission, with the whole spiritual Israel of the redeemed in all ages.[49]

The largest piece of teaching text in the NT is Romans 9–11, especially 11:11–36.[50] For Paul, Israel's restoration to the favor and blessing of God must come in "full number" or RSV "full inclusion" (*plērōma*, Rom. 11:12; cf. v. 25, *plērōma tōn ethnōn*). Thus, Israel is and remains God's link to her own future as well as the link to the future of the nations. For if their temporary loss of land and failures has fallen out to the spiritual advantage of the world and their

48. Hendrikus Berkhof, trans. Lambertus Buurman, *Christ the Meaning of History* (Richmond: John Knox, 1966), p. 153.
49. Willis J. Beecher, *The Prophets and the Promise* (Grand Rapids: Baker, 1975, reprint, 1905 Crowell edition), p. 383.
50. See H. Berkhof, *Meaning*, pp. 141–46; Also Bruce Corley, "The Jews, the Future, and God: Romans 9–11," *Southwestern Journal of Theology* 19 (1976):42–56.

reconciliation to God, what will their acceptance signal "but life from the dead"? (Rom. 11:11–15).

"And so all Israel will be saved" (Rom. 11:26) in accordance with the predictions of Isaiah 59:20–21 and 27:9. The "and so" (*kai houtōs*) probably points back to verse 25 and the "mystery" of the temporary failure of Israel until the full number of the Gentiles comes in (cf. Luke 21:24). Then, in that future moment, "all Israel will be saved" (*pas Israēl sōthēsetai*). This is not a matter of individual salvation, or worse still, a matter of converting Jews to a Gentile brand of religiosity, but it is a matter of God's activity in history when the nation shall once again experience, as days of blessing in the past, the blessing and joy of God spiritually, materially, geographically, and politically.

The main lines of Paul's argument in Romans 9–11 are clear and in complete agreement with the promise of the land to the nation of Israel in the Hebrew Bible. Therefore, we conclude that evangelicals ought to avoid any subtle temptation to detract or minimize the full force of this blunt witness to God's everlasting work on behalf of Israel. For herein lies one of the greatest philosophies of history ever produced: Israel is God's watermark on secular history that simultaneously demonstrates that: (1) he can complete in time and space what he promised to do; and (2) he, the owner and current ruler of all nations, geography, and magistrates, will deal severely with those nations that mock, deride, parcel up, and attack Israel (e.g., Joel 3:1–5). Those that attempt to do so either in the name of the church or the name of political and economic expediency will answer to the God of Israel.

Yes, Israel is the "navel"[51] of the earth (Ezek. 38:12; cf. also 5:5) in more ways than one. The mark of God's new measure of grace, not only to Israel as a nation, but also to all the nations and Gentiles at large will be Israel's return to the land.

CONCLUSION

The rest of God, then, is distinctively His own rest that He offers to share first with Israel and then through them with all the sons of men who will also enter into it by faith. While there were antecedent aspects of that final rest to come, chiefly in the divine rest provided

---

51. But see the brilliant essay by Shemaryahu Talmon, ed. Arthur L. Merrill and Thomas W. Overholt, "The 'Navel of the Earth' and the Comparative Method," *Scripture in History and Theology: Essays in Honor of J. Coert Rylaarsdam* (Pittsburgh: Pickwick, 1977), pp. 243–68. He concluded that *ṭabbûr hāʾāreṣ* does not mean a mountain peak that serves as the center of all the surrounding landscape, but it is a plateau, a level plain nestled on a mountain. The LXX *omphalos*, "navel," is unwarranted when judged by inner biblical and contextual considerations.

by the inheritance of the land of Canaan; because it was not accompanied by the inward response of faith to the whole promise of God, of which this rest was just a part, the land of Canaan still awaits Israel and the people of God. The rest of God, lost in the Fall, again rejected by the older wilderness generation, and subsequently, by their erring children is still future to us in our day.

The dead will enter into its full enjoyment after their resurrection from the dead (Ps. 116:7), therefore, it is not to be identified with heaven. Rather it is fixed by Isaiah 11:10 as being "in that day" when "the Lord will extend his hand a second time to recover the remnant of his people" (Isa. 11:11). In that eschatological setting, "his rest" (not "dwellings" as in RSV) shall be glorious. Then the Lord shall choose Jerusalem as His dwelling place, and this new David will say, "This is my resting place for ever" (Ps. 132:14).

9

Including the Gentiles
in the Plan of God

Amos 9:9–15

It is virtually impossible to find a more appropriate set of canonical texts to test such a vast array of burning questions now posed in the whole curriculum of divinity than the two selected for discussion in this chapter. The areas of debate are familiar by now: What is the relationship of the OT to the NT? What exegetical method(s) does (do) the NT quotations of the OT employ, especially in argumentation that seeks OT support? What are the elements of continuity and/or discontinuity between Israel and the church—or, to put it another way: Who are the people of God and what is the kingdom of God? Did the prophets envisage the church or even the salvation of Gentiles during the church age in their writings? Is there a single master plan or divine program involving eschatological completion for both Testaments?

INTRODUCTION

"No small dissension" on these issues still remains within the body of Christ long after some of the same questions were tackled by the Jerusalem council. The only difference is that the debate now centers around one thing that apparently was especially clear in that day—namely, the significance and meaning of the OT quotation used by James to resolve the issue under debate. But what was it in that passage that settled the controversy? Did James claim that the mission to the Gentiles, dare we even say to the Christian church, was part of the divine revelation to Amos—in any form whatever? And did James thereby also indicate that a fulfillment of Amos's prophecy had come in the day of the apostles?

AREAS OF TENSION

Erich Sauer succinctly summarized the principal differences in the interpretation of the Amos and Acts passages. It was his judgment that whenever the subject of the Davidic kingship of Messiah's kingdom is raised, especially as it relates to the Gentiles, three areas of tension emerge: (1) the *time* of the kingdom's commencement (whether it was at the ascension and Pentecost, or at the future epiphany and parousia); (2) the *form* of this rule (whether it was solely inward and spiritual, or external, visible and historical-political); and (3) the *extent* of this kingdom (whether it was over a spiritual body such as the Christian church, or a political body such as national Israel and other lands and peoples).[1] The vested interests in these questions and their answers are well known.

THE SIGNIFICANCE OF ACTS 15:13–18

The *Scofield Reference Bible*, for example, noted that "dispensationally, this [Acts 15:13–18] is the most important passage in the N.T." and "the verses which follow in Amos describe the final regathering of Israel, which the other prophets invariably connect with the fulfillment of the Davidic Covenant."[2] O. T. Allis, however, affirmed "that James declares expressly that Peter's experience at Caesarea, which he speaks of as God's visiting 'the Gentiles to take out of them a people for his name,' was in accord with the burden of prophecy as a whole, and quotes freely from Amos in proof of it."[3] Which is correct? Must we choose between a solely nationalistic and a solely spiritual interpretation? Are these the only options available?

For our part, each of Sauer's three questions on the *time, form,* and *extent* of the kingdom of Messiah already have had a long history of biblical revelation that antedated the time of James and Amos. In fact, the presence of those features can be noted in the biblical text prior to the blessing of David; yet each is part of that theology that "informs" the Amos text, and thus they are part of the background of our

1. E. Sauer, *From Eternity to Eternity* (Grand Rapids: Eerdmans, 1954), p. 185ff.
2. *Scofield Reference Bible*, p. 1343. On p. 1169, however, Scofield does not include it, saying that "the pivotal chapters, taking prophecy as a whole, are Deut. xxviii, xxix, xxx; Psa. ii; Dan. ii, vii."
3. O. T. Allis, *Prophecy and the Church* (Philadelphia: Presbyterian and Reformed, 1945), p. 147.

concern here. Such an "informing theology"[4] can be seen from both the subject matter considered and especially from the specialized vocabulary that was reiterated in Amos 9:11–12. The former may be quickly summarized in accordance with the historical canons of biblical theology as they develop from the prepatriarchal era to Davidic times.

BIBLICAL THEOLOGY

Let is be observed from the start that Genesis 1–11 can hardly be put down as a nationalist tract; indeed, the scope of the seventy nations listed in Genesis 10, when taken with the promise of Genesis 12:3 that in Abraham's seed "all the nations of the earth [viz., those just listed in Genesis 10] shall be blessed," constitutes the original missionary mandate itself. The redemptive plan of God from the beginning, then, was to provide a salvation as universal in scope as was the number of the families on the earth. Accordingly, the *object and content* of the prepatriarchal person's faith was the same as that of the post-Abrahamic or Davidic promise era: It was the man ("seed") of promise and his work (e.g., a "dwelling," a "great name," a "land," a "blessing") as witnessed by Genesis 3:15; 9:27; 12:1–3. And part of that *content* Paul equated with the "gospel"—the same[5] gospel Paul preached to the Gentiles: "In you shall all the nations be blessed" (Gal. 3:8); or the Mosaic ("!") word of Deuteronomy 30:10–14, "the word of faith which we preach" (Rom. 10:6–8); or the "gospel of God which he promised beforehand through his prophets in the holy Scriptures" (Rom. 1:1–6). Likewise, Hebrews 3:17—4:2 clearly equates the "gospel" that "came to *us*" (= believers of the first century and hence ourselves as well) as the *same* one that came to those unbelieving Jews of the forty years of wanderings, "whose carcasses fell in the wilderness." What could be clearer?

Consequently, we conclude that the *extent* of that kingdom had already in its earliest design embraced the steady absorption of Gentiles as well as Jews. Furthermore, there were numerous illustrations of this historical inclusion of the Gentiles. Witness the presence of Melchizedek, Jethro, Zipporah, Balaam, Rahab, Ruth, and possibly the Gibeonites, the Rechabites, the Ninevites, and the entire books

4. See for a provisional definition my article "The Present Status of OT Studies," *JETS* 18 (1975):69–79, esp. pp. 73–74.
5. C. Welch, *Dispensational Truth* (London: n.d.), p. 36 says, "Not only are there observable in Scripture various dispensations and purposes, but there are also in relation to these varying administrations *varying Gospels*. . . . There is a message regarding the earth and the future blessings of the earth; this is the gospel of the kingdom. There is a message of free salvation . . . ; this is the gospel of grace. . . . Let us not join together that which God has kept distinct" (italics added).

(e.g., Obadiah, Jonah, Nahum), or sections of books (e.g., prophecies to the nations in Isa. 13–23, Jer. 45–51, Ezek. 25–32, Amos 1–2), addressed to Gentiles. Moreover, many of the specific evangelistic appeals in the OT (e.g., those given through the plagues of Egypt) were so "that the Egyptians (or Pharaoh) might believe (or know) that I am the LORD" (Ex. 7:5; 8:10, 19, 20; 9:16, 20, 30; 14:4, 18).

Nevertheless even if such *content* and *extent* be agreed upon, there still remains the problem of matching such inclusions and extensions with the messianic kingdom promised to David. What was or will be the *time* of its realization? What *form* will this rule take? And did the prophets predict the church in any shape or form? Or, was this Gentile body of believers a parenthesis and gap in the plan of God deliberately left in mystery form, until the political rule of God was rejected (Matt. 13) and the spiritual kingdom was unveiled? And did God predict a future for Israel that coincided with his spiritual kingdom in any shape or form? Or, have the Israelites' promises been made over to a new Israel, the church, by some hermeneutical method such as spiritualizing?

EPANGELICAL THEOLOGY

Recently, this writer has affirmed that a rapprochement can be had between the heretofore opposite positions assumed by dispensationalists and covenantal theologians. Such a solution he calls "promise theology" or "epangelicalism." Its unifying principle is not soteriological (covenant theology) or doxological (recent dispensational theology);[6] it is, rather, the single, inclusive, everlasting plan of God announced and continuously expanded. It is what the NT writers refer to as "the promise" (hence the *epangel*), but what the OT refers to under a constellation of terms such as "blessing," "oath," and "word"[7] and/or a set of formulas such as the ubiquitous tripartite formula: "I will be your God, you shall be my people, and I will dwell in the midst of you."[8] Such a center for OT and NT theology, we alleged, is supplied inductively from the text; it is not a grid laid over the Testaments. Its growth and development (even as the perfect Christ was "made perfect") is overtly supplemented by the historic progress of revelation that consciously connects each new addition to the existing core ideas by means of explicit citation and allusion to those earlier phrases, clauses, and words that began to assume a technical status in each new supplement to the doctrine. This promise

---

6. C. Ryrie, *Dispensationalism Today* (Chicago: Moody, 1965), p. 102.
7. See W. C. Kaiser, Jr., "The Old Promise and the New Covenant: Jeremiah 31:31–34," *JETS* 15 (1972):12, nn.3–8.
8. Ibid., n.10.

spoke of one people—a "people of God," a "people for his possession." It also spoke of a single purpose—the "blessing" of God for the "kingdom of God." The "seed" of God was always collective, never plural; yet it embraced a physical and spiritual seed for Abraham under the one seed, Christ Himself. Likewise, its program was one— a veritable "charter for humanity" (*tôrat hā ādām*, 2 Sam. 7:19*b* = 1 Chron. 17:17).[9] It is our earnest contention that what David was given in his kingship and kingdom was nothing less than an updated and supplemented Edenic and Abrahamic promise which at once embraced "all the nations of the earth" (i.e., "humanity") if they would but believe in that Man of promise, the "seed." God's intention was to bless the whole earth through David. Nonetheless, He would not thereby jettison His promises to Israel as a nation. His single program was more complex and comprehensive than our either/or mentality.

But again the questions persist: When? And in what form? And did such a "charter" incorporate the believing church? Did the prophets ever speak to this question?

Evidently, James thought they had! His appeal for support on this point to Amos 9:11 promptly settled the Jerusalem council debate! Could it do the same to effect a similar peace in the latter part of the twentieth century?

It is truly amazing how little hard exegetical and contextual work has been done on these key passages. Even the journal literature on these texts of Amos 9 and Acts 15 is extremely rare. Accordingly, it must first be noted that the context of Amos had just predicted a separation of the evil from the good in the *nation* of Israel and the destruction of the wicked (Amos 9:8–9). The survivors and their descendants would one day experience a divine restoration of the dilapidated condition of the grand old house (= dynasty) of David. So extensive would this rebuilding be that it would affect all nations and all nature as well! But the text must be examined more minutely.

KEY EXEGETICAL ISSUES IN AMOS 9:11-12

THE FALLEN HUT OF DAVID

The subject of Amos 9:11, the present condition of David's *sukkâ*, the "booth" or "hut," is not to be equated with the Mosaic "tabernacle," the *miškān*, or the messianic "Branch," the *sôkâ*;[10] rather, it normally signifies the hastily constructed shelters made of branches for the

9. See the arguments of this writer in J. H. Skilton, ed., "The Blessing of David: The Charter for Humanity," in *The Law and the Prophets: OT Studies Prepared in Honor of O. T. Allis* (Philadelphia: Presbyterian and Reformed, 1974), pp. 310–18.
10. L. H. Silberman, "A Note on 4Q Florilegium," *JBL* 78 (1959):158–59.

"feast of tabernacles" (Lev. 23:40, 42; Deut. 16:13). Here, however, it stands for the dynasty of David, which is normally styled "the house of David" (2 Sam. 7:5, 11). But this dynasty with all its glorious promises of blessing will shortly be in a collapsed state with "breaches" and "ruins" in it.[11] The Hebrew active participle stresses either its *present* state ("falling") or its *impending* state ("about to fall"). Thus, the house of David would suffer, but God promises to raise it from its dilapidated condition, which raising up is described in the three following clauses.

THE INTERCHANGE OF SUFFIXES

The suffixes on three words in verse 11 are of special interest for the theology of the passage. If the Masoretic text is correct (and there is no reason to suspect it other than modern harmonistic motivations to level out the text), then the suffixes of the phrase "breaches *thereof*" (feminine plural), "*his* ruins" (masculine singular), and "rebuilt *it*" (feminine singular) take on major significance for the interpretation of this passage.

Keil is certain that "the plural suffix ('breaches *thereof*,' *pirṣêhen*) can only be explained from the fact that *sukkāh* actually refers to the kingdom of God, which was divided into two kingdoms ('these kingdoms,' ch. vi. 2)."[12] God would "wall up their rents." Thus, even before Ezekiel 37:15–28 pictured the unification of the ten northern tribes with the two southern ones, Amos had anticipated him in the eighth century. Clearly, the writer's intention had a distinctly nationalistic element as its referent.

The masculine singular suffix ("his ruins," *hărisôtāyw*) must refer to none other than David himself and not to the "hut" (which is feminine). Consequently, under that new-coming-David (= Christ) the destroyed house would rise from the ashes of "destruction."[13] But when? And how? And for whom? One thing was certain: What had affected the nation had also for the moment affected the Davidic person himself.

Only after those two acts of reconstruction are noticed does the third clause about "rebuilding it" (*bᵉnîtîha*) appear. It may well be, as Keil contends, that *bānâ* here means "to finish building, to carry on,

---

11. E. Henderson, *The Book of the Twelve Minor Prophets* (Boston: 1960), pp. 179–80 notes that "when the prosperity of that family is spoken of, the more dignified phrase *bêt Davîd*, 'the house of David,' is employed. See II Sam. iii.1; I Kings xi.38; Is. vii.2, 13. *'ōhel Davîd*, 'the tent, or tabernacle, of David,' Is. xvi.5 would seem to express an intermediate state of things."
12. C. F. Keil, *Biblical Commentary on the Old Testament: Minor Prophets* (Grand Rapids: Eerdmans, 1954), 1:330.
13. For this meaning of *hărîsâ*, cf. Isaiah 49:19.

enlarge, and beautify the building."[14] Naturally, the feminine suffix refers to the "fallen hut." But it is most important to notice also the phrase that completes this clause: "as it was in days of old." Here is one of the keys to the passage, for it points back to the promise of 2 Samuel 7:11, 12, 16 where God had promised that he would raise up David's seed after him and give him a throne and a dynasty that would endure forever. Accordingly, we note that the resurrecting of the dilapidated Davidic fortunes would involve a *kingdom*, a *seed*, and a *dynasty*. Likewise, the subject of the phrase in verse 12, "in order that *they* might inherit the remnant," is clearly the people. Therefore, it is decisively taught here: The kingdom, David, David's house (dynasty), the people, and the remnant are indissolubly linked together; one stands and falls with the other.[15] But who were the remnant these people would possess? And how was the possession to be accomplished?

EDOM AND MANKIND

For many, verse 12 appears even more problematical than verse 11—especially with its "offensive" reference to "the remnant of Edom." However, the reference is not to be understood in a negative or retaliatory sense—that is, as a punishment to Edom for one or more of its rivalries with Israel. On the contrary, "Edom" along with the other nations would be brought under that reign of the Davidic King who is to come—the Messiah. This "remnant" must also share in the covenant promise to David.

It was Gerhard Hasel[16] who pointed out that Amos employed the "remnant" theme in a threefold usage: (1) "to refute the popular remnant expectation which claimed all of Israel as the remnant" [Amos 3:12; 4:1–3; 5:3; 6:9–10; 9:1–4, all of which were bleak descriptions of doom with little hope for Israel]; (2) "to show there will indeed be a remnant *from* Israel" [Amos 5:4–6, 15, an eschatological sense]; and (3) "to include also the 'remnant of Edom' among and with the neighboring nations as a recipient of the outstanding promise of the Davidic tradition" [Amos 9:12].

Edom alone is singled out because of her marked hostility toward the people of God. Their role was similar to that of the Amalekites, the earliest nation to represent the kingdom of men (Ex. 17:8ff.; Deut.

14. Keil, *Commentary*, p. 330.
15. E. W. Hengstenberg, *Christology of the Old Testament* (Grand Rapids: Kregel, 1970), p. 549, n.3.
16. G. Hasel, *The Remnant* (Berrien Springs: Andrews U., 1972), pp. 393–94.

25:17–19), which stood violently against the kingdom of God.[17] More-over, Edom's representative role[18] is further stressed by the epexeget-ical note in verse 12, "and/even all the nations/Gentiles who are called by my name." Again, the point is not about David's or Israel's military subjugation of Edom or the Gentiles; rather, it is about their spiritual incorporation into the restored kingdom of David that is in view in Amos 9:12. Indeed, had not the promise of God to Abraham and David included a mediated "blessing" to all the Gentiles?

The verb "to take possession of" was likewise specially chosen. Balaam's prophecy in Numbers 24:17–18 had predicted that a "star" and "scepter" would rise in Israel "to take possession of Edom ... while Israel did valiantly." This "One from Jacob would exercise dominion" over all. Can serious students of Scripture fail to observe the obvious messianic reference to our Lord's first ("star") and second ("scepter" and "rule") coming? And are not the representatives of the kingdom of men present? Moab, Sheth, Edom, Amalek, and Asshur? Yet, does not Amos now deliberately add by divine revelation that God will by divine plan "take possession" of a "remnant" from all the nations—including even bitter Edom? And will they not be owned by Yahweh because they will "be called by [His] name"?

CALLED BY THE NAME OF THE LORD

This phrase,[19] no doubt, was the trigger thought that brought to the mind of James the words of Amos. He had just commented: "Symeon has related how God first visited the Gentiles to take out of them a people for his name" (Acts 15:14). This is what the prophets also agreed with, continued James, as he cited Amos 9:11–12 with the identical concept: "the Gentiles that are called by my name."

The usage of this phrase in the OT always placed each of the objects so designated under divine ownership. What God or man named, they owned, and protected,[20] whether cities (2 Sam. 12:28; Jer. 25:29; Dan. 9:18, 19), the Temple (1 Kings 8:43; Jer. 7:10, 11, 14, 30; 32:34; 34:15), or men and women (Isa. 4:1; Jer. 14:9; 15:16; 2 Chron. 7:14). When Israel walked by faith, Moses promised: "All peoples of the earth shall see that you are called by the name of the Lord" (Deut. 28:10). This constituted Israel as a "holy people of the Lord," for where the Lord

17. Note the pivotal text of Exodus 15:18: "The Lord will reign for ever and ever," with the arrangement of the two responses: (1) murmuring Israelites versus (2) fighting (Amalek) and believing (Jethro) Gentiles!
18. See the fine discussion and bibliography in M. H. Woudstra, "Edom and Israel in Ezekiel," *Calvin Theological Journal* (1968):21–35.
19. J. Morgenstern, "The Rest of the Nations," *JSS* 11 (1957):225–31.
20. See the full study by W. C. Kaiser, Jr., "Name," *Zondervan Pictorial Encyclopedia of the Bible*, ed. M. C. Tenney (Grand Rapids: Zondervan, 1975), 4:360–70.

placed his name, there was he "in the midst of [them]" (Jer. 14:9). But when they refused to believe, they were "like those who [were] not called by thy name" (Isa. 63:19). Hengstenberg observed, "One need only consider the inferior use of the phrase [in] Gen. 48:6 where [the phrase] 'over the name of their brothers shall they be called in mine inheritance' [was] the same as 'they shall be incorporated with their brothers, no one shall have an existence separate from the rest.'"[21] Consequently, the expression was, as Keil observed, practically the same as Joel 2:32 (Heb., 3:5): "all who call upon the name of the LORD." In fact, that was the precise reference used by Peter on the Day of Pentecost to inaugurate the era of the Spirit, the new covenant and the church. Therefore, we conclude that this phrase is the most crucial one in the whole passage so far. It definitely meant to teach that Gentiles will be included in some future reign of God. The only question remaining was when? Must that inclusion wait until the restoration of nature and the nation had taken place?

KEY EXEGETICAL ISSUES IN ACTS

But our concerns must now probe more deeply into the context of the parallel passage in Acts. Immediately we are asked: Was the NT in the habit of changing the literal meaning of these prophecies involving Israel into something spiritual and *more* than was intended by the original prophet's thought? Or, did the NT writers preserve the literal references to Israel without finding a single prediction of the church in the OT? Was the church, then, a parenthesis in the plan of God as announced in the OT? Had all prophetic outlines of the future and divine *eschaton* skipped over her times? These issues are so serious that they have been a major factor in dividing equally devout biblical scholars into dispensational or covenantal schools of thought.[22]

THE TIME WORDS IN ACTS 15:15-16

Two fine dispensational writers, Willard M. Aldrich and Allan MacRae, have stressed the importance of the words "first" and "after

21. E. W. Hengstenberg, *Christology*, p. 550.
22. Obviously the issue here concerns only the identity of the "people of God"; only obliquely does it touch the question of the kingdom of God or program of God. Still, as both sides agree, it is a pivotal issue.

this" for the dispensational argument.²³ "God first (*prōton*) visited the Gentiles" (v. 14); "after this (*meta tauta*) [He] will return ... and ... rebuild the tent of David" (v. 16). Thus, the argument is that the visitation of the Gentiles came first, an event not explicitly noted by the prophets. A second visitation will come to a regathered national Israel when David's house is rebuilt, but the two events must not be confounded or united.

The problem with this analysis is that it must then be admitted that the OT citation had no direct bearing on the question at stake. Was the apostle, as Keil suggests, quoting from memory the introductory words which he inadvertently altered from *tē hēmera ekeinē anastēsō* ("in that day I will raise up") into *meta tauta anastrepsō kai anoikodomēsō* ("after these things I will return, and I will rebuild"), because the point he was making in the citation did not turn on this phrase but the one about "all nations [will be] called by my name"?²⁴ Perhaps *anastēso* was recollected as *anastrepsō*—or was it instead deliberately introduced by James to clarify his point that everything the prophet Amos was saying was to take place *after* Christ had returned to the earth a second time? However, if the latter was the case, why was *anastrepsō* chosen? This would be the only use of that word to denote the second coming of Christ in the NT.²⁵ Aldrich²⁶ does cite the "great lexicographer Thayer" as one who so applied the "I will return" to the personal return of Messiah rather than to any emphatic form of "I will build *again*." But will either of those alternatives fit here?

In our judgment, the meaning "again" appears unlikely because the Hebrew of Amos would have read *ʾāšûb* instead of the present *ʾāqîm*. Furthermore, the repeated Greek prefix *ana* on *anoikodomēsō*, "I will rebuild," and *anorthōsō*, "I will raise up again," easily made the "again"

23. W. M. Aldrich, "The Interpretation of Acts 15:13–18," *Bibliotheca Sacra* 111 (1954):317–23, esp. 320ff.; A. MacRae, "The Scientific Approach to the OT," *Bibliotheca Sacra* 110 (1953):309–20, esp. 311ff. MacRae, however, appears to have vacillated in his opinion, for on p. 319 he argues that James used "after these things" to refer to the Amos context! (This article was reprinted in *Truth for Today* [Chicago: Moody, 1963]). After I had finished this chapter, I also noticed two additional adherents of this view: C. Zimmerman, "To This Agree the Words of the Prophets," *Grace Journal* 4 (1963):28–40; and the most definitive and careful work by J. E. Rosscup, *The Interpretation of Acts* 15:13–18 (Th.D. dissertation, Dallas Theological Seminary, 1966).
24. Keil, *Commentary*, p. 334, n.1. This principle is in full accord with an orthodox view of inerrancy as has been observed since Calvin's day.
25. C. E. Hayward, "A Study in Acts XV. 16–18," *EvQ* 8 (1936):162–68; see p. 165. He argues that the LXX translators, knowing the Hebrew idiom, tried to reproduce it in the sense of "again" as in Genesis 26:18, etc., according to its transitive usage.
26. Aldrich, "Interpretation," p. 322. Allis, *op. cit.*, p. 313, n.10, argues that to "return and (do something)" is rendered "again" forty-nine times in the KJV; indeed, in Amos 9:9. Furthermore, even Darby attached no meaning to the phrase as did Scofield.

point apart from any borrowed semitism. Consequently, the reference is not to the second coming, nor is it a built-up phrase about a "rebuilding *again*" of David's house. Rather, verse 14, *kathōs prōton*, "how first God visited the Gentiles," is no doubt temporal with *kathōs* referring to an indirect question, as Robertson's larger grammar suggests. The "first" was an historical fact and unrelated to the return of Christ.

But verse 16 is a different story. *Meta tauta*, "after these things," probably has reference to the Amos context which James consciously included in his citation; both the Hebrew *and* and the LXX had clearly read "in that day" (i.e., in the messianic times), yet, James purposely departed from both![27] Why? The "things" James wanted to highlight were the predicted judgments that Amos had said were to fall on Israel, causing the outward and material collapse of the "house of David." Beginning with Amos 7, God had depicted in five visions one judgment after another that would visit Israel, climaxing in a smiting and destruction of the Temple itself (Amos 9:1ff.). There would be no escape, dig or hide wherever one might. Indeed, God would sift the house of Israel in the sieve of the nations (Amos 9:9) with the result that they would be dispersed and shaken, yet not a small kernel of the true remnant would fall to the ground; they would be preserved and delivered by the same Lord who shook the sieve. The same cannot be said for Israelite sinners, however, who claimed some type of magical exemption (Amos 9:10). Their doom was sure.

Now "after these things"—the destruction of the Temple, the fact of the Diaspora, and the end of Samaria—warned James, with an eye to the Amos context, God "would turn again" (*anastrepsō*) to reestablish the house of David. To obtain the dispensational view one must assume that the "first" of verse 14 signified the "first [era]" (a clear interpolation) while the second reference was given a sequential meaning: "After this [gospel dispensation]"[28] God would "come again"

---

27. It is only partially true that James's text is "exactly identical" with that of the Qumran text of 4Q Florilegium according to J. de Waard, *A Comparative Study of the OT Text in the Dead Sea Scrolls and in the NT* (Grand Rapids: Eerdmans, 1966), pp. 25–26, because the phrase "after these things I will return" does not appear in 4Q Flor or CD. Neither can this phrase be an allusion to Jeremiah 12:15 as Nestle's *Novum Testamentum Graece* suggests (*ad loc.*, in margine), since the only word common to both is *meta*. The *tauta* is missing in LXX of Jeremiah and *epistrepsō* is common only to the D text of Acts. Rosscup, *Interpretation*, p. 148, chides Aldrich and Zimmerman for making "after these things" so strategic in their interpretations, for *meta tauta*, Rosscup observes, is also used by LXX of Joel 2:28 to translate Masoretic text *'ahărêkēn*.
28. P. Mauro, "Building Again the Tabernacle of David," *Evangelical Quarterly* 9 (1937):398–413, esp. pp. 399–401. Rosscup, *Interpretation*, pp. 143–44: "By 'these things' he [Jesus] had reference to the 'things' of the total period of Jewish dispersion which Amos describes. He was not referring back particularly to the

and restore Israel. But on these grounds neither phrase is a literal, grammatical or natural interpretation of James. Dispensationalism has thereby yielded any hermeneutical edge it possessed by so arguing.

THE INTRODUCTORY FORMULA

James summarized Peter's testimony about the Gentile conversion of Cornelius by observing that "God had visited the Gentiles in order to take out (infinitive of purpose) of them a people for his name." The English hardly conveys the surprising connection of the words "to take from the *nations*" (*ethnōn*—the word used, when a distinction is made, for heathen or Gentiles) "a people" (*laos*, a term for chosen people).[29] Even that great premillennial interpreter, Bengel, saw the sharpness of putting it in this fashion. He said: "The converts from among the Gentiles were [regarded] no less than Israel [as] the people of God"; yes, a transformation from being "heathen" to being "people"!

"With this fact" (*kai toutō*, neuter form) just stated (= the conversion of Gentiles), the prophets (plural) "agree ... as it is written." MacRae and Aldrich strenuously object to the exegesis that Amos had predicted that God would visit the Gentiles to call out a people for his name.[30] For one thing, they claimed the formula appears only here in Acts.

Indeed, this is the one time an OT quotation is introduced in Acts in this manner. But then, as Aldrich unintentionally pointed out, there was no set formula for doing so in Acts: He cited a dozen different formulae.

But did the formula only indicate a "harmony of principle"[31] but with no direct bearing on the question from the OT? Or, alternatively, did it give only "the gist of OT prophecy on the subject ... [where James] is intentionally 'spiritualizing' and broadening Amos's prophecy"?[32] Which is correct, the dispensational or covenant hermeneutic?

Neither, we answer. Both solutions miss opposite parts of the single truth. It was "the words" of the prophets that "were written" and "were in conformity with the fact" (*toutō*) just summarized. God had

'things' of Acts 15:14 ... [this] is attractive in that it avoids the necessity of leaning too heavily upon certain inconclusive arguments involving the [words] 'first' and 'after' of Acts 15:14, 16.... The suggested connection between the 'first' and the 'after' is to some degree tenuous." But Rosscup makes the "things" of Amos 9:9–10 equal to the entire period of the Jewish dispersion!

29. See the informative discussion by G. Bertram, "People and Peoples in the LXX," *TDNT*, 2:364–69.
30. MacRae, "Scientific," p. 319; Aldrich, "Interpretation," pp. 319ff.
31. Aldrich's word, ibid.
32. Hayward, "Study," p. 163.

visited Gentiles, and Gentiles had become the "people" of God! The harmony was not an application of a principle, but an explicit argument naming "Gentiles" and carrying evidential force for Jews who were resisting the idea, but who knew and accepted the authority of the inscripturated word! Nor was this a "spiritualization" of either Israel or David which thereby preserved only the gist of the original thought. Such a view must adopt some form of *sensus plenior* hermeneutic wherein the prophets are alleged to have written better (= less) than they knew. But we urge a speedy consultation of Peter 1:10ff., where the prophets are represented as most assuredly knowing what they wrote, including: (1) the Messiah; (2) His death; (3) His glorious reign; (4) the sequential order of these two events; and (5) that they wrote not only for their day, but also for those of us in the church. 1 Peter 1:12 explicitly affirms, "unto whom it was revealed, that not for themselves, but unto us they did minister the things which are now reported unto you by them that have preached the gospel unto you."[33]

REBUILDING DAVID'S TENT WHICH HAS FALLEN

Obviously, then, God intended to receive Gentiles and set David's name over them; but what had that to do with David's fallen tent? And how does that solve the circumcision issue? Is the point merely that there is an analogy between the calling of Gentiles in the dispensation of the gospel with the gathering of Gentiles during the future dispensation of the kingdom? Or, must national Israel be transmuted into the value of spiritual Israel, the church, if any connection, is to be observed?

Again, our conclusion is: neither! The former solution reads into the words "first" and "after this/these" two *eras*. This method leans too heavily, at the start, on what is believed to be the teaching of the analogy of faith. It divides Gentiles from Jews because of prior theological commitments. Such commitments are not unwise *if* they originate in a prior exegesis and develop along with the course of the history of revelation; but where they are first discerned in the NT and then subsequently used as a tool to exegete or circumscribe an OT text, the risks are high. Literal, grammatical, historical exegesis has thereby suffered a defeat, even if it is at the hands of its friends!

The alternative is not inviting either. It also uses the NT analogy-of-faith method from systematics, but with a different conclusion that emphasizes the unity of the Testaments. This also is commendable so

---

33. See our lengthy argument on this point in "The Eschatological Hermeneutics of 'Epangelicalism': Promise Theology," *JETS* 13 (1970), esp. pp. 92–96.

long as it does not drop any of the distinctives garnered from solid exegesis along the way. But if everything is judged by a spiritual soteriology, then any nascent philosophy of history in the soteriological process might be jettisoned prematurely—which this writer believes is just what has happened to the concept of national Israel for most of traditional covenantal thought. Accordingly, Hendrikus Berkhof justifiably has complained that such a view only reflects our western doceticism and secular/sacred dichotomization of God's world, rather than the results of hard exegesis.[34]

The promised rebuilding of David's tent is a brief but direct reference to the total program of God announced to David in 2 Samuel 7. Its significance was grasped by David when he exclaimed with uncontainable joy, "And this [new addition to the promise doctrine] is the charter for all mankind, O Lord GOD."[35]

Such was the theology that "informed"[36] Amos's allusion to David's house. God's plan did include the nations and Gentiles at large in the rebuilt Davidic "house." Such also had been the program and intention of God all along since Abraham had received the word. Indeed, that was the principal thing: All mankind was to be blessed in Abraham and his seed (Gen. 12:3; 18:18; 22:17–18; 26:3–4; 28:13–14). Abram was specifically promised that he would be "father of a multitude of nations" (Gen. 17:5) when he was renamed Abraham. Beecher argued that "multitude" was an unlimited word, entirely different from "assembly of nations."[37]

But no era of prophetic activity stressed this aspect of the promise doctrine more than did the eighth-century preexilic prophets. Isaiah was the master when it came to seeing the "nations" connected with the ancient and emerging promise of God. Thirty-six times he linked the "nations" with the promise in the last twenty-seven chapters of his work. Characteristically, Isaiah 42:6 affirmed: "I have given you [the Servant, Israel] as a covenant to the people, a light to the nations" while David's "everlasting covenant" made him a "witness," "leader," and "commandment giver" "to all the peoples." Furthermore, to this new David who would yet come, it was said, "Behold, you shall call

---

34. H. Berkhof, *Christ the Meaning of History* (Richmond: Knox, 1966), pp. 136–53. See W. C. Kaiser, Jr., "Old Promise," p. 15, n.24.
35. See the full argument in W. C. Kaiser, Jr., "Blessing of David," pp. 298–318.
36. J. Bright's phrase from *The Authority of the Old Testament* (Nashville: Abingdon, 1967), pp. 143, 170. Such exegesis we call the "analogy of [antecedent] Scripture," see n.4 above.
37. W. J. Beecher, *The Prophets and the Promise* (Grand Rapids: Baker, 1975), p. 201 and n.1. He also argued that Genesis 17:6 is a specification subordinate to the broader statement of verse 5 as in the other five passages about Abraham's relation to the nations cited above. Nations will descend from him "but his being father of a multitude of nations is parallel with all the nations being blessed in him . . . ," ibid.

nations that you know not, and nations that knew you not shall run to you, because of the LORD your God, and of the Holy one of Israel, for he has glorified you" (Isa. 55:3–5). Thus the invitation was open: "Turn unto me and be saved, all the ends of the earth! For I am God, and there is no other. By myself I have sworn . . . : 'To me every knee shall bow, every tongue shall confess'" (Isa. 45:22). True, the nations would dramatically figure in God's final "day of vengeance" (Isa. 60:3, 5, 11, 12, 16) as well as in His current providential disposition of nations (Isa. 41:2), but nothing can take away the obvious linkage of the Abrahamic and Davidic blessing to the nations with these references to Isaiah that promise the harvest of the days of the church.

This missionary consciousness of the OT reached its climax in Isaiah. When the Messiah ("Servant") would come at the incarnation with God's approbation of him as the one "in whom my soul delights" (Isa. 42:1), he would bring forth mišpāṭ, "justice or true, right religion" (Isa. 42:1; cf. vv. 3, 4).[38] "Justice, judgment" may mean God's gracious and favorable[39] salvation. Davidson also notes that mišpāṭ is followed by lᵉ in only one other passage, Psalm 146:7, where Yahweh "gave a decision in favor of the imprisoned"—that is, a deliverance! Also note that Isaiah 51:4 linked God's "law," his "salvation," and his "light to the peoples."

Thus, God's servant was given as "a covenant to the people, a light to the nations" (Isa. 42:6; 49:6, 8). Certainly, Israel was to be restored and preserved, but God's salvation designedly gave the seed of the covenant as "light to the nations" so that God's "salvation might reach to the end of the earth." Indeed, Jesus came with "good news for the afflicted" (Isa. 61:1; 42:6; Luke 4:18), just as was predicted. We conclude that the inclusion of the Gentiles was part and parcel of God's single plan with Israel!

Likewise, Isaiah's contemporary, Amos, had briefly but comprehensively referred to the same prospect: nations being called or owned by the name of the Lord. This was to dramatically increase "in that day," a characteristic phrase used of the messianic era—that is, of both the first coming (e.g., of Heb. 1:1 and Acts 2:17) and the second coming.

Previously, whenever God had "glorified" Israel (Isa. 55:5) and accomplished a triumph in and for his people Israel—as he did, for example, at the Red Sea and in the transjordanian battles over Sihon and Og—there the missionary work commenced as it did for the

38. See the significant discussion of R. Davidson, "Universalism in Second Isaiah," *SJT* 16 (1963):166–85. W. Zimmerli remarks that "our whole interpretation of the Servant's task will turn on our understanding of these words" [Isa. 42:1].
39. Cf. J. van der Ploeg, "Šāpaṭ and mišpāṭ," in *OTS* 2 (1943):144ff., as cited by Davidson.

Canaanite Rahab, as she testified in Joshua 2:10–11. Now it would come like "light" bursting in on the Gentiles everywhere.

CONCLUSION

JAMES'S USE OF AMOS

Here, then, is the point of our argument: James used a plain, simple and straightforward hermeneutic when he appealed to Amos. His understanding of the term "tabernacle of David" was replete with all the revelation of God that antedated that eighth-century revelation. What had been promised to Abraham was made over to David with an enlarged scope of reference: it was a veritable "charter for all humanity"! As a dynasty, it symbolized God's rule and reign on into eternity.

However, the political and national aspects of that same promise could not be deleted from Amos's truth-intention. As the suffixes in Amos 9:11 indicate, the northern and southern kingdom, the Davidic person, the people of Israel, and the remnant of humanity at large were all encompassed in that rebuilding of the "tent of David," even though its outward fortunes would appear to sag in the immediate events of the eighth century.

THE SYSTEMS CONTRASTED

Epangelical theology, then, refuses to divorce any specific word of God (such as that of Amos) from the total but antecedent "promise" of God. Moreover, the hermeneutical principle used in these passages must be without a spiritualizing tendency that reassigns converted values of the OT secular or national word signs about Israel's future (a process leading to dualism and docetic views of history)[40] or unilinear types of "literal" exegesis that bifurcate unified items by divorcing these phrases and passages from the antecedent theological context in which they were given.

To covenant theologians, we say that the inclusion of the Gentiles with Israel both throughout the history of redemption and especially after the cross may be obtained by solid grammatical-syntactical-theological exegesis without terminating God's offer to the Jews. Both were there almost from the beginning, and both continue into the gospel era revelationally (Romans 9–11) and historically (the seminal reappearance of the state of Israel in 1948).

40. See our article, "The Eschatological Hermeneutics of Epangelicalism: Promise Theology," *JETS* 13 (1970):91–99, esp. pp. 92ff.

To dispensationalists, we say that the preservation of God's promise to national Israel in the past and the future may be retained by sound grammatical-syntactical-historical exegesis without bifurcating the single plan of God into two peoples and two programs. This stress on different times, methods, and plans, while legitimately sensing an element of discontinuity in the Scriptures between Israel and the Church, has hardened into separate realities or ages what was only to be several *aspects* of the one eternal promise.

These two systems, and the dilemmas they pose for each other, can only be reconciled by meeting where the biblical writers authoritatively rested their case (viz., in the *epangelia*) to use the NT term, or in the *contents* of the covenant (not the *form* of the covenant, for there were many covenants, and stress on the form leads into the schema of looking for continuity structures in the signs, people, and the setting up of the series of old and new covenants).

ISRAEL AND THE CHURCH THEN AND NOW

What then are we to conclude about the Jerusalem council? Was circumcision necessary for Christian converts? No! God's future rested with a restoration of "David's hut" and the full promise of God, not in the perpetuation of the Mosaic ritual. So the prophets had predicted.

Was the "tabernacle of David" a type of the Christian church that transferred especially Amos's national hopes into spiritual realities of the gospel era? Again, no! For that fails to take seriously the verses that precede and follow Amos 9:11–12, much less the constant repetition of God's total program that encompassed the past, present, and future in a plan that provided for the restoration of nature itself and the calling of Gentiles in that single kingdom of God. The *new* covenant was nothing *less* than what God had promised to Abraham and David, but it was also *more*—but along those same lines of thought already traced. And the "people of God" were and still are one. That was James's point and Amos's prediction! Both Jews and Gentiles—Edomites included—would be "called by the name of the Lord."

Time fails me to recall the terminology used of believers in 1 Peter 2:5, 9, 10, which originally belonged to Israel in Exodus 19:5–6 and Isaiah 43:21. Furthermore, Gentiles have become part of the "seed of Abraham" (Gal. 3:29)—not by analogy, spiritualization, or some type of midrashic *pesher*, but by the authorial intention of the OT and NT writers and the single plan of God.

Promise theology, or epangelicalism, without setting out to be a middle way between covenant theology and dispensationalism, promises to be such, for it picks up the strengths of both systems of exegesis. If a vigorous exegetical theology and a revived biblical theology that heeds historical canons and contexts would take the lead in all future theological construction, then we would be able to witness a renascence of that biblical picture of a unified people and program of God that refuses to exclude either Israel or the church, God's kingdom in heaven or on earth. I urge my generation to hold its finger on the biblical text and context while it talks through these complex issues. May God yet grant us a reformation that will shake the foundations of our culture to the glory of God once more before the King Himself appears.

PART 5
THE PRACTICAL USE
OF THE OLD TESTAMENT
IN THE NEW

Introduction

The NT writers frequently turned to the wisdom and legal portions of the OT to reinforce a practical and ethical life-style they had commended to their readers. But the succinctness and abbreviated form of many of the proverbs and the specificity and particularity of the legal portions seem to prejudice their practical usefulness to other peoples, cultures, and times. Both of those issues need to be addressed if NT readers are to rise above their own provincialisms to hear the Word of God continuing to speak forth from these portions as well as the NT.

The issue of OT particularity (i.e., the fact that it is seemingly bound to a particular culture in a particular time and addressed to a particular person or persons) is not new to biblical studies in either Testament. Such precise specificness and particularity in the Bible was not meant to prejudice its universal usefulness; instead, it was meant to be an aid to us in identifying with that text and take it out of the realm of the abstract and put it into the real world of concrete illustration and personal attachment.

In the case of the legal portions of the OT, a good case can be made for the fact that abstract principles are to be found in the Decalogue. The subsequent sections of the Covenant Code (Ex. 21–23) and the legislation of large portions of Deuteronomy, consequently, are merely illustrations of those all-embracing principles. In fact, we have recently argued, following Stephen Kaufman, that all of Deuteronomy 12–26 is a rather highly structured composition whose major topical units are so arranged as to follow the order, contents, and the principles set forth in the Decalogue.[1]

To raise this problem of contextualization as a protest against all endeavors to make universal applications of so-called dated material is a red herring issue. The fact is that every biblical command, whether it first appeared in a biblical law code, a narrative, wisdom text, or a prophetic message, was originally addressed to someone in some place and some particular historical situation and context. Usually lurking in the background of almost all of the specific and particularized injunctions is an understood middle term, a definite universal that justifies the particular. It is that universal which we ought to search out as exegetes and readers of the text.

Some will surely object that even if such universals can be shown behind the particulars of OT texts, there is no guarantee that those same universals would have any practical relevance or application to modern problems or people. The fear is that the OT may present us with a class of situations that has no application or no examples in the present age. But surely that argument assumes that there is such strong diversity between the Testaments, books, sections, and paragraphs of the biblical text that we are left, for all practical purposes, with only a list of bare events or uninterpreted injunctions. But that is to treat the contextualized and particularized situations totally apart from any pattern of ethical thought or the universals enjoined elsewhere in that same author—if not within that section or part of the biblical canon itself. To place a priority on diversity is as much a methodological decision as is the decision to place a priority on harmony.[2]

The case for harmony can be found not only in the universal principles that undergird the concrete particulars serving as illustrations of those principles, but also in the character and nature of the God who revealed this text in the first place. Therein lies the ultimate argument for consistency and pertinency of universals across cultural and temporal barriers. Because the character of God is not susceptible to change, we are guaranteed stability and transcultural and transtemporal relevancy.

What about the proverbial form of so many of the wisdom materials found in the OT? Is it not true that these aphorisms tend to generalize to the point of excluding careful notation about real exceptions? Do

1. Walter C. Kaiser, Jr., *Toward Old Testament Ethics* (Grand Rapids: Zondervan, 1983), pp. 127–37. See also Stephen Kaufman, "The Structure of the Deuteronomic Law," *MAARAV* (1978–79):105–58.
2. This point and others in this paragraph are made by M. T. O'Donovan, "The Possibility of a Biblical Ethic," *Theological Students Fellowship Bulletin* 67 (1973):15–23 and cited in W. C. Kaiser, Jr., *Toward Old Testament Ethics*, pp. 24–29.

not many of these quotable one- or two-liners deliberately highlight certain kinds of actions or results to the exclusion of others?

Of course, these observations make valid points. But the problem here is no more difficult than it is for any other group of contemporary proverbs. It is inherent in the very literary genera itself and not a problem distinctive to the OT as such. Accordingly, the alert interpreter will notice some or all of the following characteristics as the way proverbs operate:[3]

1. Universal moral statements in proverbial literature may be limited to:
   a. only a certain tendency of some thing(s) to produce a certain effect (e.g., Prov. 15:1, "a gentle answer turns away wrath"— though there are times when it may have no effect on wicked men).
   b. only telling what generally or often takes place without making it an irreversible rule for any and all situations (e.g., Prov. 22:6, "Train a child in his way and when he is old he will not turn from it"—though some children occasionally will refuse the best of parental leadership and help).
   c. only noting what is the normal course of action without listing some implied or understood exceptions (e.g., Matt. 5:34, "Do not swear at all"—though this does not forbid us from taking legitimate oaths in court).
2. Universal moral truths in proverbial literature may often be stated as direct opposites when they are meant to be understood in terms of priorities or to be taken comparatively in such expressions as:
   a. "I desired mercy, not sacrifices" (Hos. 6:6; Matt. 9:13; 12:7).
   b. "To obey is better than to sacrifice" (1 Sam. 15:22; Ps. 51:17, 19; Jer. 7:22–23).
3. Universal moral truths in proverbial literature often assume that the correspondingly proper circumstance is also understood, thus:
   a. "Answer a fool according to his folly or he will be wise in his own eyes" (Prov. 26:5).
   b. "Do not answer a fool according to his folly, or you will be like him yourself" (Prov. 26:4).

---

3. This is a shortened version of a list in my book *Toward Old Testament Ethics* (Grand Rapids: Zondervan, 1983), pp. 64–67 where I express my indebtedness to Thomas Hartwell Horne, *An Introduction to the Critical Study and Knowledge of the Holy Scriptures*, 8th ed., rev. (New York: Carter, 1858), 1:395–99.

It must also be realized that often the interpreter of such proverbs, whether they be found in the wisdom, narrative, prophetic, or legal sections of the Bible, is dealing with poetry. In such cases, the thought is usually not completed in a single line (or what scholars usually refer to by the German word *stich*), but in a minimum of two lines (a *distich*).

There are five main kinds of *distichs* or *tristichs* that can be illustrated in the following chart (hyphenated words indicate one word in the Hebrew text):

Kind of Distich		*Example*			*Interpretation*
1. Synonymous	a. "A wicked-doer	gives-heed	to-false-lips		a. Principle Stated
	b. And a-liar	gives-ear	to-a-naughty-tongue (Prov. 17:4)		b. Principle Repeated
2. Antithetic	a. "Righteousness	exalts	a-nation		a. Principle Stated
	b. But-sin	is-a-reproach	to-any-people (Prov. 14:34)		b. Principle Contrasted
3. Artificial or Synthetic	a. "Better-is	a-dinner-of-vegetables	where-love-is		a. Principle Begun
[a debatable form][4]	b. Than-a-stalled-ox	and-hatred	therein (Prov. 15:17)		b. Principle Completed
4. Emblematic or Parabolic	a. "As cold waters	to-a-thirsty	soul		a. Illustration from Life
	b. So is good news	from-a-far	land (Prov. 25:25)		b. Analogous Principle

Kind of Tristich		*Example*			*Interpretation*
5. Climactic or Staircase	a. For lo	your-enemies	O-Lord		a. Subject Introduced
	b. For lo	your-enemies	shall-perish		b. Principle Stated
	c. They-shall-be-scattered	all-the-workers-of-iniquity			c. Principle Enlarged

Now the point for the purposes of our concern about the NT's use of the OT is this: when the OT is properly understood, it can be used by the NT believer and indeed the NT shows us how it was used. There are some clear cases where what most allege as being the distinctively high ethic of the NT actually is nothing more than a direct citation of the OT, namely,

If your enemy is hungry, feed him;
if he is thirsty, give him something to drink.
In doing this, you will heap burning coals on his head. (Rom. 12:20)

4. See our discussion and bibliography on this point in W. C. Kaiser, Jr., *Toward an Exegetical Theology* (Grand Rapids: Baker, 1981), pp. 212, 219. This kind of a *distich* is also known as a formal or constructive parallelism and it can be divided into these subclasses: reason, completion, and comparison (which is the kind illustrated here).

But this verse is a direct verbal citation of Proverbs 25:21–22a. The principle is the same for both Testaments.

But what about the use of the legal portions of the OT? Obviously the church is no longer under obligation or bondage of the numerous civil and ceremonial observances found in the Pentateuch. But has faith rendered null and void the law? Paul answered that question as decisively as one can with no uncertain tones about it—*never;* rather, "by faith we establish the law" (Rom. 3:31).

How this is to be accomplished without setting our new position and free, gracious standing in Christ in jeopardy is the subject of the final two chapters illustrating the practical use the NT makes of OT quotations.

10

Applying the Principles
of the Civil Law

Deuteronomy 25:4; 1 Corinthians 9:8–10

The most important contribution our generation could make to the whole curriculum of divinity would be to face up to the current crisis in biblical exegesis. At present, the crisis has shown very little regard for our traditional ecclesiastical categories, for it has spread like the plague from liberal to evangelical scholars and preachers alike. The only factors that will differ are the symptoms of the crisis. The sad fact remains. And it is most evident when the questions focus on how we twentieth-century Christians understand and use OT law.

REVIEW AND ANALYSIS

THE FAILURE TO DISTINGUISH MEANING AND SIGNIFICANCE

As E. D. Hirsch analyzed one aspect of this problem,[1] a decadent "subjectivism" had cast off all literary constraints and thereby ruled out the possibility of a common and determinate object of knowledge. For Hirsch, this "post-Kantian relativism"[2] that "all 'knowledge' is relative"[3] had produced "cognitive atheists"[4] who adhered to no common authority or to any shared principles, but who freely degraded

1. E. D. Hirsch, *Validity in Interpretation* (New Haven: Yale U., 1957); idem, *The Aims of Interpretation* (Chicago: U. Press, 1976).
2. Hirsch, *Aims*, p. 4.
3. Ibid., p. 36.
4. Ibid., pp. 4, 36, 49.

knowledge and value, subverted the goal of objective knowledge, and threatened the very arena of scholarship with their interpretive solipsism.

In Hirsch's judgment:

> *Meaning* is that which is represented by a text; it is what the author meant by his use of particular sign sequence; it is what the signs represent. *Significance*, on the other hand, names a relationship between that meaning and a person, or a conception or a situation.[5]

With this we agree. The theoretical eye of this storm has now been identified. Unfortunately, even Hirsch has undermined his own fine analysis of the normative power of the author's intention as found in the text by allowing the interpreter to frequently usurp the right of the author to say first what he meant to say.[6] Instead of arguing that the "meaning" is always a return to the text as it was meant to be understood by the author, he has most recently enlarged "meaning" to "simply meaning-for-an-interpreter" and comprising "constructions where authorial will is partly or totally disregarded."[7]

Whereas we applaud Hirsch for his earlier distinction between "meaning" and "significance," which, if employed, will save us from interpretive anarchy and subjectivistic relativism, we must not follow his most recent concession and abandon the principle that "meaning" is a return to what the author intended to say by his use of words in a particular text.

THE FAILURE TO LET THE BIBLE TRANSFORM HUMANITY

While dismissing objective controls in the area of meaning, most contemporary theologians have gone to extreme lengths to avoid subjectivity in another area. In the words of Jay G. Williams:

> In the [scholars'] attempts to avoid the apparently futile, sectarian quarrels of the past and arrive at certainties, [they] have attempted to rid themselves of those subjective and communal biases which divided Christian scholars and to adopt a more scientific and detached attitude [of source and form criticism].[8]

5. Hirsch, *Validity*, p. 8.
6. For a telling criticism of this flaw in Hirsch (kindly pointed out to me by Ms. D. Roethlisberger, professor of English at Trinity College, Deerfield, Illinois) see W. E. Cain, "Authority, Cognative Atheism, and the Aims of Interpretation: The Literary Theory of E. D. Hirsch," *College English* 39 (1977):333–45. He refers to a similar criticism found in S. Suleiman, "Interpreting Ironies," *Diacritics* 6 (1976):15–21.
7. Hirsch, *Aims*, pp. 79–80; see the previous seeds of dissolution in his *Validity*, pp. 24, 25, 122–23.
8. J. G. Williams, "Exegesis-Eisegesis: Is There a Difference?" *Today* 30 (1973–74):226.

But alas, commented Williams, "scarcely a word is said about the meaning of the text. It lies before the reader like an inert, dissected corpse."[9]

Even more startling was the iconoclastic frankness of Walter Wink. In his view historical criticism of the Bible was, above everything else, an evangelistic tool to convert students from fundamentalism to liberal theology.

> There can be little quarrel that the historical significance of the Graf-Wellhausen hypothesis (which no one today accepts as then formulated) was its usefulness as a method for destroying the conservative view of Biblical origins and inspiration, thereby destroying the entire ideology.[10]

> Far more fundamentally than revivalism, biblical criticism shook, shattered, and reconstituted generation after generation of students, and became their point of entree unto the "modern world"![11]

However, this drive for objectivity and scientific detachment in the form of biblical criticism, commented Wink, had "gone to seed" and was now "bankrupt" and a "dead letter":

> Simply but quite precisely put, the historical-critical approach to biblical study had become bankrupt. Not dead: the critical tools have a potential usefulness, if they can only be brought under new management. But on the whole, the American scholarly scene is one of frenetic decadence.... Most scholars no longer address the lived experience of actual people in the churches or society.[12]

Williams and Wink were not the only voices to raise this cry. O. C. Edwards, Jr., tacitly agreed:

> It has been assumed for many years in the theological seminaries of all the major denominations that responsible interpretation of the Bible is interpretation that uses the historical-critical method. Without wishing to deny that axiom completely, I do wish to propose that today the

---

9. Ibid., p. 224.
10. W. Wink, *The Bible in Human Transformation: Toward a New Paradigm for Biblical Study* (Philadelphia: Fortress, 1973), p. 12.
11. Ibid., p. 15.
12. W. Wink, "How I Have Been Snagged by the Seat of My Pants While Reading the Bible," *Christian Century* 24 (1975):816.

historical-critical method is in trouble. The particular kind of trouble is ... a failure of [the liberal scholar's] nerve.[13]

Lest we receive the impression that these criticisms are novel and without precedence in the preceding decades, let it be noted that early voices in neoorthodox theology had made the same analysis. J. N. Sanders concluded in 1941:

> The application of the methods of historical criticism to the N.T.... is proving to be inadequate to achieve the aim which the N.T. scholar sets before himself—namely, that of understanding and expounding the N.T. This does not mean [he hastened to add] that historical criticism is without value. Its value is real, but it is only the preliminary [task] to the real exposition of Scripture,... which may be said to be achieved when one hears in the language of one's own time the message which one is convinced was meant by the author of one's text.[14]

Naturally, evangelicals will have no part of a destructive historical criticism that demands philosophical and theological grid or *Vorverständnis* that cheerfully imbibes the flat-world spirit of modernity while it scales down the textual claims of the Bible to sizes more to the liking of twentieth-century secular man. However, the employment of all the tools of higher criticism cannot be an optional luxury—even for the evangelical. We cannot afford to be opposed to legitimate source criticism; on the contrary, our complaint has always been with *hypothetical* sources that exist solely in the imaginations of literary reconstructionists. Certainly Chronicles, for example, has sixty or seventy references to actual sources such as *The Vision of Iddo the Seer, The Book of the Chronicles of the Kings of Israel*, and so forth. And Luke plainly tells us (in Luke 1:1–4) that he freely consulted sources.

Accordingly, evangelicals are likewise involved in the same exegetical crisis, even if it is not of the exact shape as it is for Wink, Sanders, and Edwards. All of these background studies on date, authorship, audience, times, and sources, along with a careful parsing and translation of the original languages, while necessary and important and the first order of business for the interpreter, still leave much to be desired. But what is the missing element that has eluded evangelicals and liberals alike?

13. O. C. Edwards, Jr., "Historical-Critical Method's Failure of Nerve and a Prescription for a Tonic: A Review of Some Recent Literature," *Anglican Theological Review* 59 (1977):116.
14. J. N. Sanders, "The Problem of Exegesis," *Theology* 43 (1941):325. Notice that the last part of his quotation reflects the situation almost forty years ago, before the autonomy of a text from its author was announced!

THE FAILURE TO ARTICULATE THE THEOLOGY OF THE BIBLE

In reaction to a literary criticism that had occupied itself with everything except the finished literary product of the biblical text, one alternative has been to supplement historical criticism with theological exegesis. In the early view of Sanders, the key problem for exegesis was one of discovering "some scientific method of bridging the chasm [between the men of the first and twentieth centuries]."[15] In a moment of candor he conceded that historical criticism was too "purely phenomenological," too "closely akin in method and outlook to the natural sciences," and therefore a "fundamentally alien technique" for the study of rational beings, especially since it viewed all things "as the product of natural causes." It left out "the question of truth or relevance" of the biblical teachings. How could such academic detachment, marveled Sanders, "bring men to a decision between accepting the Gospel or rejecting it?"[16]

George M. Landes was even more emphatic: "Any exegesis which refuses to expound the theological dimensions in [the Scriptures] overlooks their d'etre."[17] For Landes, "no theological interpretation of a text is finished until it has been brought into relation with the entire theological witness of the Bible to the issues at stake in that text."[18]

Whereas we agree that theological exegesis is the missing part of the agenda on most exegetical guides that normally take the exegete through an enormous mass of data in higher and lower criticism, we still do not believe we have been given any steps by which we might truly validate what the writer's theology of that passage was when he wrote it under the inspiration of God. Landes's use of the words "theological witness" handicaps the truth-asserting force of that theology in favor of its experiential force. Furthermore, by failing to consider the theology of each textual unit in its diachronic setting (i.e., by failing to limit one's consideration of those theological themes raised by the text's key words, phrases, quotes, or allusions to those Scriptures that had appeared already and were known to the writer and audience of the book under consideration for exegesis) that exegesis opens itself to the charge of subjectivism, for once again meaning is tied to something other than the words as the writer of that text intended those words to be understood. In the hands of the

15. Ibid., p. 329.
16. Ibid., pp. 330–31.
17. G. M. Landes, "Biblical Exegesis in Crisis: What Is the Exegetical Task in a Theological Context?" *USQR* 26 (1970):276.
18. Ibid., p. 280. In B. S. Childs's terminology, this is called "canonical exegesis"; see his *Biblical Theology in Crisis* (Philadelphia: Westminster, 1970), pp. 99–114. See also Childs's most recent discussion, "The Canonical Shape of the Prophetic Literature," *Interpretation* 32 (1978):46–55.

friends of Scripture, this method prematurely imported meaning and overloded earlier texts with the subsequent progress of revelation— even when the subjects had been correctly matched. But in the hands of the careless scholar, the whole procedure was a travesty on any fair hermeneutic.

THE FAILURE TO LOCATE THE PRESENT NORMATIVENESS OF THE BIBLE

The burning question of the hour, then, is this: In whose hands does the final court of appeal rest for deciding normative theology for contemporary readers of Scripture? Even for hypothetical-source critics and historical reconstructionists of the mild variety, such as the Jesuit scholar Norbert Lohfink, the agony of identifying where this final court of appeal resides, given the acceptance of the Wellhausenian hypothesis, is apparent. At first he conjectures that inspiration must now be restricted to the "final redactor." Thus, "even though [this final author] possibly did not make a single alteration" in the earlier composition that he reused, this text will now assume the new meaning, which meaning may also be said to be "inerrant."[19] However, he quickly shifted the grounds for what was normative to that which the "whole Bible" taught. In his judgment:

> The Bible is inerrant only as a unity and as a whole ... to ... the degree to which within the whole pattern of the meaning of the Scripture [the individual parts] contribute to the formation of its total statement. In this sense it is both possible and obligatory to say that every statement of the Bible is inerrant.[20]
>
> Scripture is only inerrant when it is read as a unity, and when individual statements are critically related to the whole.[21]

Lohfink makes it abundantly clear that Joshua, for example, could "hardly have destroyed"[22] the cities of Jericho and Ai as Joshua 6–8 claims, yet, he also argues that that text is inerrant! And if you ask, with amazement, "How so?" Lohfink has an answer:

> Over and above the establishing of the original sense of an utterance, one must erect a further process of exegesis, which goes on to give the total statement of the scripture. Only at this point do we enter the

19. N. Lohfink, *The Christian Meaning of the Old Testament*, trans. R. A. Wilson (London: Burns and Oates, 1969), p. 32.
20. Ibid., p. 40.
21. Ibid., p. 46.
22. Ibid., p. 47.

region where the scripture is God's word to us, and where it is therefore inerrant.[23]

But has Lohfink solved our problem? How do we validate that teaching that constitutes the whole? It cannot be that which the sacred writers or the inspired "final authors" or "redactors" or even the single books themselves taught; it can only be what is taught in the whole of the Bible, Lohfink assures us.[24]

But what is it that is in the whole or unity of Scripture that is not also in the individual books or in the grammar and syntax of the sacred writings? Lohfink, trapped by his own logic, turns like some evangelicals also do (for entirely different reasons, at least for this present generation) to a *sensus plenior* or "fuller sense" that goes beyond the consciousness of the original author.[25]

This theory, however, which would make the inspired writer the mere instrument of God while God, the principal author, is viewed as meaning more than the human author did—both using the very same words—misuses the old scholastic analogy of instrumental causality, according to Bruce Vawter's brilliant analysis.

> If this fuller or deeper meaning was reserved by God to Himself and did not enter into the writer's purview at all, do we not postulate a Biblical word effected outside the control of the human author's will and judgment and therefore not produced through a truly *human* instrumentality? If, as in the scholastic definitions, Scripture is the *conscriptio* of God and man, does not the acceptance of a *sensus plenior* deprive this alleged scriptural sense of one of its essential elements, to the extent that logically it cannot be called scriptural at all?[26]

23. Ibid., p. 49.
24. Ibid., p. 39.
25. Ibid., p. 43. P. B. Payne, "The Fallacy of Equating Meaning with the Author's Intention," *JETS* 20 (1977):243–52, confuses the issue by (1) including what is properly termed "significance" in his enlarged definition of "meaning" (pp. 244–46); (2) insisting that because writers did not know the "full import" of their own words, they must not be made the final court of appeal for exegesis (p. 248)—a confusion of the larger topic of subject matter with a legitimate and adequate contribution to that subject by an author—and (3) identifying the wrong antecedent for the clause "to which the Spirit of Christ ... was pointing" in 1 Peter 1:10–12 (p. 249). The prophet's search was not "that which the Spirit was revealing through them"—a most unsure word of prophecy!—but rather "the time" when these things should happen. To prove this, I would urge the syntax of verse 11 and ask Payne to identify "not themselves alone" to whom it was *revealed* that they were serving when they also served *us!*
26. B. Vawter, *Biblical Inspiration* (Philadelphia: Westminster, 1972), p. 115. See my own analysis of some related problems in "The Fallacy of Equating Meaning with the Reader's Understanding," *Trinity Journal* 6 (1977):190–93; also my article, "The Single Meaning of Scripture," in *Evangelical Roots in Memoriam of Wilbur Smith*, ed. Kenneth S. Kantzer (Nashville: Thomas Nelson, 1978), for a discussion of the key biblical passages urged against our view.

Vawter slams the door shut on that kind of *sensus plenior.* God's meaning, on that view, no matter whatever else it is, cannot be equated with Scripture. The words of Scripture will act as little more (if that) than a catalyst in speeding up our reaction to meeting with God and directly receiving our own new revelations.

But a more sophisticated contention avoids the dilemma just posed by announcing that language has a life of its own, independent of its user. In its extreme form this view announces that a literary work of art is totally autonomous of its author and must be understood apart from the intentions of the writer or the circumstances of its origin. In a more modified form, David J. A. Clines states:

> Once it is recognized that the text does not exist as a carrier of information, but has a life of its own, it becomes impossible to talk about *the* meaning of a text, as if it had only *one* proper meaning.... Meaning is seen to reside not in the text, but in what the text becomes for the reader.... Thus the original author's meaning, which is what is generally meant by *the* meaning of a text, is by no means the only meaning a text may legitimately have (or rather create). We cannot even be sure that a literary text (or any work of art) "originally"— whatever that was—meant one thing and one thing only to its author; even the author may have had multiple meanings in mind.... [Therefore] ... it is not a matter of being quite wrong or even quite right: there are only more and less appropriate interpretations ... according to how well the world of the [literary piece] comes to expression in the new situation.[27]

Of course, the most effective answer to this suggested solution is to use its own hermeneutic on its own writings and to claim some of the very things such interpreters wish to fight as part of the meaning we are receiving from their pens. It is strange how this hermeneutical circle wishes to be temporarily broken and excused from its own position long enough to be understood on the grounds of the position it attacks—namely, that what these new interpreters write has a single meaning exactly as they meant it and as indicated by the use of the words they selected!

But more to the point of the matter: What is this but a surreptitious way of returning to the "four senses" of Scripture as practiced by many of the patristic and medieval exegetes? Let the merits of the Alexandrian school be weighted by the best practices of the Antiochian school to settle this debate. Whether the argument takes the

27. D. J. A. Clines, *I, He, We, and They: A Literary Approach to Isaiah 53, Journal for the Study of the Old Testament, Supplement Series, 1* (Sheffield: JSOT, Sheffield, 1976):59–61. See also his "Notes for an Old Testament Hermeneutic," *Theology, News and Notes* (March 1975):8–10.

form of linguistic analysis—with its stress on the fact that language has a force and meaning of its own even apart from man as its user— or a Whiteheadian process form of understanding language—where language is important "not [for] its presentation of certain truths as logical relationships, but for its capacity to elicit in the reader a number of 'lures for feeling'"[28]—the bottom line will still be: Which meaning? Which use of language? Which lure and personally inter- esting feature of the text is the valid one and, therefore, normative and divinely authoritative for our generation?

Those questions immediately spoil everything for some. It brings them back to precisely those questions that the modern ethos had hoped to escape. Admittedly, those propositions identified with the text's meaning as indicated by the author's use of linguistic symbols will need to be the source for making any normative decisions. Barry Woodbridge, however, will weakly complain that such a retrogression constitutes "what Toynbee foresaw as the idolatry of worshiping the past."[29]

We cannot agree. The exegetical question will remain regardless of what our personal preferences are. What is true? What is normative? Should the descriptively true simply be equated with that which is normative and significant for our generation? And can we evangelicals claim that we have escaped our own crisis in exegesis? For is not the current evangelical crisis—commonly referred to as "the battle for the Bible"—at its roots actually one involving just these issues?

Evangelicals have tried, with varying degrees of success, to face up to the chasm that lies between the B.C. or first-century A.D. setting of the biblical text and the problem of developing a method for appro- priating those same texts so that contemporary men and women could also respond to them. Unfortunately, some evangelicals have also explored and, in some cases, sadly adopted some or all of the methods already examined above and found wanting.

Still others have attempted to base their novel methods for identi- fying secondary or deeper meanings in the practice of the NT writers' quotations of the OT. Paul's alleged allegorical interpretation of the OT has been one favorite way of bridging this chasm. Paul Jewett, for one, argues for an allegorical interpretation of Scripture. In his view, the allegorical understanding of the text will supply something

> more than the ordinary grammatico-historical exegesis of the Old Tes- tament will yield. We do not say that [this conclusion] is reached apart

28. B. Woodbridge, "Process Hermeneutic: An Approach to Biblical Texts," in *Society of Biblical Literature 1977 Seminar Papers*, ed. P. J. Achtemeier (Missoula, Mon- tana: Scholars, 1977), p. 80.
29. Ibid., pp. 82–83.

from such exegesis, much less in contradiction to it; but we would emphasize that the attitude of the interpreter to the question of the unity of Scripture determines to a large extent his hermeneutical methods, especially in the area of allegorical or typical interpretation.[30]

But whether that allegorical interpretation is bound to the literal meaning of that text and to the truth-intention of the author of that original text seems to be optional for Jewett.[31]

It would appear that when judged by these standards the oft-repeated judgment of Cardinal Newman would be the consensus of many evangelicals as well: "It may be almost laid down as an historical fact, that the mystical interpretation and orthodoxy will stand or fall together."[32] That thesis we seriously doubt. In fact, there may be enough evidence to suggest just the opposite conclusion.

An Evangelical Solution: 1 Corinthians 9:8-10

In an attempt to bring partial relief to the exegetical crisis as defined here, we propose to examine Paul's use of the Mosaic civil law from Deuteronomy 25:4 ("you shall not muzzle the ox that threshes") in 1 Corinthians 9:8-10 to determine how Paul used the OT with a new but related application of a divinely authorized principle.

THE PROBLEM OF PAST PARTICULARITY AND PRESENT SIGNIFICANCE

Of course, careful students of the Scripture have long since recognized that older biblical texts were applied to subsequent generations of listeners by the prophets and apostles. For example, Hosea 12:3-4 clearly refers to the Jacob-and-Esau struggle at birth in Genesis 25:26 and to Jacob's contest with the angel of God in Genesis 32:24ff. and boldly concludes: "[Jacob] met God at Bethel and there God spoke with *us*" (Hos. 12:4). Some modern versions are so surprised by the final pronoun "us"—in light of the one thousand intervening years—that they arbitrarily emend the text to "*him*." The same first person plural pronoun again appears in Hebrews 6:18 even though the promise and oath spoken of there were not—or so it would appear on a careless reading—directed to "*us*" but instead were announced to Abraham in Genesis 12 and 22! Likewise, Paul assigns the significance

---

30. P. Jewett, "Concerning the Allegorical Interpretation of Scripture," *WTJ* 17 (1954):15. See also M. W. Bloomfield, "Allegory as Interpretation," *New Literary History* 3 (1971–72):301–17; G. W. Olsen, "Allegory, Typology and Symbol: the *Sensus Spiritualis*," *Communio* 4 (1977):161–79.
31. Ibid., pp. 4–5.
32. J. H. Newman, *An Essay on the Development of Doctrine* (Baltimore: Penguin, repr. 1974), p. 340.

of "what was written in former days" in the OT as being for "*our instruction*" so that "*we* might have hope" (Rom. 15:4).[33]

In a similar manner, Paul clearly asserts in 1 Corinthians 9:8–10 that the instruction prohibiting the muzzling of oxen when they are threshing was addressed to the Corinthian church and thus also to "*us.*" How, then, was Paul able to facilely jump the very chasm that has created in a large measure the current exegetical crisis? That is our question here.

THE VARIOUS ESTIMATES OF PAUL'S METHOD IN 1 CORINTHIANS 9:8–10

Usually Paul is credited with accomplishing his exegetical feat by departing from the literal sense of Deuteronomy 25:4 and using one of three aberrant methods of exegesis.

Allegory. A good number of scholars like W. Arndt[34] have concluded that Paul's argument was an allegorical or mystical understanding of Deuteronomy which, while not violating the literal meaning, was not dependent on it either. Thus, this text and Galatians 4:21–31[35] are usually considered to be the two prime examples of the Pauline use of allegory.

According to A. T. Hanson, an allegory in this situation would mean either "interpreting a text in a sense which completely ignores its original meaning, or in a sense whose connection with its original meaning is purely arbitrary."[36] In Hanson's view Paul may be acquitted of deliberately designing an allegorical use of the OT, for the literal meaning of Deuteronomy 25:4 has not completely disappeared. 1 Corinthians 9:8–9 is only "formally" an example of allegory, but "not consciously" constructed to be so.[37]

Richard Longenecker, however, takes a harder line. In his opinion, Paul "seems to leave the primary meaning of the injunction in Deu-

---

33. See also Romans 4:23ff.; 1 Corinthians 10:11; Matthew 15:7; 22:31; Mark 7:6; Acts 4:11; Hebrews 10:15; 12:15–17. See P. Fairbairn, "The Historical Element in God's Revelation," in *Classical Evangelical Essays on OT Interpretation*, ed. Walter C. Kaiser, Jr. (Grand Rapids: Baker, 1972), pp. 72–79.
34. W. Arndt, "The Meaning of I Cor 9:9, 10," *CTM* 3 (1932):329–35.
35. For a good discussion of this text by my former colleague, see R. J. Kepple, "An Analysis of Antiochene Exegesis of Galatians 4:24–26," *WTJ* 39 (1977):239–49.
36. T. Hanson, *Studies in Paul's Technique and Theology* (Grand Rapids: Eerdmans, 1974), p. 159. H. A. Wolfson, *Philo* (Cambridge: 1947), pp. 1, 134, defined it this way: "The allegorical method essentially means the interpretation of a text in terms of something else, irrespective of what that something else is." P. Jewett, however, cautions that it must be in terms of "something else" which has organic or analogical relationships, "Allegorical," p. 11. Jewett rejects Philo's allegories because he interpreted Scripture by analogy with Greek philosophy, and this disregarded the unity of Scripture and was, therefore, an illegitimate type of allegorical interpretation.
37. Ibid., p. 166.

teronomy 25:4 ... and interprets the OT allegorically."³⁸ For him the
point hinges on the word *pantōs* ("it is written *pantōs* for our sakes").
If *pantōs* is to be translated "altogether" or "entirely," then Paul ruled
out the literal meaning. But if the word is to be translated "certainly"
or "undoubtedly," then Paul merely claims a second meaning is to be
found alongside the literal meaning of Deuteronomy 25:4. More on
this later.

Adolf Deissmann was caustic in his espousing this position:

> With Philo, as also with Paul, allegorical exegesis ... was more a sign of
> freedom than of bondage, though it led both of them to great violence
> of interpretation.
>
> [Among the] instances of such violence [is] ... the application of the
> words about the ox, which was not be muzzled while threshing, to the
> Apostles. Paul ... speaks in these strangely unpractical and feeble words
> as a man from the city, who does not regard animals.³⁹

Notice that Deissmann did not hesitate to charge Paul with a grossly
erroneous use of the OT Scriptures because of his alleged allegorical
interpretations.

Rabbinic type of argument. The Anchor Bible took another stance.
For Orr and Walther, Paul here employed "the Rabbinic principle of
argument from the lesser to the greater (*qal wāḥōmer*)" and thus his
"citation is much less precise than modern hermeneutical standards
allow."⁴⁰ Most of these examples from the Talmud are analogical
applications of this law, which must have gained great popularity if
one may judge from the number of its occurrences in this literature
and from Paul's use of it again in 1 Timothy 5:18.⁴¹ Nevertheless,
C. K. Barrett concluded that Paul's argument was not of a *minori ad
majas* (*qal wāḥōmer*) sort.⁴²

38. R. Longenecker, *Biblical Exegesis in the Apostolic Period* (Grand Rapids: Eerdmans, 1975), p. 126. H. A. W. Meyer also argued that "the apostle *sets aside* the
actual *historical sense* of that prohibition ... in behalf of an allegorical sense,
which ... is not but an *application* made 'a minori ad majus'.... But this need not
surprise us, considering the freedom used in the typico-allegorical method of
interpreting Scripture, which regarded such an application as the *reference* of
the utterance in question designed by God, and which from *this* standpoint did
not take the historical sense into account along with the other at all" (*A Critical
and Exegetical Handbook to the Epistles to the Corinthians* [New York: Funk and
Wagnalls, 1884], p. 201).
39. A. Deissmann, *Paul: A Study in Social and Religious History,* trans. W. E. Wilson
(New York: Harper, 1957), pp. 102–3.
40. W. Orr and J. A. Walther, *I Corinthians,* The Anchor Bible Series (Garden City,
N.J.: Doubleday, 1976), pp. 238, 241.
41. For an easily accessible digest and discussion of most of these rabbinic references
see Hanson, *Studies,* pp. 163–65.
42. C. K. Barrett, *A Commentary on the First Epistle to the Corinthians* (New York:
Harper, 1968), p. 206.

Hellenistic Jewish exegesis. A third school of opinion is exhibited by Hans Conzelmann. Paul, he explained, expounded "according to the Hellenistic Jewish principle that God's concern is with higher things" so that the literal sense has been abandoned because it expressed something unworthy of God.[43] The detailed prescriptions of the law may therefore be treated allegorically.

Literal theological exegesis. In spite of all the assurances to the contrary, it will be our contention here that Paul has neither abandoned the literal meaning nor taken liberties with the Mosaic legislation to obtain divine authorization for ministerial honoraria. No one has seen this better than F. Godet.[44] He pointed to the total context of Deuteronomy 24–25: the command to restore the poor man his garment (24:10–13), to pay the poor laborer his wages on the same day (24:14–15), to leave the corners of the fields for widows and strangers to glean (24:19–22), and so forth. The whole Deuteronomic context, he argued, showed that Moses' concern was not for oxen alone, but to develop gentleness and gratitude in their owners. "It was the duties of *moral beings* to one another that God wished to impress" on mankind.[45] With convincing logic and excellent methodology, Godet explained:

> Paul does not, therefore, in the least suppress the historical and natural meaning of the precept.... He recognizes it fully, and it is precisely by starting from this sense that he rises to a higher application.... Far from arbitrarily allegorizing, he applies, by a well-founded *a fortiori,* to a higher relation what God had prescribed with reference to a lower relation.... The precept has not its full sense except when applied to a reasonable being....
>
> It is difficult to suppress a smile when listening to the declamations of our moderns against the allegorizing mania of the Apostle Paul.... Paul does not in the least allegorize.... From the literal and natural meaning of the precept he disentangles a profound truth, a law of humanity and equity.[46]

Calvin is even more insistent:

> We must not make the mistake of thinking that Paul means to explain that commandment allegorically; for some empty-headed creatures make this an excuse for turning everything into allegory, so that they

43. H. Conzelman, *A Commentary on the First Epistle to the Corinthians,* trans. J. W. Leitch (Philadelphia: Fortress, 1975), p. 155, n.38.
44. F. Godet, *Commentary on the First Epistle of St. Paul to the Corinthians,* trans. A. Cusin (Grand Rapids: Zondervan, 1957), pp. 2, 11.
45. Ibid.
46. Ibid., pp. 13, 16.

change dogs into men, trees into angels, and convert the whole of Scripture into an amusing game.

But what Paul actually means is quite simple: though the Lord commands consideration for the oxen, He does so, not for the sake of the oxen, but rather out of regard for men, for whose benefit even the oxen were created. Therefore that humane treatment of oxen ought to be an incentive, moving us to treat each other with consideration and fairness.[47]

What, then, about the oxen? "Does God care for [them]?" (1 Cor. 9:9b).[48] What would appear at first to be a flat Pauline denial of God's care for oxen is, as Arthur P. Stanley correctly observed,

> one of the many instances where the lesson which is regarded as subordinate is denied altogether as in Hos. vi. 6, "I will have mercy and not sacrifice," and Ezek. xx. 25, "gave them statutes which were not good."[49]

Thus, it was not so much for animals as it was for men that God had spoken, but both were definitely involved in God's directive. This should solve the *pantōs* problem.[50]

But did Paul give Deuteronomy 25:4 a meaning the words did not possess? The solution to that question is to be found in Paul's answer to his own query: "Is not [God] speaking simply[51] (*pantōs*) for our sakes?" (1 Cor. 9:10). "Yes (*gar*)," Paul continued, "it was written for

47. J. Calvin, *The First Epistle of Paul to the Corinthians*, trans. J. W. Fraser (Grand Rapids: Eerdmans, 1960), pp. 187–88. See also *The Works of St. Chrysostom* in the *Nicene and Post-Nicene Fathers of the Christian Church* (First Series). ed. P. Schaff (New York: Christian Literature, 1889), 12:120–21.

48. G. M. Lee, "Studies in Texts: I Cor 9:9–10," *Theology* 71 (1968), pp. 122–23, is worried about a possible callousness on God's part for oxen. But Philo referred to Deuteronomy 25:4 as an example of the law's concern for animals (*De Virtutibus*, 146). Yet, in *De Offerentibus*, 251, Philo says God speaks only on behalf of creatures with reason and sense. Again in *De Specialibus Legibus* I, 26, he comments, "For you will find all this elaborate detail indicates indirectly (*antittomenan*) the improvement of your morals. For the law is not concerned with irrational creatures, but with those who possess mind and reason"[!]. The citation and translation is from A. T. Hanson, *Studies*, p. 164.

49. A. P. Stanley, *The Epistles of St. Paul to the Corinthians*, 4th ed. (London: John Murray, 1876), p. 142. We might also add the further examples of Jeremiah 7:21; Hosea 6:6; Matthew 9:13; 12:7; cf. 1 Peter 1:12, "not for themselves, but for you [the prophets] were ministering." E. W. Bullinger, *Figures of Speech Used in the Bible* (Grand Rapids: Baker, reprint 1968), p. 24, argues (along with Rückert and Tholuck) that there is a figure of speech called ellipsis here involving the omission of the word "only" ("is God concerned [only] about oxen?") as perhaps also in Luke 14:12.

50. R. Jamieson, A. F. Fausset and D. Brown, *Commentary on the Whole Bible* (Grand Rapids: Zondervan, n.d.), pp. 2, 278, follow Grotius and translate *pantōs* "mainly" or "especially." It certainly conveys the sense in this context.

51. C. K. Barrett's happy rendering of *pantōs*, *Commentary*, p. 205.

our sakes." And then comes the crucial word in the translation: the Greek word *hoti.*

Three different ways of rendering this word have been suggested: (1) in a declarative or explicative sense, giving the substance of the Deuteronomy command in different words (H. A. W. Meyer, C. F. Kling); (2) in a recitative sense, introducing a quotation from a non-canonical source (Rückert, Weiss, Conzelmann); or (3) in a causal sense, giving the reason why God gave this figurative command (Godet, Calvin, Alford, Hodge, Stanley).

Because Paul's reference to "it is written" (especially with the affirmative *gar,* "yes") can only be to the preceding quotation from Deuteronomy, the notion that he is introducing a quote from an apocryphal book is ruled out immediately. Likewise, the declarative or explicative sense will not fit; his purpose is not to give the contents of the Mosaic command. Deuteronomy had nothing specifically to say about oxen plowing or that the ox that threshes is the same one that had plowed those very fields. Paul wants to give the reason *why* he said that law was written for our sakes. The meaning of the command is a principle for all men: The workman, be he man or animal, is to be rewarded for his labor. And to whom is the command directed? Only to men.

What, then, is Paul's reasoning? It is not that plowing and threshing are two parallel works each worthy of reward. Rather, it is that the one who has been on the job working (or, in Paul's continuing agricultural metaphor, plowing in hope) ought to be the one who is there when the recompense for that labor is passed out (i.e., at the threshing of the harvest thus yielded).

Paul has not given a different meaning or a secondary and hidden sense to the Mosaic command. He has expertly taken from its temporary wrapping a permanent principle, as Moses intended.

THE MODERN USE OF SCRIPTURE

Thus, both the literal meaning and the theological significance of Deuteronomy 25:4 were preserved by the apostle without resorting to any of our contemporary substitutes. This text may serve then as a graphic illustration as to how we too may begin to bridge that notorious chasm between the B.C. text and the A.D. needs of men and end the exegetical crisis in our day.

Paul argues his case for the rights of pastoral support on four separate levels: (1) the level of illustration from experience: the soldier, vinegrower, and herdsman—1 Corinthians 9:7; (2) the level of the authority of Scripture: Deuteronomy 25:4 (cf. 1 Timothy 5:18 in subsequent usage)—verses 8–11; (3) the level of illustration from current practice in the church and in pagan religions—verses 12–13; and (4) the authoritative teachings of Jesus—verse 14.

Paul grounds his argument in the authority derived from Scripture and the teaching of Jesus. His reading of the text was not done at the expense of the literal meaning. However, neither was he so taken with materials on animal husbandry and background studies that he had no message for the contemporary situation.

How, then, did Paul make any legitimate connection between the Mosaic requirement of rewarding the labors of oxen and urging that the Corinthians supply material rewards to the missionary or preacher in their midst? Does Scripture have a "hidden meaning" known only to God, which eludes the original authors and most readers? If it has, then whatever else that "hidden meaning" is, it is not Scripture as we have already argued above. And our concern, like the apostle's, must be with what God has communicated by means of the truth intentions of his human authors. To allow a "pastoral meaning" that may mean something in addition to the grammatical-syntactical-theological meaning (as does I. Howard Marshall[52]) or an "exegesis" that approaches the text from a separate level of understanding than the grammatical-historical meaning (as David Kelsey did[53]) is likewise unwarranted and ultimately devoid of the authority it seeks.

Without consuming more time with the history of the discussion, we affirm that the connection between rewarding oxen and pastors is textually derived and is to be found in E. D. Hirsch's earlier distinction between "meaning" and "significance."

The textual connection is simple: Moses spoke primarily for the benefit of the rational beings who owned the oxen. The whole immediate context of Deuteronomy 24–25 and its larger setting was but a series of precedent-setting examples in the realm of civil law that illustrated the rightful divine demands that the moral law made on men. While it is remarkable that Paul did not appeal directly to Deuteronomy 24:15—"You shall give the hired servant his wages on the day he earns them"—nevertheless, the wisdom of embarrassing God's reluctant people to give to preachers who served them well what they would have given to dumb animals is apparent. Furthermore, the illustration suited his other examples from the sphere of agriculture in verse 7 very well.

52. I. Howard Marshall: "I would be prepared to accept a 'pastoral' interpretation of John 4, even if it were not in the author's mind.... It could be that in scripture too there was a meaning different from that intended by the author." *JETS* 17 (1974):67–73, esp. p. 72.
53. D. H. Kelsey, *The Uses of Scripture in Recent Theology* (Philadelphia: Fortress, 1975), pp. 199–201.

"Meaning" is clearly distinguished from "significance" in Paul, yet, they are not so distinctive as not to be in touch with one another. For the first, Paul establishes the principle that God spoke to men (not oxen) primarily for their moral growth in attitudes of fairness and generosity. "Meaning" here is specifically limited to the text and that which Moses meant by his use of these words. Only in this case will Paul's citation gain any status of authority in persuading men.

"Significance," in E. D. Hirsch's terms, names a relationship between that meaning and a person, a concept, or a situation. Consequently, Paul does proceed to name one specific area where a relationship between that meaning and the persons under consideration exists—namely, the fair remuneration of preachers. In this case, the relationship was made on the basis of its contextual setting and its antecedent theology. The examples given by Moses, in Deuteronomy were not meant to be an exhaustive listing or even ends in themselves; they were only illustrations that were to serve as incentives to fairness and generosity. And rational beings did not exist for the benefit of nonrational creatures, but vice versa. Earlier Mosaic teaching in the creation account had already determined that animals were created for man's benefit. Neither was the mere performance of the civil law or even the ceremonial law the object of God's commandment, but rather the moral law that was the embodiment of the nature and being of God. All of these arguments can be established exegetically in a diachronic biblical theology of the OT[54] but for our purposes here will be only stated.

Paul arrived at this unique application of his text by first preserving Moses' right to say what he intended to say by his own words before he established any new relationships of the same principle. Paul did *not* (1) allegorize (Hanson, Longenecker), (2) establish typico-allegorical counterparts for the OT (H. A. W. Meyer), (3) contend only for what loosely belonged to the whole of Scripture as his inerrant grounds (Lohfink), (4) try to draw on the entire theological corpus of Scripture as "witness" (Sanders, Lohfink), or (5) claim that he had God's meaning (a *sensus plenior* or new hermeneutic) that was over and above or in addition to whatever the original meaning might have been.

Christian ministers had the right to expect that their hearers and congregations would support them and provide for their material needs much as soldiers receive pay, the vineyard planters eat the fruit

---

54. See Walter C. Kaiser, Jr., *Toward an Old Testament Theology* (Grand Rapids: Zondervan, 1978). See the fine discussion of the patristic use if *skopos* (by which they meant the unifying theological purpose for each biblical book) in A. F. Johnson, "The Methods and Presuppositions of Patristic Exegesis in the Formation of Christian Personality," *Dialog* 16 (1977):186–90.

from their vines, and shepherds enjoy the milk supplied by their herds. For "does not the law say the same thing? [Wasn't] it written in the law of Moses?" (1 Cor. 9.8*b*–9*a*). If the principle that all workers have a right to be paid for their services (be they animal or human) is what is written, and that is what Moses meant, then that is what God meant. The issue was settled. New relationships where the identical principle could be established for the same reasons were all that was left for the interpreter to do. And these relationships were to be established along the same contextual and theological lines as they had been in the original passage quoted. Accordingly, so must modern exegetes operate if we are going to end the current crisis in exegesis.

Again, we insist on asking, in whose hands does the final court of appeal rest for deciding normative theology for contemporary readers? There can be only one legitimate answer if communication is to continue and if men are going to be able to declare the Word of God with authority: in the original writers' hands, in their single meaning and principle for each text, in their contextual settings, in the theology that informs their writings, and in the faithful naming of new relationships between that original meaning and contemporary persons, conceptions, and situations.

11

Applying the Principles of the Ceremonial Law

Leviticus 19; James

It is not uncommon for some Christians to be puzzled, if not out-rightly disturbed (e.g., Martin Luther), over the contents of the NT letter of James. This letter, which has traditionally been ascribed to the half-brother of Jesus, does not appear to fit in with the rest of the NT. It appears to lay such stress on obedience as a proof or evidence that a believer is actually what he or she claims to be. What is it about this book that has generated such vehement discussion and, at times, outright opposition?

One of the key reasons for all the feelings of discomfort may have been identified in an unusually insightful article by Luke T. Johnson.[1] His thesis is that James may have used Leviticus 19:12–18 as one of his key sources for the series of paraeneses in his book.

What is certain about the thesis is that James definitely knew and quoted directly from the LXX version of Leviticus 19:18b in James 2:8. This is what James labeled as the "royal law of law." It read: "Love your neighbor as yourself."

But not only is the citation an accurate rendering of the Greek version of the text, but as Johnson also pointed out, James placed this citation clearly in the same contextual setting that it had in Leviticus:

---

1. Luke T. Johnson, "The Use of Leviticus 19 in the Letter of James," *Journal of Biblical Literature* 101 (1982):391–401. See also, P. W. van der Horst, *The Sentences of Pseudo-Phocylides* (Leiden: E. J. Brill, 1978) and O. J. F. Seitz, "James and the Law" in *Studia Evangelical* II, Part I. *The New Testament Scriptures*, ed. Frank L. Cross (Berlin: Akademie-Verlag, 1964), pp. 472–86.

that of not showing partiality when rendering a judgment (cf. James 2:9 and Lev. 19:15).[2]

However, there is more. According to Johnson, six other thematic or verbal allusions exist between the book of James and this section from what is generally called the "Law of Holiness" (Lev. 18–20). Thus, from the heart of what many would regard as the ceremonial law comes the basis for the practical, ethical, and moral nurturing of NT believers! Our chart of these passages, based on Johnson's work, is as follows:

The New Testament Order of the Texts
(with Pseudo-Phocylides)

James	Leviticus 19:12–18	Pseudo-Phocylides
2:1: μὴ ἐν προσωπολημψίαις ἔχετε "Do not show favoritism"	**19:15:** οὐ λήμψῃ πρόσωπον "Do not show partiality..."	**10ᵇ:** μὴ κρίνε πρόσωπον "...judge not partially"
2:9: εἰ δὲ προσωπολημπτεῖτε "if you show favoritism"	**19:15:** οὐ λήμψῃ πρόσωπον "Do not show partiality..."	**10ᵇ:** μὴ κρίνε πρόσωπον "...judge not partially"
2:8: Ἀγαπήσεις τὸν πλησίον σου ὡς σεαυτόν "You shall love your neighbor as yourself"	**19:18ᵇ:** ἀγαπήσεις τὸν πλησιόν σου ὡς σεαυτόν "You shall love your neighbor as yourself"	
4:11: Μὴ καταλαλεῖτε ἀλλήλων ἀδελφοί "Do not slander (speak boisterously against) one another, brothers"	**19:16:** οὐ πορεύσῃ δόλῳ ἐν τῷ ἔθνει σου "Do not go about spreading slander among your people" לא תלך רכיל = "do not go about as a slander"	**21:** μήτ' ἀδικεῖν ἐθέλῃς μήτ' οὖν ἀδικοῦντα εἄσῃς "Neither wish to do injustice, not therefore allow another to do injustice"
5:4: ἰδοὺ ὁ μισθὸς τῶν ἐργατῶν τῶν ἀμησάντων τὰς χώρας ὑμῖν ὁ ἀπεστερημένος ἀφ' ὑμῖν κράζει "Behold, the wages you failed to pay the workman who mowed your fields are crying out against you"	**19:13:** οὐ μὴ κοιμηθήσεται ὁ μισθὸς τοῦ μισθωτοῦ παρὰ σοὶ ἕως πρωί "Do not hold back the wages of a hired man overnite" cf. also Deut. 24:14; Mal. 3:5	**19:** μισθὸν μοχθησοντι δίδου "Give the laborer his pay" cf. also Isa. 5:9, LXX
5:9: μὴ στενάζετε ἀδελφοὶ κατ' ἀλλήλων "Don't take out your resentments on each other, brothers"	**19:18a:** καὶ οὐκ ἐκδικᾶται σου ἡ χείρ καὶ οὐ μὴ νιεῖς τοῖς υἱοῖς τοῦ λαοῦ σου "And thy hand shall not avenge thee, and thou shalt not be angry with the children of thy people"	
5:12: μὴ ὀμνέτε ἵνα μὴ ὑπὸ κρίσιν πέσητε "Do not swear ... so that you will not be condemned"	**19:12:** οὐκ ὀμεῖσθε τῷ ονοματί μου ἐπ' ἀδίκῳ καὶ οὐ βεβηλώσατε τὸ ὄνομα τοῦ θεοῦ ὑμῖν "Do not swear falsely by my name and profane the name of your God"	**16:** μὴ δ' ἐπιορκήσῃς μήτ' ἀγνως μήτε ἑκοντι "Do not commit perjury neither, ignorantly nor willingly" cf. James's use of ἐλέγχω

5:20: γινώσκετω ὅτι ὁ
ἐπιστέψας ἁμαρτωλὸν ἐκ
πλάνης ἰδοῦ αὐτοῦ σώσει ψυχὴν
αὐτοῦ σώσει ψυχὴν αὐτοῦ ἐκ
θανάτου καὶ καλύψει πλῆθος
ἁμαρτίας
Remember: Whoever turns a
sinner away from [his] error,
lo, he will save him from
death and cover a multitude
of sins.

19:17b: ἐλεγμῷ ἐλεγξεις τὸν
πλησίου σου καὶ οὐ λήμψῃ δι᾽
αὐτον ἁμαρτίαν
"Rebuke your neighbor
frankly so you will not share
in his guilt"

In the Leviticus 19 Order of the Texts

Leviticus 19:12–18	*James*
19:12: Do not swear falsely by my name and profane the name of your God.	**5:12:** Do not swear … so that you will not be condemned.
19:13: Do not hold back the wages of a hired man overnight.	**5:4** Behold, the wages you failed to pay the workman who mowed your fields are crying out against you.
19:14	no parallel
19:15: Do not show partiality.	**2:1:** Don't show favoritism. **2:9:** If you show favoritism....
19:16: Do not go about spreading slander among your people.	**4:11:** Do not slander one another, brothers
19:17b: Rebuke your neighbor frankly so you will not share in his guilt.	**5:20:** Know that whoever turns a sinner back from his error will save him from death and cover a multitude of sins.
19:18a: And your hand shall not avenge you and you shall not be angry with the children of your people.	**5:9:** Don't take out your resentments on each other, brothers.
19:18b: You shall love neighbor as yourself.	**2:8:** You shall love your neighbor as yourself.

Note that only verse 14 is without a parallel, but not because it is too ceremonial or culturally related. In fact, it urges: "Do not curse the deaf or put a stumbling block in the path of the blind, but fear your God! I am the Lord" (NIV).

Therefore, we conclude that four of the six thematic or verbal parallels are fairly certain. Only two, Leviticus 19:17 and 19:18a, are less likely. But the situation may even be as Johnson[3] suggested; that the apodictic commands of Leviticus 19:11, which reflect the Decalogue as much as the included verse 12, are included in substance along with Leviticus 19:12–18 in James 3:13—4:10. Leviticus 19:11 reads:

Do not steal,
Do not lie,
Do not deceive one another. (NIV)

3. Ibid., p. 399, n.29.

It is even more interesting to reflect on James's phrase in 2:8, *kata tēn graphēn,* "according to the Scriptures." In his inspired mind, the "fulfilling of the law" must be carried out "according to the Scriptures" and these Scriptures are here preeminently the contents of OT law! Harsh as the truth may seem to us, James appears to link the "royal law of love" in verse 8 with a warning against being guilty of being a "lawbreaker" in verse 9 by the use of the Greek correlatives *mentio* (v. 8) and *de* (v. 9). Thus, Christians must sense a legitimate obligation to render obedience to the law (not for their salvation, mind you) or be found guilty of sin! And this law must be that which is found in the inscripturated writings of the OT (*kata tēn graphēn*). Johnson concludes:

> ... Keeping the law of love involves observing the commandments
> explicated in the Decalogue (2:11) and Lev. 19:12–18 in their entirety.
> ... For James, Lev. 19:12–18 provides an accurate explication of the law
> of love which should be obtained in the Church.[4]

Such an analysis will agree with Paul's conclusion. The OT "law is holy, just, good, and spiritual" (Rom. 7:13–14) "... if we use it rightly" (1 Tim. 1:8). Thus, the Christian is called to "the obedience of faith" (Rom. 1:5; 16:26). There is an obedience that simply accepts God's gift of salvation that in turn opens us up to truly serve God out of the obedience of faith (Deut. 8:2; 30:51, 11–16).

Love is an essential part of a Christian's ethic, but it is a *how* word, not a *what* word. It will tell us *how* we ought to do what we need to do, but we need to go to Scripture to learn more precisely *what* we are to do, otherwise, there is no difference between situational ethics and the Christian ethic. We will be left to the anarchy of everyone protesting that whatever they are doing, they have done it out of love. But who or what will supply us with the practical principles by which we can live? And we answer: only the Scriptures can fill that need. Yes, *all* Scripture is given by the inspiration of God and it *all* is profitable. One of the functions of the legal and proverbial passages is to fill in the lacunae of our understanding as to "how then shall we live."

4. Ibid., p. 400.

12

Conclusion

The frequency with which the NT writings appeal to the OT must be judged by all to be most impressive. The fact remains that, "At the most there are in the NT only four quotations from [nonbiblical] Greek authors, and virtually all the NT parallels with extracanonical Jewish writings can be explained as arising from a common dependence on an OT source."[1] Accordingly, interpreters of the NT can ill afford to relegate study of the OT to a secondary position behind mastery of intertestamental or extra-canonical literatures. The impact of the OT on the NT will always remain a major consideration in coming to terms with the meaning of the NT. Unfortunately, the wisdom of this advice is not frequently observed in NT exegesis today.

This is not to say, however, that the relationships between the two Testaments has always been a simple matter devoid of any complications. Nor have we maintained that we have supplied the reader with a comprehensive treatment of each of the various uses of the OT found in the New.

Instead, we have attempted to focus primarily on those NT citations of the OT that had an apologetic reason for their appearance in the NT, that is, those that wished to show that what was being preached by the apostles was not in every case some brand new idea, but an

1. Henry M. Shires, *Finding the Old Testament in the New* (Philadelphia: Westminster, 1974), pp. 180–81. On p. 20 Shires lists the Greek authors as Aratus, Menander, and Epimenides, which are reflected in Acts 17:28; 1 Corinthians 15:33; and Titus 1:13.

idea that had been anticipated in the OT when judged by any fair interpretation of the OT grammar and syntax. If we limit our discussion to this one class of citations, It Is our contention that the NT did not find, nor did they attach new or different meanings to the OT verses they used. On the contrary, we have argued that all such reassessment of the OT texts were not only unwarranted, they will in all the cases we have tested here (to limit, for the moment, our discussion to certain of the more troublesome texts and various approaches) yield the same basic meaning in both Testaments when patiently exegeted by the methods that assign a priority to the human author's own single truth-intention.

Of course, it is true that Scripture is not frozen, as if we possessed a "flat" Bible devoid of any real progress in revelation.[2] We would agree that "It is of the essence of Scripture to put forward God's truth so that its meaning will be understood with increasing clarity,"[3] but we cannot agree that we have found evidence that the Scriptures are "forever changing."[4] The only change that we have detected in the NT use of the Old is in application—not in meaning. However, this fact should not have surprised us, for once the meaning, truth-intention, or principle of the OT text has been established, the interpreter *must* continue the *exegetical* procedure by continuing to take that single meaning/principle and begin naming a number of pertinent situations, places, persons, or areas where that text may be applied. It is at this point where the horizon of meaning, in the sense of meaning as significance, or value, or entailment, may be merged with the horizon[5] of the author's original meaning; not in the sense that the historical or syntactical meaning of the original writer is "overtaken," but in the sense that the interpreter's horizon flows easily out of the principles already patiently established in the meaning of the text.

Now such a position as set forth in these pages runs counter to some of the major contributions made by biblical scholars in this century. Perhaps Krister Stendahl, C. H. Dodd and E. Earl Ellis can illustrate the diversity of answers being given to this question.

Krister Stendahl's major contribution was to suggest that there was a school of interpretation in the early church that differed from the methods used by the rabbis or even from the traditional grammatical-

2. For a discussion of progressive revelation, see W. C. Kaiser, Jr., *Toward Old Testament Ethics* (Grand Rapids: Zondervan, 1983), pp. 60–64.
3. Shires, *Finding the Old Testament*, p. 181.
4. *Ibid.*
5. This concept of a merging of horizons comes from Hans Georg Gadamer, *Truth and Method* (New York: Crossroad, 1982), pp. 269–89. He writes, "The projecting of the historical horizon, then is only a phase in the process of understanding, and does not become solidified into the self-alienation of a past consciousness, but is overtaken by our own present horizon of understanding," p. 273.

historical approach to exegesis. Instead, NT writers appropriated a method that closely "approaches what has been called the _midrash pesher_ of the Qumran sect, in which the OT texts were not primarily the source of rules, but prophecy that was shown to be fulfilled [in the contemporary events of Qumran]."[6] Thus, the _pesher_ method of utilizing quotations emphasized the application of the OT texts apart from their historical context. Usually, the values of OT words were immediately reassigned in light of whatever was on the minds of the subsequent generations of readers. In actual practice, this appeared to be little more than a sophisticated form of allegorizing or spiritualizing of the OT text with this one exception: it was usually restricted to equating historical personages, nations, movements, and events with past personages, nations, movements, and events in the OT.

C. H. Dodd, on the other hand, correctly called attention to the entire context from which the OT quotation was taken, as we pointed out in our introductory chapter. But he added one other feature: the NT writers also shared "a certain understanding of history, which is substantially that of the prophets."[7] And the central event in that history of God's people and of all humanity was the death and resurrection of Jesus Christ. Except for limiting the sphere of the concern to OT texts, Dodd's method did not appear to leave any major damaging effects on NT interpretation, for the greater proportion of OT texts did, as a matter of fact, focus on a prophetic view of history and, more particularly, on Jesus Christ Himself.

However, Earle Ellis began to shift the focus away from the historical context once more and called instead for a method in Paul's use of the OT, which was "grammatical-historical plus.... The grammar and the historical meaning are assumed; and Pauline exegesis, in its essential character, begins where grammatical-historical exegesis ends."[8] Thus, whereas there was some similarity between Pauline and rabbinic exegesis of the OT, Ellis found more evidence for the Qumranian _pesher_ method of quoting the OT. In this method, the interpretation or exposition was incorporated into the body of the text itself thereby shaping not only the textual form, but often creating an _ad hoc_ interpretive paraphrase of the text.[9]

What is common to those three men is that each in his own way tended to remove the locus for the search for meaning away from the

---

6. Krister Stendahl, _The School of St. Matthew_ (Lund: C. W. K. Gleerup, 1954), p. 35.
7. C. H. Dodd, _According to the Scriptures: The Substructure of New Testament Theology_ (London: Nisbet, 1952), p. 120.
8. E. Earl Ellis, _Paul's Use of the Old Testament_ (Grand Rapids: Eerdmans, 1957), p. 147.
9. E. Earl Ellis. _Prophecy and Hermeneutic in Early Christianity_ (Grand Rapids: Eerdmans, 1978), p. 179.

human writer of Scripture: Standahl related it to Qumran, Dodd to the prophet's understanding of history (though with heavy emphasis on the context of the passage and the author's truth-intention), and Ellis on a kind of surplusage that exceeded the grammatical-historical interpretation. But to the degree that the results of those methods conclude that the NT writers indulged in doubtful, unnatural, or forced interpretations of the OT, we cannot agree having tested such claims against the hard evidence of the texts examined in this work. Even when this conclusion is moderated by the disclaimer that "such instances of strained interpretations are the exception rather than the rule,"[10] we still cannot agree. Henry Shires does go on to caution that:

> The great bulk of the quotations are careful reproductions or translations of the original Scripture. In most instances the historical sense is carefully preserved, and often the source of the quotation is accurately acknowledged even though such reference was not the normal practice at that time.[11]

THE CASE FOR THE APOLOGETIC USE OF THE OLD TESTAMENT IN THE NEW

Such conclusions, even when they are carefully circumscribed by moderate language, still raise the issue as to whether the OT language has been fairly interpreted and applied to Jesus and the NT fulfillments when the NT writers were attempting to convince their listeners (and readers) that the events connected with Jesus and this new "way" were not an afterthought and an imposition of values on their part.

The impression is much too frequent that "the ideology that Christians brought to Scripture ... [is what] contributed most to their distinctive interpretation of them."[12] But once again, even though Goldingay qualifies that sweeping assertion by saying, "Many scholars find the NT more contextual in its approach," he will go on to water down that conclusion by allowing that "there is a number of standard examples of less literal interpretation (e.g., Matt. 22:32; 1 Cor. 9:9; Gal. 3:16; 4:21–31; Eph. 4:8; Heb. 7:1–3)."[13]

But that is precisely the point in tension here. Did the reapplication of the OT texts by the NT writers involve the creative use of imagination or the revelation by the Holy Spirit of a meaning *separate* and *different* from that revealed to the OT text? Certainly the claim cannot be made, if this argument is true, that the word of God had clearly

10. Shires, *Finding the Old Testament*, p. 38.
11. *Ibid.*
12. John Goldingay, *Approaches to Old Testament Interpretation* (Downers Grove, Ill.: InterVarsity, 1981), p. 155.
13. *Ibid*, p. 152.

anticipated the events that came later, for no one knew that that word was capable of being pressed into service for that point until the NT writers' imagination or belated revelation was imposed on that text.

The rationale, then, for NT writers going to the trouble to cite in a situation where the apostles were struggling to assert the fact that Christianity was not a brand new invention is missing. How could such a line of reasoning carry any weight, especially with a hostile Jewish audience that was more than skeptical about the illegitimate use of their Scriptures? True, the Jewish interpreters freely indulged in situational midrash in which they created a bridge between the biblical text and life with all its practical questions and needs, but there were limits to the employment of this technique. Just as contemporary evangelicals will indulge in a good deal of spiritualizing and allegorizing the text for devotional purposes (I report this with a note of deep sadness), yet they will tolerate no nonsense when it comes to such doctrinal texts as John 3:16 or statements such as, "The just shall live by faith" (Rom. 1:17). Is it not fair to assume that the same would be true of the Jewish community as well? Every time that an arbitrary interpretation was offered, or one that went contrary to the natural grammatical syntactical meaning of the text, there would be every reason for resistance rather than acceptance by the Jewish community.

But the argument is more than the mere requirements and necessities of logic we have pressed into service here; it is also an exegetical argument. Modern interpreters are overly affected by what they have learned from Jewish or Qumranian "exegetical" practices. Why do we insist that these intertestamental methodologies are more normative and more closely approximate the style of the NT writers? True, Paul was the student of Gamaliel, but then why was it necessary for him to make a major point of the fact that upon his conversion he "did not consult with any man, nor did [he] go up to Jerusalem to see those who were apostles before [he] was, but [he] went immediately into Arabia and later returned to Damascus [and] went up to Jerusalem [only] after three years [had elapsed]" (Gal. 1:16–18)? If his theology and especially his scriptural methodologies already were fixed, he had only to begin his ministry. But it is clear that there is a major break. Surely this must mean, in part, that he had much to learn, if not relearn, about the way he had understood and approached the Scriptures.

If anything, the repeated and frequent use of the OT ought to be a strong indication that it was the OT text itself that had made a stronger impression on them. And if the argument is pressed further with a "Yes, but how did they interpret these texts?" we will answer with the NT writers' own claims and Jesus' expectation for even the ordinary lay person or disciple. Jesus roundly rebuked the two on the road to Emmaus for not knowing what they ought to have realized from reading the OT (Luke 24:25–27). Likewise, the NT apostles argue that they are finding in the OT texts precisely what the original writers understood them to say (e.g., Acts 2:29–34).

Only by relentlessly pursuing this argument in each and every passage where modern interpreters claim that something less than the original OT sense was used in a NT context that was attempting to argue apologetically, will the issue finally be settled. In the meantime, we have offered a sample exegesis of some of the most notoriously difficult passages as an illustration of NT apologetic use of the OT.

THE CASE FOR THE PROPHETIC USE OF THE OLD TESTAMENT IN THE NEW

Closely allied with the apologetic use of the OT is the prophetic use. In fact, it is difficult to know where to place some texts, for indeed they do fit both categories. Therefore, what we have argued in the preceding case equally applies here and we can, as a result, be much briefer.

Nevertheless, the issue of a single meaning or a single truth-intention for prophecies that obviously have multiple fulfillment events in history has been the main problem. It is our hope that the church will cease confusing the alleged "double sense/meaning" of these prophecies with the legitimate observation that there often are multiple realizations in history and the eschaton of that same single prophetic word and meaning.

There is no doubt that the references to which these one and the same prophetic word applies are multiple. But to infer from this phenomenon that the prediction was therefore ambivalent or open-ended in the number of possible meanings that could be attached to each OT prophecy is to miss the generic or corporate nature of many OT as well as NT prophecies.

A generic prophecy, we have argued in the introduction to Part 2, is one that envisages an event as occurring in a series of parts, often separated by intervals of time, yet, expressed in such a way that the language of the OT may legitimately apply either to the nearest, remoter or climactic event. Thus, the same word, with the same sense or meaning of the OT author, may apply at once to the whole complex of events or to any one of its parts in any particular era without destroying what the author had in mind when he first gave that word.

It is only such a generic prediction or corporate solidarity to their words that can begin to account for the phenomena of the text. There are so many singular collective terms such as "seed," "Servant of the Lord," and "firstborn" that one is forced to think within a Semitic

framework rather than in an occidental way. Furthermore, it is likewise clear that whereas both Testaments anticipate the arrival of the
antichrist or even Elijah the prophet, it is just as clear when it is
unblushingly asserted that indeed already many antichrists have
come (1 John 2:18) and some Elijahs have already come, even if only
in "the Spirit and power of Elijah" (Luke 1:17).

In a similar manner, "the Day of the Lord" has had many realizations and fulfilments already in history (witness the locusts of Joel 1–
2, the destruction of Jerusalem in Lamentations, or the onslaught of
the Babylonians in Zephaniah), but this in no way diminishes the
expectation that that day is still a final day in the eschaton. Thus the
writers see a wholeness, singleness, and unity to the series without
lapsing into dual or a plurality of meanings or senses. And that is
where the key issue resides in the discussion.

Instead, 2 Peter 1:19–21 sets the tone for the interpreter of OT
prophecies in the New. Because all believers are urged to give heed to
the light of the OT prophecies shining as in a dark place, inasmuch as
the Spirit of God has already revealed through these prophets what
is certain, plain, and intelligible, we conclude that that prophecy is not
so enigmatic and mysterious that no one can understand it until a
further revelation in the NT arrives. If that were so, how then could
Peter's listeners have ever been expected to give heed to what they
knew not? On the contrary, they and we could have an adequate
enough idea of what was intended that we should be able to respond
to that word.

THE CASE FOR THE TYPOLOGICAL USE OF THE OLD TESTAMENT IN THE NEW

There is nothing approaching a consensus within the believing or
scholarly communities either on the definition or the ways typology
is to be used in biblical studies. In its earliest usage in the first two
centuries of the church, typology had an almost exclusive apologetic
purpose. But his purpose gave way to using typology to edify believers.
These interpreters were the successors of Origen and Clement at
Alexandria. This edification purpose in turn was followed by a "con-
strictive" use of typology during the middle ages to buttress theological systems.[14] But all three usages had their excesses and therefore
fell into disfavor and eventually were all but abandoned.

Even in the current revival of interest in the subject of typology
among scholars in Germany and Great Britain, a debate of significant
proportions rages. Originally, the debate began between Martin Noth

---

14. J. R. Darbyshire, "Typology," *Encyclopedia of Religion and Ethics,* ed. James
   Hastings, XII (1922), pp. 502–03.

and Gerhard von Rad, on the one hand, and A. A. van Ruler and Friedrich Baumgartel on the other hand. The first pair affirm the possibility of typological interpretation whereas the latter two men outrightly reject it.

But each man had an agenda in mind from which he gave his answer to this question. For example, Martin Noth argued that past events could be contemporized in many of their details simply by retelling them in a process he called *re-presentation*. Noth said, "God and his action are always present, while man in his inevitable temporality cannot grasp this present-ness except by 're-presenting' the action of God over and over again in his worship."[15] Von Rad, on the other hand, argued that correspondences were "an elementary function of all human thought and interpretation."[16] Therefore, it was legitimate for the interpreter to look for "the eschatological correspondence between beginning and end."[17]

Contrary to those two opinions, van Ruler and Baumgartel rejected typology in a very outspoken manner, but for different reasons. For van Ruler, there were too many promises in the OT for Christ to be the fulfillment of them all. Furthermore, the OT provided for multiple solutions to some problems (e.g., ways of reconciliation) whereas the NT only provided for one.[18] Likewise, Baumgartel rejected typology because for him the OT must remain the *Old* Testament and confined to its time-bound aeon.[19]

We have argued, instead, that typology may be used as a tool for exegesis of OT texts if the types can be shown to have been intended by the OT authors. Its key characteristics are:

1. Historical correspondence
2. Escalation in the antitype (in the NT)
3. Divine intent and designation (in the OT)
4. Prefiguration or a *devoir-etre* quality

When exegesis will observe those characteristics, it will be clear that there are some large sections of biblical truth intended by God to be prophecies. Especially helpful are the five NT passages that explicitly

15. Martin Noth, "The 'Re-presentation' of the Old Testament in Proclamation," *Essays on Old Testament Interpretation*, ed. Claus Westermann, trans., James Luther Mays (Richmond: John Knox, 1791), p. 85.
16. Gerhard von Rad, "Typological Interpretation of the Old Testament," in *Essays on Old Testament Interpretation*, p. 17.
17. *Ibid*, p. 19.
18. Arnold A. van Ruler. *The Christian Church and the Old Testament*, trans. Geoffrey W. Bromiley (Grand Rapids: Eerdmans, 1971), pp. 37, 45, 52, 62–73.
19. Friedrich Baumgartel, "The Hermeneutical Problems of the Old Testament," *Essays*, pp. 147–48.

employ the *tupos* terminology and structures: 1 Corinthians 10:1–13; Romans 5:12–21; 1 Peter 3:18–21; Hebrews 8:5; and Hebrews 9:24.

If our argumentation in 1 Corinthians 10:11 is correct, then it is clear that many of the events in the OT, as qualified by the list of characteristics discussed above, happened in the OT as "types *of us*" rather than as "types *for us*."

Typology is one of the results of the unity between the Testaments and a further affirmation of the unchanging character of God. But it is also one of the marks of divine revelation and we believe our two texts clearly illustrate such a usage: 1 Corinthians 10:6, 11.

THE CASE FOR THE THEOLOGICAL USE OF THE OLD TESTAMENT IN THE NEW

The church still struggles, as it must, to identify the amount of continuity and discontinuity between the two Testaments. But one thing is clear: the church must not give way to the deeply ingrained incipient Marcionite tendency in our circles; one that deliberately silences, avoids, twists, or devalues the contribution that the OT makes to the theology derived from the Bible. To limit ourselves only to the NT is to demean the fullness and richness of God's revelation, not to mention His unchanging nature and will.

There is a desparate need to bring the OT into the discussion of the NT's theological themes. And those who distrust that unity must feel the burden of proof on their shoulders to demonstrate from an in-depth exegesis of key teaching passages (we must get over our pension to summarily employ at will numerous prooftexts without demonstrating that that is indeed the writer's identical point of view) that there are stronger reasons for observing discontinuity between the Testaments.

Naturally, if discontinuity is more prevalent than unity, then the church is correspondingly freed of any obligation to derive her doctrinal teachings from the OT. But we feel the reverse situation is the case here and thus we must not constantly erect walls of partition between the doctrines in the OT and the NT. If there were no other passage, certainly the teaching passage of Jeremiah 31:31–34 would warn us against such a facile erection of dichotomies.

THE CASE FOR THE PRACTICAL USE OF THE OLD TESTAMENT IN THE NEW

The final case we wish to make is that the wisdom and legal portions of the OT are a rich source of extremely practical advice on a believer's life-style and system of values. Rather than being more didactic and abstract in its teaching, these sections of the OT tended to be more illustrative, proverbial, and concrete.

It is at once as amusing as it is sad to see how many believers will flock to seminars that inculcate practical hints from such proverbial books as Proverbs. But those same believers have a strong built-in antipathy for the law-grace question. Why is it that no one has realized that Proverbs, for example, is a veritable patchwork of allusions or partial citations of Deuteronomy, Exodus, and other portions of the Law.

Even when the law is from the so-called ceremonial or civil sections, there remain underlying principles from which Paul and James illustrate the durability of their usefulness in the two essays we have included above. It is our hope that those samples may open up even a larger scope of God's neglected Word.

And so the case goes on. We have only scratched the surface of this most intriguing subject. But we cannot help but feel that the tone we have set here is a more authentic representation of the way that the OT was used by the NT writers than the majority opinion currently being offered in most scholarly circles. If this question had no major implications for other exegetical or critical questions, perhaps we could have spared the world one more volume to print, catalogue, read, and review. Alas, the issue is no longer an innocent one merely illustrating the results of few hermeneutical blunders; it has tended to provide all sorts of excuses for methodologies carrying a vast amount of freight.

Perhaps we should give at least one concrete example of this argument in action. In a most sweeping article arguing for a broad type of contextualization, Charles R. Taber mused:

> I also wonder about the relationship of our whole approach to hermeneutics to other, also culturally conditioned views. For instance, the New Testament writers used a hermeneutic in relation to many Old Testament citations which was derived from rabbinic interpretation but was at the opposite pole from what we would consider legitimate today. In our terms, some of the Old Testament passages cited are clearly taken out of context.... But the fact of the matter is that what they considered proper hermeneutics was part and parcel of their cultural heritage."[20]

Taber then turns, what we believe is an inaccurate depiction of the NT writer's practice, against us and uses that as a lever to soften up a waiting church for a pluralistic theology.

It is the fervent hope of this writer that the line of argumentation used here and the depth of hard exegesis will correct this problem at

20. Charles R. Taber, "Is There One Way to Do Theology?" *Gospel in Context* 1 (1978):8.

its source. Rather than there being a plurality of meanings or hermeneutical methodologies, there was only one. And that is the one that the NT used, especially when they used the OT in an apologetic, prophetic, typological, theological, or practical way.

Bibliography

GENESIS

Davids, Peter H. "Tradition and Citation in the Epistle of James." In
Scriptura, Tradition, and Interpretation, pp. 113–26. Edited by W.
Ward Gasque and William S. LaSor. Grand Rapids: Eerdmans, 1978.
Hahn, Ferdinand. "Genesis 15:6 im Neuen Testament (James 2:23,
Galatians 3:6, Romans 4)." In *Probleme Biblischer Theologie*. pp. 90–
107. Edited by Hans W. Wolff. Munich: Kaiser Verlag, 1971.
Lincoln, Andrew T. "The Use of the Old Testament in Ephesians (Gen
2:24, Ex 20:12, Isa 57:19, & Ps 68:18)." *Journal for the Study of the
New Testament* 14 (1982):16–57.

EXODUS

Bretscher, P. G. "Exodus 4:22–23 and the Voice from Heaven." *Journal
of Biblical Literature* 87 (1968):301–11.
Davids (see GENESIS).
Dunn, J. D. G. "2 Corinthians III,17: The Lord is the Spirit (Ex 34)."
Journal of Theological Studies 21 (1970):309–20.
Kee, Howard C. "The Function of Scriptural Quotations and Allusions
in Mark 11–16." In *Jesus und Paulus*, pp. 165–85. Edited by E. Earle
Ellis and Erich Grässer. Göttingen: Vandenhoeck & Ruprecht, 1975.

———. "Scripture Quotations and Allusions in Mark 11–16." In *Society of Biblical Literature: 1971 Seminar Papers*, pp. 475–502. Edited by J. White et al. Society of Biblical Literature, 1971.

Lincoln (see GENESIS).

Meeds, W. A. "'And Rose Up to Play': Midrash and Paraenesis in 1 Corinthians 10:1–22." *Journal for the Study of the New Testament* 16 (1982):64–78.

Piper, Otto A. "Unchanging Promises: Exodus in the New Testament." *Interpretation* 11 (1957):3–22.

Richter, Georg. "Die alttestamentlichen Zitate in der Rede vom Himmelsbrot John 6:26–51a." In *Schriftauslegung: Beiträge zur Hermeneutik des Neuen Testamentes und im Neuen Testament*, pp. 193–279. Paderborn: Verlag F. Schöningh, 1972.

Ronen, Yochanan. "Mark 7:1–23: 'Traditions of the Elders.'" *Immanuel* 12 (1981):44–54.

Smith, Robert Houston. "Exodus Typology in the Fourth Gospel." *Journal of Biblical Literature* 81 (1982):329–42.

Snodgrass, Klyne R. "1 Peter 2:1–10: Its Formation and Literary Affinities." *New Testament Studies* 24 (1977):97–106.

Westermann, Claus. "Alttestamentliche Elements in Lukes 2:1–20." In *Tradition und Glaube: das frühe Christentum in seiner Umwelt. Festgabe für Karl Georg Kuhm zum 65. Geburtstag*, pp. 317–22. Edited by Gret Jeremias, Heinz-Wolfgang Kuhn, & Harmut Stegeman. Göttigen: Vandenhoeck & Ruprecht, 1971.

LEVITICUS

Davids (see GENESIS).

Johnson, Luke T. "The Use of Leviticus 19 in the Letter of James." *Journal of Biblical Literature* 101 (1982):391–401.

Kaiser, Walter C., Jr. "Leviticus 18:5 and Paul." *Journal of the Evangelical Theological Society* 14 (1970):19–28.

Ronen (see EXODUS).

Stern, Jay B. "Jesus' Citation of Dr 6:5 & Lv 19:18 in the Light of Jewish Tradition." *Catholic Biblical Quarterly* 28 (1966):312–16.

Westermann (see EXODUS).

DEUTERONOMY

Davids (see GENESIS).

Kaiser, Walter C., Jr. "The Current Crisis in Exegesis and the Apostolic Use of Deuteronomy 25:4 in 1 Corinthians 9:8–10." *Journal of the Evangelical Theological Society* 21 (1978):3–18.

Katz, Peter. "Quotations from Deuteronomy in Hebrews." *Zeitschrift für die neutestamentliche Wissenschaft* 49 (1958):213–23.

Kee (see EXODUS).

Kölichen, Johann C. von. "Die Zitate aus dem Moseleid Deut 32sten im Romerbrief des Paulus (Rom 10:19, 12:19, 15:10)." In *Theologische Versuche 5*, pp. 53–69. Berlin: Evangelische Verlagsanstalt, 1975.

Ronen (see EXODUS)

Stern (see LEVITICUS).

Taylor, A. B. "Decision in the Desert. The Temptation of Jesus in the Light of Deuteronomy." *Interpretation* 14 (1960): 300–309.

Wilcox, Max. "Upon the Tree: Deut 21:22–23 in the New Testament (Gal 3:13, Acts 5:30, 10:39, 13:28–30)." *Journal of Biblical Literature* 96 (1977):85–99.

2 SAMUEL

Goldsmith, D. "Acts 13:33–37: A Pesher on II Samuel 7." *Journal of Biblical Literature* 87 (1968):321–24.

Kaiser, Walter C., Jr. "The Blessing of David: The Charter for Humanity." In *The Law and the Prophets: in Memory of O. T. Allis*, pp. 298–318. Edited by J. Skilton. Philadelphia: Presbyterian & Reformed, 1974.

PSALMS

Allen, Leslie C. "Psalm 45:7–8 (6–7) in Old and New Testament Settings." In *Christ the Lord: Studies in Christology Presented to Donald Guthrie*, pp. 220–42. Edited by Harold H. Rowden. Downers Grove: InterVarsity, 1982.

Best, E. "1 Peter II,4–10: A Reconsideration." *Novum Testamentum* 11 (1969):270–93.

Beutler, Johannes. "Psalms 42/43 Im Johannesevangelium (John 11:25)." *New Testament Studies* 25 (1978):33–57.

Boers, H. W. "Psalm 16 and the Historical Origin of the Christian Faith." *Zeitschrift für die alttestamentliche Wissenschaft* 80 (1968):105–10.

Callan, T. "Psalm 110:1 and the Origin of the Expectation that Jesus Will Come Again." *Catholic Biblical Quarterly* 44 (1982):622–36.

Crossan, J. D. "Redaction and Citation in Mark 11:9–10 and 11:17." *Biblical Research* 17 (1972):33–50.

———. "Redaction and Citation in Mark 11:9–10, 17 and 14:27." In *Society of Biblical Literature: 1972 Seminar Papers*, pp. 17–61. Edited by Lane C. McGaughy. Society of Biblical Literature, 1972.

Emerton, J. A. "The Interpretation of Psalm 82 in John 10." *Journal of Theological Studies* 11 (1960):329–32

Fisher, Loren R. "Betrayed by Friends: An Expository Study of Psalm 22." *Interpretation* 18 (1964):20–38.

Fitzmeyer, Joseph. "David, Being Therefore a Prophet (Acts 2:30)." *Catholic Biblical Quarterly* 34 (1972):332–39.

Glenn, Donald R. "Psalm 8 and Hebrews 2: A Case Study in Biblical Hermeneutics and Biblical Theology." In *Walvoord: A Tribute*, pp. 39–51. Edited by Donald K. Campbell. Chicago: Moody, 1982.

Hanson, A. T. "John's Citation of Psalm LXXXII." *New Testament Studies* 11 (1965):158–62.

———. "John's Citation of Psalm LXXXII Reconsidered (John 10:33–36 11QMelch)." *New Testament Studies* 13 (1967):363–67.

Harmon, Allan M. "Aspects of Paul's Use of the Psalms." *Westminster Theological Journal* 32 (1969):1–23.

Juel, Donald. "Social Dimensions of Exegesis: The Use of Psalm 16 in Acts 2." *Catholic Biblical Quarterly* 43 (1981):543–56.

Kaiser, Walter C., Jr. "The Abolition of the Old Order and the Establishment of the New: Psalm 40:6–8 and Hebrews 10:5–10." In *Tradition and Testament: Essays in Honor of Charles Lee Feinberg*, pp. 19–37. Edited by John Feinberg and Paul Feinberg. Chicago: Moody, 1981.

———. "The Promise to David in Psalm 16 and Its Application in Acts 2:25–33 and 13:32–37." *Journal of the Evangelical Theological Society* 23 (1980):219–29.

Kee (see EXODUS, *bis*).

Kistemaker, Simon. *The Psalm Citations in the Epistle to the Hebrews.* Amsterdam: Van Soest, 1961.

Lambrecht, J. "Paul's Christological Use of Scripture in 1 Corinthians 15:20–28." *New Testament Studies* 28 (1982):502–27.

Lange, H. D. "The Relationship Between Psalm 22 and the Passion Narrative." *Concordia Theological Monthly* 43 (1972):101–9.

Lincoln (see GENESIS).

McCullough, John C. "Melchizedek's Varied Role in Early Exegetical Tradition." *Theological Review* 2 (1979):52–66.

Richter (see EXODUS).

Russell, S. H. "Calvin and the Messianic Interpretation of the Psalms." *Scottish Journal of Theology* 21 (1968):37–47.

Sampley, J. P. "Scripture and Tradition in the Community as Seen in Ephesians 4:25ff." *Studia Theologica* 26 (1972):101–9.

Schmitt, A. "Psalm 16:8–11 als Zeugnis der Auferstehung in der Apg." *Biblische Zeitschrift* 17 (1973):229–48.

Smith, Gary V. "Paul's Use of Psalm 68:18 in Ephesians 4:8" *Journal of the Evangelical Theological Society* 18 (1975):181–89.

Snodgrass (see EXODUS).

Trudinger, L. P. "Cry of Dereliction: Some Further Observations." *The Springfielder* 38 (1974):232–35.

Wallis, Wilber B. "The Problem of an Intermediate Kingdom in 1 Corinthians 15:20–28 (Ps 8:6, 110:1)." *Journal of the Evangelical Theological Society* 18 (1975):229–42.

PROVERBS

Beardslee, William A. "Uses of the Proverb in the Synoptic Gospels." *Interpretation* 24 (1970):61–73.

Davids (see GENESIS).

Laws, S. S. "Does Scripture Speak in Vain? A Reconsideration of James 4:5." *New Testament Studies* 20 (1974):210–15.

ISAIAH

Aus, Roger D. "The Relevance of Isaiah 66:7 to Revelation 12 and 2 Thessalonians 1." *Zeitschrift für die neutestamentliche Wissen schaft* 67 (1976):252 68.

Best (see PSALMS).

Crossan (see PSALMS, *bis*).

DeCock, P. B. "The Understanding of Isaiah 53:7–8 in Acts 8:32–33." *Neotestamentica* 14 (1981):111–33.

Dubarle, André. "La Conception Virginale et la Citation: d'Is 7:14 dans l'evanglie de Matthieu." *Revue Biblique* 68 (1981):362–80.

Dupont, J. "TA 'ΟΣΙΑ ΔΑΥΙΔ ΤΑ ΠΙΣΤΑ (Ac XIII:34 Is LV:3)" *Revue Biblique* 68 (1961):91–114.

Evans, Craig A. "The Function of Isa 6:9–10 in Mark and John." *Novum Testamentum* 24 (1982):124–38.

———. "A Note on the Function of Isaiah 6:9–10 in Mark 4." *Revue Biblique* 87 (1981):234–35

Flamming, J. "The New Testament Use of Isaiah." *Southwestern Journal of Theology* 11 (1968):89–103.

Grogan, Geoffrey W. "The Light and the Stone: A Christological Study in Luke and Isaiah." In *Christ the Lord: Studies in Christology Presented to Donald Guthrie*, pp. 151–67. Edited by Harold H. Rowden. Downers Grove: InterVarsity, 1982.

Kee (see EXODUS, *bis*).

Koehler, L. "Zum Verstädnis vos Jes 7:14." *Zeitschrift für die alttestamentliche Wissenschaft* 67 (1955):48–50.

Lincoln (see GENESIS).

MacRae, Allan A. "Paul's Use of Isaiah 65:1." In *The Law and the Prophets*, pp. 369–76. Edited by John H. Skilton, Milton C. Fisher, and Leslie W. Sloat. Phillipsburg, N.J.: Presbyterian & Reformed, 1974.

McNeil, Brian. "The Quotation at John 12:34 (Isa 9:5)." *Novum Testamentum* 19 (1977):22–33.

Neyrey, J. H. "The Thematic Use of Isaiah 42:1–4 in Matthew 12." *Biblica* 63 (1982):457–73.

Richter (see EXODUS).

Sanders, James A. "Isaiah in Luke." *Interpretation* 36 (1982):144–55.

———. "From Isaiah 61 to Luke 4." In *Christianity, Judaism, and Other Greco-Roman Cults*, pp. 75–106. Edited by Jacob Neusner. Leiden: Brill, 1975.

Schmitt, J. "L'oracle d'Is, 61:1ss et sa Relecture par Jesus." *Revue des Sciences Religieuses* 54 (1980):97–108.

Schnackenburg, Rudolph. "John 12:39–41: zur Christologischen Schriftauslegung des vierten Evangelisten." In *Neues Testament und Geschichte: Historisches Geschehen und Deutung im Neuen Testament*, pp. 167–77. Edited by Heinrich Baltensweiler and Bo Reicke. Zurich: Theologischer Verlag, 1972.

Snodgrass (see EXODUS).

Tannehill, Robert C. "The Mission of Jesus According to Luke 4:16–30." In *Jesus in Nazareth*, pp. 51–75. Edited by Erich Grässer, et al. Berlin: DeGruyter, 1972.

Thorton, Timothy C. G. "Stephen's Use of Isaiah 66:1." *The Journal of Theological Studies* 25 (1974):432–34.

Wolf, H. M. "Solution to the Immanuel Prophecy in Isaiah 7:14—8:22." *Journal of Biblical Literature* 91 (1972):449–56.

Young, F. W. "A Study of the Relation of Isaiah to the Fourth Gospel." *Zeitschrift für die neutestamentliche Wissenschaft* 46 (1955).

JEREMIAH

Crossan (see PSALMS, *bis*).

Dahlberg, Bruce T. "The Typological Use of Jeremiah 1:4–19 in Matthew 16:13–23." *Journal of Biblical Literature* 94 (1975):73–80.

France, Richard T. "The Formula-Quotations of Matthew 2 and the Problem of Communication." *New Testament Studies* 27 (1980–1981):233–51.

Kaiser, Walter C., Jr. "The Old Promise and the New Covenant." In *The Bible in Its Literary Milieu*, pp. 106–20. Edited by John Maier and Vincent Tollers. Grand Rapids: Eerdmans, 1979. Reprinted from the *Journal of the Evangelical Theological Society* 15 (1972):11–23.

Kee (see EXODUS).

Kuhr, F. "Römer 2:14f und die Verheissung bei Jeremia 31:31f." *Zeitschrift für die neutestamentliche Wissenschaft* 55 (1964):243–61.

Lindars, Barnabus. "Rachel Weeping for Her Children—Jeremiah 31:15–22." *Journal for the Study of the Old Testament* 12 (1979):47–62.

Petersen, David L. "The Prophecy of the New Covenant in the Argument of Hebrews." *The Reformed Theological Review* 38 (1979):74–81.

Richard, Earl. "Polemics, Old Testament, and Theology: A Study of II Cor III:1—IV:6." *Revue Biblique* 88 (1981):340–67.

Sparks, H. F. O. "St. Matthew's References to Jeremiah." *Journal of Theological Student* 1 (1950):155–56.

Upton, J. A. "The Potter's Field and the Death of Judas." *Concordia Journal* 8 (1982):213–19.

EZEKIEL

Grassi, J. A. "Ezekiel XXXVII:1–14 and the New Testament." *New Testament Studies* 11 (1965):162–64

Mackay, C. "Ezekiel in the New Testament." *Church Quarterly Review* 162 (1961):4–16.

Vanhoye, A. "L'utilisation du Livre d'Ezechiel dans l'Apocalypse." *Biblica* 43 (1962):436–76.

DANIEL

Kee (see EXODUS).

HOSEA

Baumstark, A. "Die Zitate de Mt—Evangeliums aus dem Zwölfprophetenbuch" *Biblica* 37 (1956):296–313.

France (see JEREMIAH).

Hill, David. "On the Use and Meaning of Hosea 6:6 in Matthew's Gospel (Hos 6:6, Matt 9:13, 12:7, Mk 2:13–17, 23–27)." *New Testament Studies* 24 (1977):107–19.

Leving, Etan. "The Sabbath Controversy According to Matthew." *New Testament Studies* 22 (1976):480–83.

JOEL

Kaiser, Walter C., Jr. "The Promise of God and the Outpouring of the Holy Spirit: Joel 2:28–32 and Acts 2:16–21." In *The Living and Active Word of God: Essays in Honor of Samuel Schultz*, pp. 109–22. Edited by Morris Inch and Ronald Youngblood. Winona Lake: Eisenbraun, 1982.

AMOS

Kaiser, Walter C., Jr. "The Davidic Promise and the Inclusion of the Gentiles (Amos 9:9–15 and Acts 15:13–18)." *Journal of the Evangelical Theological Society* 20 (1977):97–111.

MICAH

Baumstark (see HOSEA).
France (see JEREMIAH).

HABAKKUK

Johnson, S. L. "The Gospel That Paul Preached (Rom 1:16–17; Hab 2:3–4)." *Bibliotheca Sacra* 128 (1971):327–40.
Moody, R. M. "The Habakkuk Quotation in Romans 1:17." *Expository Times* 92 (1981):205–8.

ZECHARIAH

Barnicki, Roman. "Das Zitat Von Zach 9:9 und die Tiere im Bericht von Mätthaus über dem Einzug Jesu im Jeresalem (Mt 21:1–11)." *Novum Testamentum* 18 (1976):161–66.
Baumstark (see HOSEA).
Bernard, J. H. "The Death of Judas." *The Expositor* 9 (1904):422–30.
Crossan (see PSALMS).
Kee (see EXODUS, *bis*).
Luke, K. "The Thirty Pieces of Silver (Zch 11:12f)." *Indian Theological Studies* 19 (1982):15–32.
Roth, C. "The Cleansing of the Temple and Zechariah xiv:21." *Novum Testamentum* 4 (1960):174–81.
Schnackenburg, Rudolph. "Das Schriftzitat in John 19:37 (Zech. 12:10)." In *Wort, Leid, und Gottespruch: Beiträge zu Psalmen und Propheten*, pp. 239–47. Edited by Josef Schreiner. Würtzburg: Echter Verlag, 1972.
Upton (see JEREMIAH).

MALACHI

Baumstark (see HOSEA).
Kaiser, Walter C., Jr. "The Promise of the Arrival of Elijah in Malachi and the Gospels." *Grace Theological Journal* 3 (1982):221–33.

MATTHEW

Albright, W. F. "The Names 'Nazareth' and 'Nazoraean'." *Journal of Biblical Literature* 65 (1946):397–401.

Bartnick (see ZECHARIAH).

Baumstark (see HOSEA).

Beardslee (see PROVERBS).

Brown, Raymond E. *The Birth of the Messiah,* pp. 98–99, 213–28. Garden City: Doubleday, 1977.

Cave, C. H. "St. Matthew's Infancy Narrative." *New Testament Studies* 9 (1962–1963):382–90.

Coleman, Robert O. "Matthew's Use of the Old Testament." *Southwestern Journal of Theology* 5 (1962):29–39.

Dahlberg (see JEREMIAH).

Derrett, J. Duncan M. "Further Light on the Narratives of the Nativity." *Novum Testamentum* 17 (1975):81–108.

Dodewaard, J. A. E. van. "La Force Évocatrice de la Citation: Mise en Lumière en prenant pour base l'Evangile de S. Matthieu." *Biblica* 36 (1955):482–91.

Down, M. J. "The Mathean Birth Narratives: Matthew 1:18—2:23." *Expository Times* 90 (1978–79):51–52.

Dubarle (see ISAIAH).

France, Richard T. "Herod and the Children of Bethlehem." *Novum Testamentum* 21 (1979):98–120.

————. (see JEREMIAH).

Gibson, Edgar C. S. "Our Lord's Use of the Old Testament: St. Matthew xxiv.29–34." *The Expositor* 1 (1881):292–304.

Goldingay, J. "The Old Testament and the Christian Faith: Jesus and the Old Testament in Matthew 1–5, Part 1." *Themelios* 8 (1982):4–10.

Goulder, M. D. *Midrash and Lection in Matthew.* London: SPCK, 1974.

Gundry, Robert. *The Use of the Old Testament in St. Matthew's Gospel.* Leiden: E. J. Brill, 1967.

Hill (see HOSEA).

Hillyer, N. "Matthew's Use of the Old Testament." *Evangelical Quarterly* 36 (1964):12–26.

Johnson, Sherman E. "The Biblical Quotations in Matthew." *Harvard Theological Review* 36 (1943):135–53.

Kaiser (see MALACHI).

Kent, Homer A., Jr. "Matthew's Use of the Old Testament." *Bibliotheca Sacra* 121 (1964):34–43.

Koehler (see ISAIAH).

Langee (see PSALMS).

Leving (see HOSEA).

Lindars (see JEREMIAH).

Luke (see ZECHARIAH).

McCasland, S. V. "Matthew Twists the Scriptures." *Journal of Biblical Literature* 80 (1961):143–48.

McConnell, Richard S. *Law and Prophecy in Matthew's Gospel: the Authority and Use of the Old Testament in the Gospel of Matthew.* Basel: Friedrich Reinhardt, 1972.

Neyrey (see ISAIAH).

O'Rourke, J. J. "Fulfillment Texts in Matthew." *Catholic Biblical Quarterly* 24 (1962):394–403.

Pesch, R. "Eine alttestamentliche Ausführungsformel im Matthäus—Evangelium: Redaktionsgeschichtliche und Exegetische Beobachtungen." *Biblische Zeitschrift* 10 (1966):220–45.

Prabhu, George M. Soares. *The Formula Quotations in the Infancy Narrative of Matthew: an Enquiry into the Tradition History of Mt. 1–2.* Analecta 63. Rome: Biblical Institute Press, 1976.

Sanders, J. A. "ΝΑΖΩΡΑΙΟΣ in Matt 2.23." *Journal of Biblical Literature* 84 (1965):169–72.

Segbroeck, F. van. "Citations d'accomplissement dans l'Evangile selon Matthieu d'après trois ouvrages récents." In *L'Evangile selon Matthieu: Redaction et Théologie*, pp. 107–30. Edited by M. Didier et al. Gembloux: J. Duculot, 1972.

Senior, Donald. "A Case Study in Matthean Creativity: Matthew 27:3–10." *Biblical Research* 19 (1974):23–36.

Smith, Wilbur M. "Out of Egypt Did I Call My Son." In *Egypt in Biblical Prophecy*, pp. 125–30. Boston: W. A. Wilde, 1957.

Sparks (see JEREMIAH).

Stendahl, Krister. "Quis et Unde? An Analysis of Mt 1–2." In *Judentum Urchristentum Kirche: Festschrift für Joachim Jeremias*, pp. 94–105. Edited by Walther Eltester. Berlin: Alfred Töpelmann, 1964.

———. *The School of Matthew and Its Use of the Old Testament.* 2d ed. Philadelphia: Fortress, 1968.

Stern (see LEVITICUS).

Taylor (see DEUTERONOMY).

Thomas, Kenneth. "Torah Citations in the Synoptics." *New Testament Studies* 24 (1977):85–96.

Unnick, Willem C. van. "The Death of Judas in Saint Matthew's Gospel." *Anglican Theological Review*, Supplementary Series 3 (1974):44–57.

Upton (see JEREMIAH).

Wolf (see ISAIAH).

MARK

Beardslee (see PROVERBS).

Crossan (see PSALMS, *bis*).

Evans (see ISAIAH, *bis*).

Hill (see HOSEA).

Kee (see EXODUS).

Lange (see PSALMS, *bis*).

Ronen (see EXODUS).

Schultz, S. "Markus und das Alte Testament." *Zeitschrift für Theologie und Kirche* 58 (1961):184–97.

Stern (see LEVITICUS).

Thomas (see MATTHEW).

Vorster, W. S. "The Function and Use of the Old Testament in Mark." *Neotestamentica* 14 (1981):62–72.

LUKE

Beardslee (see PROVERBS).

Grogan (see ISAIAH).

Sanders (see ISAIAH, *bis*).

Schmitt (see ISAIAH).

Tannehill (see ISAIAH).

Taylor (see DEUTERONOMY).

Thomas (see MATTHEW).

Westermann (see EXODUS).

JOHN

Buetler (see PSALMS).

Emerton (see PSALMS).

Evans, Craig A. "On the Quotation Formulas in the Fourth Gospel." *Biblische Zeitschrift* 26 (1982):79–83.

———. (see ISAIAH).

Freed, Edwin D. *Old Testament Quotations in the Gospel of John.* Leiden: E. J. Brill, 1965.

Hanson (see PSALMS, *bis*).

McNeil (see ISAIAH).

Morgan, R. "Fulfillment in the Fourth Gospel: Old Testament Foundations." *Interpretation* 11 (1957):155–65.

Richter (see EXODUS).

Schnackenburg (see ISAIAH; see ZECHARIAH).

Smith (see EXODUS).

Tenney, Merrill C. "The Old Testament and the Fourth Gospel." *Bibliotheca Sacra* 120 (1963):300–308.

Young (see ISAIAH).

ACTS

Bass, W. H. "Acts 2:28 and Psalm 16:11." *Expository Times* 29 (1917–18):523ff.

Bernard (see ZECHARIAH).

Boers (see PSALMS).

DeCock (see ISAIAH).

Dupont, J. "La Destinée de Judas Prophétisée par David (Actes 1, 16–20)." *Catholic Biblical Quarterly* 23 (1961):40–51.

————. "The Use of the Old Testament in the Acts." *Theological Digest* (1955):61–64.

Goldsmith (see 2 SAMUEL).

Juel (see PSALMS).

Kaiser (see PSALMS; see JOEL; see AMOS).

Kilpatrick, George D. "Some Quotations in Acts." In *Les Actes des Apôtres*, pp. 81–87. Edited by J. Kremer. Gembloux: J. Duculot, 1979.

Mare, W. H. "Acts 7: Jewish or Samaritan in Character?" *Westminster Theological Journal* 34 (1971):1–21.

Richard, Earl. "The Old Testament in Acts: Wilcox's Semitisms in Retrospect." *Catholic Biblical Quarterly* 42 (1980):330–41.

———— (see AMOS).

Ross, Martin. "Die Funktion der alttestamentlichen Zitate and Anspie-lungen in den Reden der Apostelgeschichte." In *Les Actes des Apôtres*, pp. 61–79. Edited by J. Kremer. Gembloux: J. Duculot, 1979.

Schmitt (see PSALMS).

Thornton (see ISAIAH).

Wilcox, Max. "The Judas-Tradition in Acts 1:15–26." *New Testament Studies* 19 (1972–73):438–52.

————. (see DEUTERONOMY).

ROMANS

Hahn (see GENESIS).

Johnson (see HABAKKUK).

Kaiser (see LEVITICUS; see DEUTERONOMY).

Kölichen (see DEUTERONOMY).

Kuhr (see JEREMIAH).

Moody (see HABAKKUK).

1 CORINTHIANS

Kaiser, Walter C., Jr. "The Weightier and Lighter Matters of the Law: Moses, Jesus, and Paul." In *Current Issues in Biblical and Patristic Interpretation: Studies in Honor of Merrill C. Tenney*, pp. 176–92. Edited by Gerald F. Hawthorne. Grand Rapids: Eerdmans, 1975.

Lambrecht (see PSALMS).

Malan, F. S. "The Use of the Old Testament in 1 Corinthians." *Neotes-timentica* 14 (1981):134–70.

Meeks (see EXODUS).
Wallis (see PSALMS).

2 CORINTHIANS

Dunn (see EXODUS).
Grassi (see EZEKIEL).
Hooker, Morna D. "Beyond the Things That Are Written: St. Paul's Use of Scripture (2 Cor 3)." *New Testament Studies* 27 (1981):295–309.
Richard (see JEREMIAH).

GALATIANS

Hahn (see GENESIS).
Wilcox (see DEUTERONOMY).

EPHESIANS

Lincoln (see GENESIS).
Sampley (see PSALMS).
Smith (see PSALMS).

2 THESSALONIANS

Aus (see ISAIAH).

HEBREWS

Barth, Markus. "The Old Testament in Hebrews: An Essay in Biblical Hermeneutics." In *Current Issues in New Testament Interpretation: Essays in Honor of Otto A. Piper.* Edited by William Klassen and Graydon F. Snyder. pp. 53–78. New York: Harper & Row, 1962.
Combrink, H. J. "Some Thoughts on the Old Testament Citations in the Epistles to the Hebrews." In *Ad Hebraeos: Essays on the Epistle to the Hebrews,* pp. 475–502. Edited by F. C. Fensham et al. Pretoria: Die Nuwe-Testamenties Werkgemeenskap van Suid-Afrika, 1971.
Glasson, T. F. "Plurality of Divine Persons and the Quotation in Hebrews." *New Testament Studies* 12 (1966):270–72.
Glenn (see PSALMS).
Howard, G. "Hebrews and the Old Testament Quotations." *Novum Testamentum* 10 (1968):208–16.
Kaiser, Walter C., Jr. "The Promise Theme and the Theology of Rest." *Bibliotheca Sacra* 130 (1973):135–50.
———. (see PSALMS, see JEREMIAH).
Kistemaker (see PSALMS).

McCullough (see PSALMS).
Petersen (see JEREMIAH).
Rendall, Robert. "The Method of the Writer to the Hebrews in Using Old Testament Quotations." *Evangelical Quarterly* 27 (1955):135–50.
Thomas, Kenneth J. "Old Testament Citations in Hebrews." *New Testament Studies* 11 (1965):303–25.

JAMES

Davids (see GENESIS).
Johnson (see LEVITICUS).
Laws (see PROVERBS).

1 PETER

Best (see PSALMS).
Snodgrass (see PSALMS).

REVELATION

Aus (see ISAIAH).
Trudinger, L. P. "Some Observations Concerning the Text of the Old Testament in the Book of Revelation." *Journal of Theological Studies* 17 (1966):82–88.
Vanhoye (see EZEKIEL).

GENERAL WORKS

Allen, E. L. "Jesus and Moses in the New Testament." *Expository Times* 67 (1956):104–6.
Archer, Gleason L., and Chirichigno, G. C. *Old Testament Quotations in the New Testament: A Complete Survey.* Chicago: Moody, 1983.
Atkinson, B. F. C. "The Textual Background of the Use of the Old Testament by the New." *Journal of the Transactions of the Victorian Institute* 79 (1947):39–69.
Aune, D. E. "Early Christian Biblical Interpretation." *Evangelical Quarterly* 41 (1969):79–96.
Balentine, Samuel E. "The Interpretation of the Old Testament in the New Testament." *Southwestern Journal of Theology* 23 (1981):41–57.
Bartling, V. A. "Christ's Use of the Old Testament with Special Reference to the Pentateuch." *Concordia Theological Monthly* 36 (1965):567–76.
Bates, William H. "Quotations in the New Testament from the Old Testament." *Bibliotheca Sacra* 77 (1920):424–28.

Black, Matthew. "The Christological Use of the Old Testament in the New Testament." *New Testament Studies* 18 (1971–72):1–14.

Blaser, Peter. "St. Paul's Use of the Old Testament." *Theology Digest* 2 (1954):49–52.

Bratcher, Robert, ed. *Old Testament Quotations in the New Testament.* London: United Bible Societies, 1961.

Braun, H. "Das alte Testament im neue Testament." *Zeitschrift für Theologie und Kirche* 59 (1962):16–31.

Carr, G. Lloyd. "The Old Testament Love Songs and Their Use in the New Testament." *Journal of the Evangelical Theological Society* 24 (1981):97–105.

Clements, Ronald F. "Messianic Prophecy or Messianic History?" *Horizons in Biblical Theology* 1 (1979):87–104.

Dodd, C. H. *According to the Scriptures.* London: Lowe & Brydone, 1952.

———. *The Old Testament in the New.* Philadelphia: Fortress, 1965.

Edgar, S. L. "Respect for Context in Quotation from the Old Testament." *New Testament Studies* 9 (1963):55–62.

Ellis, E. Earle. "How the New Testament Uses the Old." In *New Testament Interpretation,* pp. 199–219. Edited by I. Howard Marshall. Exeter: Paternoster, 1977.

———. *Paul's Use of the Old Testament.* London: Oliver & Boyd, 1961.

———. "Quotations (in the New Testament)" In *The New Bible Dictionary,* p. 1071. Edited by J. D. Douglas. Grand Rapids: Eerdmans, 1962.

———. "Saith the Lord (Quotations from the Old Testament in the New Testament)." *Evangelical Quarterly* 29 (1957):23–28.

Fitzmeyer, Joseph A. "'4Q Testimonia' and the New Testament." *Theological Studies* 18 (1957):513–37.

———. "The Use of Explicit Old Testament Quotations in Qumran Literature and in the New Testament." *New Testament Studies* 7 (1961):297–333.

Gardner, Frederic. "The New Testament Use of the Old." In *The Old and New Testament in Their Mutual Relations,* pp. 310–11. New York: James Pott, 1885.

Grogan, G. W. "The New Testament Interpretation of the Old Testament: A Comparative Study." *Tyndale Bulletin* 18 (1967):54–76.

Hagner, Donald. "The Old Testament in the New Testament." In *Interpreting the Word of God,* pp. 78–104. Edited by Samuel J. Schultz and Morris A. Inch. Chicago: Moody, 1976.

Hanson, A. T. *Jesus Christ in the Old Testament.* London: SPCK, 1965.

———. "The Use of the Old Testament in the Pastoral Epistles." *Irish Biblical Studies* 3 (1981):203–19.

Harmon, A. M. "Aspect of Paul's Use of the Psalms." *Westminster Theological Journal* 32 (1969):1–23.

Hebert, A. G. *The Throne of David: A Study of the Fulfillment of the Old Testament in Jesus Christ and His Church.* New York: Morehouse-Gorham, 1941.

Hebert, Gabriel. "Hope Looking Forward: The Old Testament Passages Used by the New Testament Writers as Prophetic of the Resurrection of Jesus Christ." *Interpretation* 10 (1956):259–69.

Johnson, S. Lewis. *The Use of the Old Testament in the New.* Grand Rapids: Zondervan, 1980.

Kuyper, L. J. "The Old Testament Used by New Testament Writers." *Reformed Review* 21 (1967):2–13.

Lindars, Barnabus. *New Testament Apologetic: The Doctrinal Significance of the Old Testament Quotations.* Philadelphia: Westminster, 1962.

Longenecker, Richard. *Biblical Exegesis in the Apostolic Period.* Grand Rapids: Eerdmans, 1975.

Lys, D. "L'appropriation del'Ancien Testament." *Etudes Théologiques et Religieuses* 41 (1966):1–12.

Major, H. D. A. "According to the Scriptures." *Modern Churchmen* 45 (1955):49–53.

Manson, T. W. "The Old Testament in the Teaching of Jesus." *Bulletin of the John Rylands Library* 34 (1951–52):312–32.

Marcel, Pierre Ch. "Our Lord's Use of Scripture." In *Revelation and the Bible,* pp. 121–34. Edited by Carl F. H. Henry. Grand Rapids: Baker, 1958.

Mead, R. T. "A Dissenting Opinion About Respect for Context in Old Testament Quotations." *New Testament Studies* 10 (1962–64):279–89.

Murray, J. "Christ and the Scriptures." *Christianity Today* 1 (13 May 1957):15–17.

Nicole, Roger, "The New Testament Use of the Old Testament." In *Revelation and the Bible,* pp. 135–51. Edited by Carl F. H. Henry. Grand Rapids: Baker, 1958.

———. "The Old Testament in the New Testament." In *The Expositor's Bible Commentary,* 1:617–30. Grand Rapids: Zondervan, 1979.

———. "Old Testament Quotations in the New Testament." *Gordon Review* 1 (1955):7–12, 63–68.

———. "Old Testament Quotations in the New Testament." In *Hermeneutics,* pp. 41–53. Edited by Bernard Ramm. Grand Rapids: Baker, 1971.

Oudersluys, Richard C. "Old Testament Quotations in the New Testament." *The Reformed Review* 14 (1960–61).

Rendall, R. "Quotation in Scripture as an Index of Wider Reference." *Evangelical Quarterly* 36 (1964):214–21.

Sauer, A. von R. "Problems of Messianic Interpretation." *Concordia Theological Monthly* 35 (1964):566–74.

Schaller, Berndt. "Zum Textcharakter der Hiobzitate im paulinischen Schriftum." *Zeitschrift für die neutestamentliche Wissenschaft und die Kunde der alteren Kirche* 71 (1980):21–26.

Shires, H. M. *Finding the Old Testament in the New.* Philadelphia: Westminster, 1974.

Smith, D. Moody, Jr. "The Use of the Old Testament in the New." In *The Use of the Old Testament in the New and Other Essays*, pp. 3–65. Edited by James M. Efird. Durham, N.C.: Duke University, 1972.

Smith, S. M. "New Testament Writers' Use the Old Testament." *Encounter* 26 (1965):239–50.

Stamm, J. J. "Jesus Christ and the Old Testament." In *Essays in Old Testament Interpretation*, pp. 200–210. Edited by Claus Westermann. Translated by James Luther Mays. Atlanta: John Knox, 1960.

Sundberg, Albert C., Jr. "On Testimonies." *Novum Testamentum* 3 (1959):208–81.

———. *The Old Testament of the Early Church.* Cambridge: Harvard, 1972.

Tasker, R. V. G. *The Old Testament in the New Testament.* 2d edition. London: SCM, 1954.

Toy, C. H. *Quotation in the New Testament.* New York: Scribner's, 1884.

Thomson, J. G. S. S. "Christ and the Old Testament." *Expository Times* 67 (1955):18–20.

Vielhauer, Philipp. "Paulus und das Alte Testament." In *Studien zue Geschichte und Theologie der Reformation: Festschrift für Ernst Bizer,* pp. 33–62. Edited by Luise Abramowski and J. F. Ferhard Gocters. Neukirchen-Vluyn: Neukirchener Verlag, 1969.

Vos, Geerhardus. "The Idea of 'Fulfillment' of Prophecy in the Gospels." In *Redemptive History and Biblical Interpretation: the Collected Shorter Writings of Geerhardus Vos,* pp. 352–54. Edited by Richard Gaffin. Phillipsburg, N.J.: Presbyterian and Reformed, 1980.

Weir, Jack. "Analogous Fulfillment: The Use of the Old Testament in the New Testament." *Perspectives in Religious Studies* 9 (1982):65–76.

Wilcox, Max. "On Investigating the Use of the Old Testament in the New Testament." In *Text and Interpretation,* pp. 231–43. Edited by Ernest Best and Robert Wilson. Cambridge: U. Press, 1979.

Wood, Leonard. "Manner of Quoting from the Old Testament by the Writers of the New." In *The Works of Leonard Wood,* 1:116–33. Boston: John P. Jewett, 1851. (Contained in "Microbook Library of American Classics." LAC 22218.)

Subject Index

Epangelicalism, promise theology,
180–81, 192, 193
Erfühlungszitate, or fulfillment
citations, 44
Escalation, or *Steigerung*, 106, 107–
8, 110
Eschatology
context, 57
inbreaking of, 55
signals of, 55
Exegesis
definition of, 103
theological, 115
Extracanonical writings, 225

Florilegia, 10, 187
Formula, citations, 43, 44, 45
Fulfillment
climatic, 67, 71, 85, 86
continuous, 62, 94
disjoined, 171
double, 62, 230
initial, 94
multiple, 62, 230
NT, 70
of OT, 21, 25, 52
partial, 62, 94
ultimate, 94
Fusion of horizons, 28

Generic promise, or prediction, 68,
70, 100, 230
definition of, 67
foci of, 88
Generic prophecy, 15, 29, 51
definition of, 56, 84, 85, 230
Generic term, 68
Grammatico, historical method,
103, 120, 226–27

Haraz method, 4
Historia, 71
Historical criticism, 205–6, 207
Historical, theological reflection,
106, 107
Homology, 121
Human instrumentality, 209
Huponia, or occult sense, 65, 105

Illumination, 28

Informing theology, 31, 57, 106, 178,
179, 190
Intensification. See Escalation
Intention
author's, 14, 124, 125, 151, 193,
204, 226
divine, 108–10, 232
Introductory formula, 2, 91, 93,
188–89

Kingdom of God, 178, 180, 189
content of, 179, 180
extent of, 178, 179, 180
form of, 178, 180
time of, 178, 180

Legend, rabbinic, 115, 116
Letterism, 150
Logia, 11

Masoretic text, 5, 34, 51, 137, 182
Meaning(s), 203, 210, 218, 219
definition of, 204
double, 63, 64
fourfold, 210
hidden, 218
horizons of, 226
multiple, 39
pastoral, 218
single, 25–26, 29, 85, 88
surface, 46
syntactical, 106
types of, 85, 226
Midrash, 14, 138, 193, 227, 229

New (renewed) Covenant, 147–49,
193
Novissima, 84

Oriental negative, 165

Paraenesis, 119, 121, 221
Particularity, 197, 198, 212
Pesher, 6, 9, 12, 13, 14, 46, 47, 50,
138, 193, 227
definition of, 227
formula of, 44
methodology of, 45
Peshitta, Syriac, 51
Prediction, 61

Author Index

Scripture Index